POLITICAL TURBULENCE

POLITICAL TURBULENCE

HOW SOCIAL MEDIA SHAPE COLLECTIVE ACTION

HELEN MARGETTS, PETER JOHN,
SCOTT HALE & TAHA YASSERI

PRINCETON UNIVERSITY PRESS
Princeton and Oxford

FOR

OSCAR,

MIKE,

YUKO,

&

FARZANEH

CONTENTS

LIST OF ILLUSTRATIONS

LIST OF TABLES

ACKNOWLEDGEMENTS

The data for this book come from many different sources, and we have many people and organizations to thank for helping to supply it. The majority of the research was supported through Helen Margetts's Professorial Fellowship, funded by the UK Economic and Social Research Council (grant RES-051-27-0331), which provided us with a great opportunity to amass large-scale, long-range data resources as well as to conduct experiments. We thank the ESRC, particularly for trusting in a research programme that promised to collect big data before the term was invented. Early on, we collaborated with the Rediscovering the Civic and Achieving Better Outcomes in Public Policy project, funded by ESRC, the Department of Communities and Local Government, and the North West Improvement and Efficiency Partnership (grant RES-177-025-0002), and an experiment that formed part of this programme is reported in Chapter 4. In that same chapter, we report the result of an experiment carried out with mySociety, and we thank Paul Lenz for his work on the trial and Tom Steinberg for his enthusiasm and support. Most of the research for the book was carried out at the Oxford Internet Institute, the perfect multidisciplinary environment for this endeavour. In what other social science department could two political scientists, a physicist, and a computer scientist come together to coauthor a book? We thank all our colleagues there for support, comments, constructive criticism, and much else besides. We thank David Sutcliffe in particular for copyediting, proofreading, and his invaluable comments.

We thank Princeton University Press for its support of the book, in particular the interest of the former editor, Chuck Myers, and then his successor Eric Crahan. We thank the press's anonymous reviewers for their engagement with the project and very helpful suggestions for revisions. We are very grateful to the editorial and marketing staff for the smooth processing of our manuscript.

We thank Tobias Escher and Stéphane Reissfelder for the major part they played in the quasi-field experiment reported in Chapter 4, and Stéphane Reissfelder for his important and innovative contribution to the design and running of the laboratory experiment reported in Chapters 5, 6, and 7.

We thank the House of Commons Procedure Committee and the Government Digital Service in the UK Cabinet Office for data discussion and sharing, and the opportunity to feed research insight into policy practice.

Our ideas progressed in the context of the Collective Action Online: Theories and Methods workshop at the ECPR Joint Sessions in Mainz 11–16 March 2013 and the APSA panel on Collective Action and Social Media in Washington, 28 August 2014 (both convened by Lance Bennett and Helen Margetts), and we thank all the participants for their interest and discussion and reactions, particularly Mako Hill and Aaron Shaw.

We thank also the many researchers who have read early pieces or drafts, attended seminars or conference panels, or had important conversations with us about the research, particularly Jean-Luc Barbanneau (also for copyediting), Lance Bennett, Bruce Bimber, Josep Colomer, Patrick Dunleavy, Sandra González-Bailón, Philip Howard; participants in the panel on Contemporary Collective Action Dilemmas at the European Consortium Political Research general conference in Potsdam, 10 September 2009; participants at a seminar at IN3, Open University of Catalonia, Barcelona, 7 October 2010 (particularly Rosa Borge and Jaume López); participants in the Internet, Politics and Policy Conference on Big Data in Oxford in September 2012; and participants at the Paul Hirst

Memorial Lecture given by Helen Margetts at Birkbeck College on 11 February 2014.

Finally, we thank deeply our families and friends for helping us to survive the turbulence that writing a book inevitably brings to everyday life.

POLITICAL TURBULENCE

CHAPTER 1

COLLECTIVE ACTION GOES DIGITAL

'Everyone out against everything' ran the headline of the leading Brazilian newspaper of 21 June 2013 in response to mass protests in over one hundred cities.[1] Starting as a demonstration against increased bus fares, the protests grew into a movement against a range of deep issues in Brazilian society: inequality, corruption, lack of public services, and spiralling expenditure on the country's commitment to host the 2016 Olympic Games as well as the 2014 World Cup. To the surprise of the world, the movement appeared to rise from the grassroots with no coordinating organization. Demonstrators refused to allow the flying of traditional political party flags in the protest marches, chanting, 'The people united don't need parties'. When the president, Dilma Rousseff, asked to meet with the leaders of the demonstration, she was told, 'there are no leaders'. This is not to say that such forms of collective action are not organized. Far from it, they are surprisingly well coordinated through the use of social media and other Internet-based platforms that allow users to generate and share content. In this way, states are being challenged by groups of citizens who have as their main weapon an ability to communicate and coordinate the resources of large numbers of people.

From wherever in the world you are reading this book, you are likely to have been touched by a mobilization that shares something with the one in Brazil; that is, having social media as a key tool of coordination. Movements like this have become a central feature of twenty-first-century politics, driving policy change, highlighting weaknesses in public services, bringing new political forces to the fore, acting as a focal point for dissatisfaction and discontent, campaigning for social rights, and challenging both democratic and non-democratic regimes.

From 2002, when large networks of young activists proved a major force in bringing the previously unknown Roh Moo-hyun to presidential power in South Korea, there has been a continual stream of examples. In 2003 millions of people were mobilized in eight hundred cities across the world, including two million in London on 15 February, to demonstrate against their states' involvement in the Iraq War, the largest protest in human history until that time. In 2008 the United States elected its first black president, with record levels of turnout (particularly among black and first-time voters), community support, popular engagement, and large-scale fund-raising from the general public. Mass demonstrations took place in Iran in protest at allegedly rigged election results in 2009, organized and beamed across the world through digital communications.

There have been dramatic developments in political activity for democratic and social rights. On issues of gender, mobilizations have ranged from a successful petition calling for the depiction of women on banknotes in the United Kingdom to global campaigns against the practice of female genital mutilation. In the United States in 2014, large-scale protests against perceived racism in policing started after the shooting of an unarmed black man in Ferguson, Missouri, in the summer and resurfaced at each new shocking incident. In the same year, students and other protesters calling themselves the Umbrella Revolution campaigned for democratic change in Hong Kong, using social media extensively to organize and to connect in a global movement. Even where Internet usage is low or there is heavy censorship, social media have played a role in the dissemination of images of demonstrations or state violence to the outside world.

In many countries, the financial crash of 2008 and subsequent economic crisis brought social backlash, demonstrations, protests, and even riots against banks and their leaders. Protesters highlighted state retrenchment, corruption, and public-sector cutbacks as key issues. In Spain, the 15-M (Indignados) movement carried out a series of demonstrations from May 2011, campaigning against unemployment, welfare cuts, and Spanish politicians as well as the general political system, capitalism, and political corruption. Between 6.5 and 8 million people participated, with the support of over 500 associations, but they rejected political party or labour union collaboration. Inspired in part by the Indignados, the international protest movement Occupy has campaigned against social and economic inequality, particularly the disproportionate power of large corporations, since a high-profile demonstration in New York in September 2011 (Occupy Wall Street) that quickly spread to over eighty countries and six hundred local communities in the United States. In Greece, protests, demonstrations, and riots have become common occurrences since the summer of 2011, directed against an enfeebled state and determined to overturn the deep austerity programme required by the EU in return for a succession of bailouts. These protest movements continue in their countries of origin and have spread across the world. Some have seen the rise of far-right and anti-Islamist groups, as in Germany where protests by the Patriotic Europeans Against the Islamization of the Occident (PEGIDA) have been attended by thousands, matched by a counter-movement of anti-Nazi activists who use social media and mobile apps to find where extremists are planning protests and organize counter-protests.

Autocratic regimes have fallen into disarray and even collapsed in the face of mass demonstrations, mobilizations, protests, and generalized unrest. In Tunisia in December 2010, decades of discontent erupted when a young unemployed man, Tarek al-Tayeb Mohamed Bouazizi, was forbidden from selling vegetables in the street and set himself on fire, sparking off the Arab Spring of 2011.

President El Abidine Ali fled from Tunisia in January; a month later the Egyptian president Hosni Mubarak had also gone. Protests spread across the region to twenty countries including Yemen, Bahrain, Libya, Algeria, Morocco, Jordan, Oman, and Syria. Social media were heavily implicated in much of this activity, particularly in the so-called Facebook Revolution of Egypt. The movements and uprisings that characterized the Arab Spring have proved unstable and often unsustainable, some dissipating almost as soon as they began in the face of brutal suppression, some erupting into civil war and chaos, others reverting back to regimes as autocratic and repressive as those they sought to depose. But these movements changed the practice of politics by illustrating starkly both the potential and the risks of large-scale mobilization without formal organization. Across the region, such mobilizations—or the possibility that such mobilizations will erupt—have become a permanent feature of political life.

These are just some of the more prominent examples of a general phenomenon that ranges from global political movements to neighbourhood campaigns: the emergence of mobilization coordinated by social media as a political force. Use of social media and the nature of mobilizations may be distinct depending on the context and country, but there are common patterns too. In all there has been a surge of activity among those seen traditionally as the socioeconomic groups least likely to participate politically, such as the young and members of ethnic minorities. Such mobilizations periodically burst into public awareness and headlines. But in many ways, we know little about them, beyond the self-evident fact that the nature of collective action is continually shifting and evolving. Political movements based on digital coordination seem to gather momentum rapidly, yet many have proved to be unstable and difficult to sustain as in the Brazilian example with which we opened. The Arab Spring and the other events described above took the world by surprise, evidenced by articles by prominent commentators that predicted the mobilizations would have little lasting impact, such as 'Why the Revolution Will Not Be Tweeted' and (even after the Tunisian president had fled) 'Why the Tunisian

Revolution Won't Spread'.[2] Each new wave of demonstrations and protests seems to rise up from nowhere and defy prediction.

These mobilizations pose a challenge to social science. We do not yet understand their ecology: How do they get started, and how do they operate? Why do some succeed in achieving sustainability and policy and regime change against high odds, while others fail, even where the contexts seem similar? Given this protean context, this book's main task is to examine the relationship between social media and contemporary collective action. We ask how the widespread and growing use of social media affects the operation and functioning of contemporary politics. We will be able to answer this question only by examining the patterns, trends, numbers, and causal mechanisms behind the mobilizations that have surprised the world during the past decade. We use new data and new methods to delve into the changed environment within which citizens make decisions whether or not to participate politically. We believe that understanding this new environment and outlining the association between social media and collective action are the most significant (and exciting) challenges facing political science today. Only by developing that understanding will we acquire any predictive capacity or avoid the bemusement that surrounds each new mobilization.

SOCIAL MEDIA COMES OF AGE

Up until this point we have used the term 'social media' liberally, but it requires definition. Basically, social media are Internet-based platforms that allow the creation and exchange of user-generated content,[3] usually using either mobile or web-based technologies. They can take many forms, including blogs and micro-blogs (such as Twitter or Weibo); social networking sites (such as Facebook, Twitter, Tumblr, Tuenti, Instagram, Snapchat, or Orkut); content-sharing sites (such as YouTube, Flickr, and Vine); social bookmarking sites (such as Digg, Reddit, or Delicious); projects to produce online goods (such as Wikipedia or Baidu Baike); and virtual worlds for gaming or socializing (such as Minecraft and Second Life). All these social media applications rely on the Internet. But as their use has grown to become the way that most users experience the Internet (discussed in Chapter 2), 'social media' is the more useful term to describe the kind of Internet-based interactions that impact upon collective action. Some of the Internet-based applications we discuss in this book are not by some definitions social media, such as the range of civic activism guided by email, apps, or websites, or government-initiated platforms that allow users to join campaigns with political goals. But they do allow the user to contribute some kind of content (such as signing a petition or sending an email to a political leader), and the boundary between these applications and social media is increasingly blurred as any mobilization (a demonstration, a petition, an email campaign) will be disseminated and shared on social media, exposing those considering whether to participate to the signals and influences that these media provide. We use the term to encapsulate these applications as well.

At this point, we should also clarify our use of the terms 'Internet' and 'web' due to the potential for confusion. The Internet is a global system of interconnected computer networks, while the World Wide Web, or the web for short, is a system of interlinked documents, navigated via hyperlinks and accessed via the Internet. Although for some computer science scholars the distinction is of enormous importance,[4] these terms are frequently conflated, and indeed in some languages (such as Greek and Spanish) one word is often used for both concepts. For our purposes, we select the Internet as the more relevant and widely used term because it is possible to access social media without the web, via an application on a mobile telephone, for example, but to use the web one must use the Internet. However, we do use the term 'web' where we reference research specific to the web, such as analysing the hyperlink structure of the World Wide Web.

Most early social media platforms were used primarily on computers connected to the Internet, and Figure 1.1 shows over-time usage of the Internet. In North America, usage had started to pla-

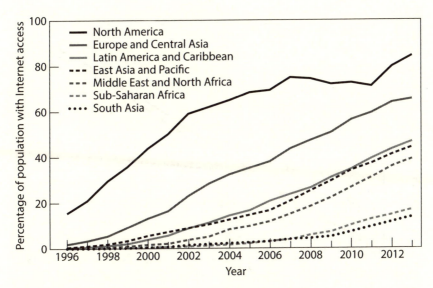

FIGURE 1.1 Internet usage across the world, 1996–2013

teau in the mid 2000s, but widespread use of Internet-enabled devices other than computers, such as smartphones and tablets, seems to have boosted acceleration again so that by 2013 usage was around 83 percent and is still rising. At 346 million, mobile phone subscriptions in the Arab world nearly matched the region's population by the end of 2011,[5] and increasingly the majority of these are for Internet-enabled devices. Even in sub-Saharan Africa and South Asia, the figures are nearing 20 percent.

Almost all major social media platforms now have native applications for mobile telephones and several newer platforms (such as Instagram and Pinterest) started on mobile devices directly. The availability of social media on mobile telephones has provided a massive injection of usage, as social media become available to users 'on-the-go', and even to new populations who do not have regular access to Internet-connected computers. At the time of writing, the number of mobile phones in the world that could access the Internet had outstripped the number of Internet-connected PCs and is contributing to the already dramatic rise in the use

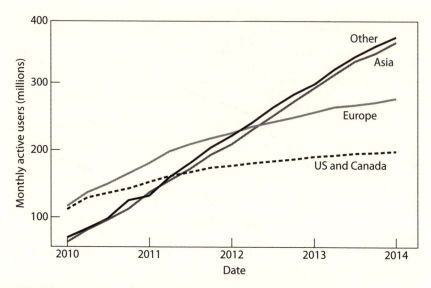

FIGURE 1.2 Facebook usage over time, across the world
Source: Facebook's annual reports (http://investor.fb.com/annuals.cfm). Monthly active users denote registered Facebook users who logged in and visited Facebook through the website or a mobile device or shared content with Facebook connections via a third-party website, in the past thirty days as of the date of measurement.

of social networking and micro-blogging sites.[6] Usage of just one prominent social media platform is shown in Figure 1.2, which shows a regional breakdown of Facebook's 1.2 billion users from 2010 to 2014. While growth in North America and Europe was reasonably steady during this period, having started from a base of over 200,000 in 2010, the rise in other regions in the world has been dramatic (note that this growth has occurred despite Facebook being blocked in one of the largest Internet markets, China). For example, by May 2014 the total number of Facebook users in the Arab world was over 81 million, up from 54.5 million in May 2013,[7] with a quarter of these users in Egypt. Other platforms showed different growth curves as they waxed and waned in popularity. By 2014, social media clearly represented the most popular part of the Internet, with Americans spending more time on social media than any other Internet-based activity and with most applications being used for social and political activity, making 'social media' the term most appropriate to use in the context of collective action.[8]

WHAT COUNTS AS COLLECTIVE ACTION?

A book about collective action also must include a working definition of this term. By 'collective action', we mean any activity undertaken by citizens with the aim of contributing to public goods: goods that are both non-excludable and non-rivalable—that is, they have benefit but cannot be sold to private buyers.[9] Because public goods have these properties—that no individuals can be excluded from their use and use by one individual does not reduce their availability to others—they are subject to the free-rider problem, in that people not contributing to the good may still continue to use it.[10] Because of this, any individual deciding whether to contribute to collective action may decide to free ride or face the possibility that people who will ultimately benefit may not contribute or may make negative contributions that detract from the public good itself. Much of political science is devoted to understanding what motivates people to contribute to public goods and how they may be encouraged to do so in spite of these in-built problems, so that public goods such as a sustainable environment, basic rights, a democratic society, social welfare (funded through taxes), transport, and security continue to be provided. Any individual deciding whether to participate will weigh up the costs of participating and the expected benefit to herself of accessing the public good, factoring in the likelihood of her participation making a difference.[11]

What counts as collective action? There are some acts that uncontroversially fall within this definition, such as voting. Other political activities are also forms of collective action. Most academic commentators perceive some kind of 'ladder' of participation, all rungs of which are aspects of collective action.[12] They range from small acts such as signing a petition, voting, attending political meetings or demonstrations, donating money to a political cause, and protesting or demonstrating, right up to political violence and armed struggle (although there has been much debate over the blurred edges at either end of the ladder).[13] The use of the Internet across all spheres of political life means that some of these acts have moved largely to Internet-based settings (signing petitions, for example), some remain largely offline but are usually coordinated through Internet-based means (voting, boycotting products, demonstration, and political violence), and some new acts enter the repertoire. As discussed in Chapter 2, these include posting a status; supporting or 'liking' something on Facebook, Tumblr, or Pinterest; tweeting or retweeting a political message on Twitter; and disseminating a photograph or video of police or military violence on YouTube, Facebook, or Twitter—all tiny acts of participation adding rungs to the bottom end of the ladder. We include all these activities in our definition of contemporary collective action.

The reader should note, however, that this is not an uncontroversial definition. Many commentators think that collective action primarily happens face-to-face or in closely allied activities and that online activities are inevitably peripheral and less important. There is a 'politics as pain' principle that pervades much of mainstream political culture, particularly in the United Kingdom, which is the view that contributing to politics should involve hard work and some kind of rite of passage. As a result, online participation is still often regarded as inferior to offline participation. This viewpoint was well encapsulated by the chair of the UK Public Administration Select Committee in 1999, during a hearing on online political participation, and in response to one of the authors' suggestion that party supporters might use the Internet at home late in the evening to participate in party business: 'If you describe it in that casual incidental way that gives a picture of people in a sense of having nothing better to do than to press buttons, not because they have anything in particular to contribute but because it is dead easy to do'.[14] In spite of all that has happened since these words were spoken, from the election of Barak Obama to the Arab Spring and the Occupy movement, we believe many in politics today share these sentiments when they hear about political activity taking place on Facebook or Twitter. Indeed, the original source of the quotation above nodded in agreement when it was quoted back to him in 2013. Similar views have led, from the early days of the Internet, to a nascent literature on 'slacktivism' (a conflation of the terms 'slacker' and 'activism'). There are many political acts that seem to have little effect and that require minimum effort. Slacktivism originally had positive connotations,[15] as it was thought to be a low-cost, small-scale route into political participation, but was later discussed in pejorative terms by a whole host of commentators, such as Morozov.[16] Most notably, Gladwell, in his widely cited *New Yorker* article, argued that the small-scale actions and weak ties facilitated by social networking platforms such as Twitter could never engender the strong relationships that characterized the civil rights movement.[17]

If, as we claim, Internet technologies are now central to collective action, then understanding online collective action will be the clue to understanding collective action more generally, allowing us to reevaluate and develop mainstream collective action theories in the light of the possibilities enabled by new forms of digital technology. In this book, we show how Internet-based social media reshape the context within which citizens operate and influence their decisions about whether to participate politically. Changes to the information environment affect the way that citizens seek and find political information, affect the nature of the information that they receive, and reduce the costs of interacting with each other; they change the scale and shape of individuals' social and information networks and their positions within them, impacting upon the costs in the collective action decision. Such changes vary across the ever-increasing range of social media that have become available to citizens over the past decade—Facebook, Twitter, Tumblr, LinkedIn, Instagram, Pinterest, Weibo, Mixi, Cyworld, and Orkut—as well as the dedicated civic activist platforms run by, for example, Avaaz, Kiva, MoveOn, and mySociety, and national electronic petition sites. Through their selection process regarding which social media platforms to use, and how long to spend there, individuals personalize information streams that they receive, which in turn influence the scope and limitations of their political behaviours.

UNDER THE INFLUENCE OF SOCIAL MEDIA

We investigate two key forms of social influence that social media exert on people deciding whether and when to join collective activity. First, in digital environments we can get to know accurately and in real time what other people are doing politically. By providing real-time information about what other people are doing, social media affect the perceived viability of political mobilizations and hence the potential benefits of joining, thereby altering the incentives of individuals to participate. We call this social information, the knowledge that helps people decide what they are going to do with reference to a wider social group and that, in so doing, has the potential to activate people's social norms. The abundance of social information in the digital world is in contrast to the offline world, where someone considering whether to sign a petition in the street will have very little idea of how many other people have signed. We investigate the influence of social information in Chapter 4, building on the work of Salganik et al. and Salganik and Watts, who performed experiments showing how changes to social information on the popularity of cultural artefacts (songs) changed the way that people viewed the quality of those songs.[18] We test these social information effects in a political context.

Second, social media environments allow other people to know what we ourselves are doing by making us visible. Visibility has great appeal to many, as demonstrated by the 'selfie' phenomenon, where individuals or groups take photographs of themselves with mobile phones and upload them to social media websites. 'Selfie' was word of the year in the *Oxford English Dictionary* in 2013, when usage of the word increased by over 17,000 percent. Visibility has less narcissistic uses also. As never before, we can disseminate images or video clips, express our views, put our names to contributions or donations, and publicize our experiences of interactions with the state or any other organizations. This new visibility expands our possibilities for undertaking collective action in terms of how we might try to spread ideas or information and draw in other people. In the strongest form of visibility, we identify ourselves by our names, our faces, and our social media profiles, and with the actions we undertake, as in the Ice Bucket Challenge of the summer of 2014 when people posted videos having ice-cold water poured over themselves to raise money for research into motor neurone disease. This form of visibility has been shown to have a strong effect on people's willingness to participate politically: for example, to vote,[19] to give to charity,[20] or to undertake a sponsored bicycle ride.[21] In other contexts, we might want our actions to be visible but our identity to remain anonymous. In the protests that swept Egypt and Tunisia in 2011, anonymity was crucial to the participation of many, particularly in the early demonstrations, but their visible actions formed a crucial conduit of social information to other people. In Chapter 5, we compare the effects of visibility with social information, looking at how these two kinds of social influence differentially affect people's willingness to contribute to collective goods.

Social media do not provide a homogeneous environment: platforms have particular designs and interfaces that offer (or do not offer) varying amounts of social influence. These various features of interaction on the many commercial social media sites and applications create different kinds of communities and information environments. Some platforms engender the creation of network structures, provide distinct types of social information, allow or do not allow feedback, and offer varying levels of visibility and anonymity. In so doing, they exert varying forms of social influence on their users, making them more or less conducive to political participation. Links across platforms create 'networks of networks',[22] allowing information relating to any one mobilization to travel across platforms, with the potential for the shape of networks on one platform to influence information dissemination and ultimately collective action on another. Many studies of Internet-based activism have focused on individual platforms in isolation.[23]

In contrast, in this book we focus on the effects of social information and visibility as generic influences on participation (particularly in Chapters 4, 5, and 6), which we hope will contribute to the understanding of behaviour on any social media platform that exerts these influences in some form.

As well as creating distinct information environments across alternative social media platforms, social media affect the behaviour of different people in different ways. Some types of people will be more susceptible than others to the social influence exerted by social media, such as being made visible or receiving information about what others are doing. We explore this heterogeneity in susceptibility to social influence in Chapter 6. Classical explorations of political participation have focused on socioeconomic variables as a way of explaining differences in levels of participation,[24] finding, for example that white, higher income individuals from older age groups with higher levels of educational attainment are more likely to be involved in collective action. Although some of these differences remain for some kinds of online participation,[25] widespread use of social media challenges these long-held assumptions, with participation rising among younger groups and the low costs of participation reducing the importance of income levels in determining people's decisions to participate or not. We turn therefore to another source of individual difference—personality—which has been shown in recent political science work to be as important as demographics in shaping political behaviour and attitudes.[26] In Chapter 6, we explore the relationship between personality and susceptibility to social influence, discovering that some personality types are more influenced by social information and visibility.

Differential reactions to social influence could help to explain why some mobilizations succeed and others fail, an idea we explore in Chapter 7. We are inspired by work from the 1970s when the economist Thomas Schelling and the sociologist Mark Granovetter argued that people have different thresholds for joining mobilizations in terms of the number of other participants they require before they themselves will join in.[27] Under this view, people with low thresholds will be willing to join a mobilization at an early stage when there are few signals of viability; people with high thresholds will join only at the later stages when the majority of potential participants have already joined in. These differences will affect the type of collective action that results. Some people with very low thresholds are needed to start a mobilization, which will encourage the followers with slightly higher thresholds, and so on, until the tipping point where most people's thresholds lie is reached and there will be a flood of followers. In an Internet-based environment, people are likely to know how many other people are joining in real time so they can match their joining point to their own threshold. Schelling and Granovetter developed models of how the distribution of thresholds would be critical to the success or failure of mobilizations. But they did not explore what causes individuals to have the threshold that they do. In Chapter 7, we investigate the relationship between personality and threshold, attempting to identify the personality types associated with low thresholds and willingness to start and whose participation is crucial to propel a mobilization towards a tipping point and some kind of success. The well-known idea of the tipping point has been popularized by writers such as Gladwell,[28] but only by examining mobilizations in detail using the kind of direct, empirical evidence afforded by digital systems can we ascertain whether and when such actions will take place.

If the distribution of thresholds is what matters for a mobilization, then leadership in the traditional sense is not so important. What is needed is a number of starters, people with low thresholds for starting and joining a mobilization and who are good at dissemination so that people know that an event or mobilization is happening. Under this model, charismatic leadership is not necessarily required to recruit burgeoning numbers of followers; people willing to carry out micro-acts of participation by disseminating an image, clicking 'like' on an influential photograph or Facebook page, or retweeting a political viewpoint, and who can carry the movement forward to a tipping point. This pattern is summed up by one of the Egyptian activists in the 2011 revolution: '[Mobilizations] of the past have usually had charismatic leaders. . . . But the revolution in Egypt was different. . . . It was like an offline Wikipedia, with everyone anonymously and self-lessly contributing efforts towards a common goal. . . . Ultimately it was the great middle of the population that needed to overcome its fears and believe that change was possible'.[29] Ghonim could be describing a normal distribution of thresholds. For example, in the early days of the Egyptian revolution, nearly half a million people supported the Facebook page We Are All Khaled Said, showing images of a young man brutally killed by Egyptian police. To attain this number would have required people with low thresholds to join at the beginning while those with higher thresholds would have joined later. All played an individually small part in showing the rest of Egypt (particularly the five million Egyptian Facebook users at that time) that the revolution was gaining traction and ultimately in removing Mubarak from power. As Mason put it, 'to stop the revolution he would have had to close down the Khalid Said page, hunt down its members and round up the protest networks'.[30]

UNCERTAINTY AND TURBULENCE IN ONLINE COLLECTIVE ACTION

The onslaught of Internet-based collective action discussed above might give the impression that use of social media is a surefire way for mobilization to succeed. But most online mobilizations fail. In fact, a higher proportion of online than offline mobilizations probably fail due to the very low start-up costs of initiating (say) an online petition or an email campaign or a Facebook group, which means that many non-viable initiatives get started. While those that succeed may reach millions (a petition calling for fair trade attained eighteen million signatures in 2009), 43 percent of petitions posted on the UK government site for three or more months by 1 March 2013 had five or fewer signatures.

Such skewed distributions are reported for many Internet-based human activities.[31] These distributions are generally referred to as fat-tailed. The right tail decays more slowly for large values compared to a normal, bell-shaped distribution, resulting in a thicker or 'fat' tail. In the world of social media above all, a few sources will be extremely successful in attracting links and users, while the rest do very much less well in terms of attracting attention,[32] and this is often described as exhibiting a power law, a specific case of fat-tailed distributions where the distribution takes the form of the quantity, x, raised to some negative power ($x^{-\alpha}$). We observe such a pattern in the petitions data gathered from all petitions submitted to the UK government petition platform between 2010 and 2013, which we discuss in Chapter 3. Figure 1.3 compares the distribution of signatures to petitions with what a normal distribution or bell curve would look like, showing how a few petitions receive a very high number of signatures (far higher than in a normal distribution) while most receive very few (far more than in a normal distribution). The actual petition data exhibit a classic fat-tail distribution, contrasting strongly with the classic bell shape of the normal distribution.

These kinds of distributions have been observed many times, not only in Internet-based settings, but also for some natural phenomena,[33] such as the distribution of time intervals between earthquakes, which have a non-normal distribution. Similar distributions have been identified as characterizing policy change in liberal democracies by the political scientists Frank Baumgartner and Bryan Jones, who have mapped the frequency distributions of changes in the US policy agenda in different policy sectors and found the same non-normal pattern.[34] Baumgartner and Jones argue that such a distribution is evidence of a 'punctuated equilibrium' model of policy change, where policy attention proceeds through long periods of equilibrium or stasis, punctuated by bursts of activity and positive feedback during short periods of rapid change. By identifying a similar pattern for the attention of citizens as evidenced by petition signing behaviour, as we do in Chapter 3, we identify a possible role for online collective action in policy agenda setting. That is, where political mobilizations using social media fail, they do not interrupt the period of stasis, and on the

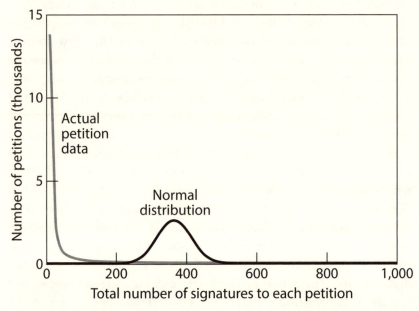

FIGURE 1.3 Distribution of petition signing in the United Kingdom

Note: The line labelled 'actual petition data' shows the actual data for 19,789 petitions to the UK government petitions platform, created between 5 August 2011 and 22 February 2013: comparing the number of petitions (y-axis) with a given number of signatures (x-axis) shows that the data are very skewed with a fat tail. The line labelled 'normal distribution' shows what a normal distribution would look like for the same quantities for a same-sized sample with the same average number of signatures (365 signatures per petition) and a standard deviation 100 times smaller than the one of the actual data (for the sake of diagram clarity).

few occasions where they take off, they initiate or contribute to punctuations. In this way, such mobilizations could inject more turbulence into the policy making process.

Distributions of this kind make it difficult to predict punctuations. Just as it is difficult (but not impossible) to know when and where the next earthquake will happen, it will be difficult to know where the next demonstration or revolution is likely to take off. There are many nascent protest movements across the world; most may never succeed in attaining public prominence, but it will be difficult to predict those that do. If in later chapters we find evidence of thresholds and tipping points as we suggest above, then this unpredictability will be even greater, as tipping points introduce extra instability and volatility. If, as we hypothesize in Chapter 6, personality rather than demographic difference is structuring thresholds, in terms of the way that people respond to social influence on social media, then contemporary collective action may become even more difficult to model and predict. Whereas we may to some extent predict behavioural change based on demographics where we know the distribution of socioeconomic variables within a population, personality is part of the hidden, unchangeable world of individual difference, not routinely collected on censuses or official statistics, as demographics are.

In summary, social media inject turbulence into political life. They facilitate a non-normal distribution of mobilizations, where most fail and a few succeed dramatically, oiled by social information and visibility and propelled forward by individual thresholds and tipping points. In the rest of this book, we investigate the dynamics behind the success and failure of mobilization via social media, and thereby uncover ways that the small number of extreme events might be understood and even predicted.

COULD PEOPLE MOBILIZE TODAY WITHOUT SOCIAL MEDIA?

On 7 January 2015, two Islamist gunmen burst into the Paris offices of the French satirical magazine *Charlie Hebdo*, and killed ten staff and two police officers, claiming provocation by the magazine's publication of cartoons of the prophet Muhammad. Shortly after the attack, the slogan 'Je suis Charlie', a statement of belief in freedom of expression and solidarity with the cartoonists who died, trended on Twitter and quickly spread to other social media around the world, with Facebook users using it to replace their profile pictures. By the evening, hundreds of thousands of people had gathered in the main squares of Paris in solidarity with *Charlie Hebdo*. One photo posted on Twitter bore the caption, 'This morning, none of these people knew they would be here tonight!'. On

11 January, about 2 million people gathered in Paris for a rally of national unity, with 3.7 million joining demonstrations across France. Could this kind of rapid popular response have happened without social media?

In spite of the plausibility of Internet-based social media having brought about the rash of collective action that has characterized the twenty-first century, it is very hard to pose the counterfactual. After all the French Revolution of 1848 and the wave of revolutions that followed across Europe, the student protests and general strike of 1968 in France, and the revolutions that broke authoritarian control in Central and Eastern Europe in 1989 all occurred without these forms of electronic communication. In the case of the Arab Spring, there seems to be a sense of change bubbling up from the bottom rather than being triggered by changes at the top, as occurred in 1989. As one commentator put it, 'there is something in the air that defies historical parallels; something new to do with technology, behaviour and popular culture'.[35] But we cannot prove that the type of mobilization today is due to social media, rather than any of the other factors that have been identified, such as the intensity of domestic or global financial crises in the aftermath of 2008, or the culmination of decades of declining trust in political institutions. What can be done is to investigate the effects of specific forms of social influence exerted by social media on collective action; to explore how different types of people respond to these influences; and thereby to investigate the mechanics of contemporary collective action. If we cannot always pose the counterfactual, we can at least make a case for a plausible set of relationships.[36]

Whether or not the demonstrations in Brazil or Hong Kong or the uprisings of the Arab Spring would have happened without social media, such platforms clearly played an important role in shaping the kind of transition that followed. After the Egyptian and Tunisian revolutions, the first elections were dominated by the Muslim Brotherhood, a long-standing institution in the region that had played only a minor role in the revolutions, but was one of the only organizations capable of acting as a political party straightaway. In post-revolution Egypt, the election of Muslim Brotherhood candidate Mohamed Morsi as president soon evoked widespread dissatisfaction among the protest movement of 2011 as he granted himself unlimited powers to 'protect' the nation and the power to legislate without judicial oversight. As one scholar commentating on the failure of the opposition movement to stand up to President Morsi's restrictive constitutional reforms put it,

> In a matter of days during the uprisings of January 2011, these same activists found their status transformed from protestors, demonstrators and strikers, who were members of loosely structured networks, to that of 'revolutionaries'. . . suddenly confronted with the expectation that they would either capture or renegotiate state power. . . . The activists/revolutionaries, however, had no ready plan, grand or otherwise, for the day after. Despite their fearless efforts to challenge the Mubarak regime and its institutions, they had never intended to replace it by themselves. Their focus was on perfecting tools and tactics to change the nature of traditional politics. Along this journey, they did not develop the kinds of skills, including organizational ones that could one day equip them to match the might of the military establishment or the iron discipline and mass base of the Muslim Brothers, whose organization has been in existence since 1928.[37]

These words illustrate how Internet-based activity has the potential to produce disruptive social and political change without the normal organizational trappings of revolutionary change, such as political leaders in the wings, resistance organizations or institutions such as political parties that would otherwise help to sustain anti-system activities and then can help coordinate bureaucracies once the old regime has gone. The interesting question is not whether mass mobilization of the kind that took place in Egypt could have happened without the Internet and social media, but how the nature of the mobilization shaped the nature of the revolution and its aftermath. After mass demonstrations against Morsi in 2012–13, the military moved in, arrested Morsi, rounded up the Muslim Brotherhood, and established a new administration. By May 2014, the former head of the Egyptian Armed forces, Abdel

Fattah el-Sisi, had been elected as president, presiding over a regime that many consider to be as repressive as that of Hosni Mubarak.

NEW METHODS FOR NEW MOVEMENTS

We use two key research methods to investigate the relationship between social media and collective action in this book. First, as well as being a major site for collective action, social media provide new ways to research it. Every participatory act, however small, carried out on social media leaves a digital imprint. So mobilizations produce digital trails that can be harvested to generate large-scale data, which can be retrieved and analysed with software, text- and data-mining tools, and network analysis.[38] These are so-called big data, a trend in the corporate world that has received a great deal of attention since 2012 from journalists, academic commentators, and entrepreneurs.[39] The much-debated term 'big data' typically refers to real-time, transactional data too large to be manipulated in a desktop computing environment. At the time of writing, the term itself was widely considered to be overhyped and losing currency, but the phenomenon remains an important one for social and political science. These are a new kind of data for social science, real-time transactional data that tell us what people in some population are really doing or have done, as opposed to survey data, the traditional staple of social science, that tell us what people think they did or might do in the future. They are more like the data that characterize the physical and life sciences and offer great potential for understanding human behaviour, offering a new lens on the social world. Some claim that tools based on such data will revolutionize the future of social science: 'Just as the microscope and telescope revolutionized the study of biology and astronomy, socioscopes in living labs will revolutionize the study of human behaviour'.[40]

These data also present new challenges, in terms of the technical skills, multidisciplinary expertise, ethical and legal procedures, and computing resources required to harvest, store, and analyse them.

These challenges are being tackled through the field of data-driven computational social science, which has been 'spearheaded by a few intrepid computer scientists, physicists, and social scientists' and the nascent field of social data science.[41] Collective action research has never before had the possibility of data like these, so we consider this a rich approach for this book. In Chapters 2 and 3 we report a new big dataset of all the petitions created on the UK and US governments' petition platforms over three years as well as data from a range of social media such as Facebook, YouTube, Wikipedia, and Twitter.

Computational social science approaches can give us an understanding of the shape of collective action in terms of the network structure or mobilization curves, for example, but (in contrast to a survey) digitally generated data of this kind do not come with demographics attached. When we look at real-time transactional data relating to mobilizations, we do not know who the participants are in terms of their socioeconomic status or indeed any variables of individual-level difference. Other methods are required to study in detail individual behaviour and motivations and the effect of different kinds of application and information environment. So the second method we use to explore the mechanics of collective action is experimentation. In the social sciences, an experiment occurs when the researcher randomly allocates subjects to treatment and control conditions in a randomized controlled trial, the common method in medicine and health evaluations. They are carried out either in laboratory conditions, where there is high degree of control over the environment in which experiments take place and with subjects who are recruited for the research and incentivized via payments,[42] or in the field, where some treatment is applied in a real social setting and many more people can participate. More recently, the Internet itself has been used for experiments, blurring the distinction between laboratory and field, for example where network analysts use experiments to understand the spread of collective activity through online social networks.[43]

Experiments can provide unbiased estimates of how different kinds of information affect participation by randomly varying the information provided to subjects and observing the effect on their behaviour. Any differences—both observed and unobserved—between a treatment and control group have been removed by randomization meaning that any difference in outcome between the treated and control groups can only be attributed to the intervention. Provided experiments have been implemented without threats to internal validity, they can offer a causal inference of the effect of one variable on another. Partly for these reasons, experimentation is in fashion in the social sciences, and political science is no exception.[44]

The other big development in experimental methods is the use of natural experiments, where observational differences in the real world sometimes can be treated 'as if random'.[45] A regression discontinuity (RD) design can be implemented to appraise the impact of such random differences on the outcome of interest. An RD design uses cut-off points or other random breaks in the generation of outcomes, such as eligibility criteria or boundaries, with the assumption that there is a random distribution of observations around these points that can be analysed as if they are in a randomized experiment. Natural experiments can be useful when it is very hard to randomize treatments and also have a special place for the Internet where many of the designs of platforms vary how citizens see information as if by chance. There are also so-called quasi-experiments, where the differences over time or place are not as if random but can be analysed like experiments.[46] Examples include interrupted time series where breaks in programme inputs can be evaluated using a statistical model of their change over time in comparison to other groups.

We use four experiments in this book. In Chapter 3, we take advantage of a change in the UK government's petition platform to include information about which petitions are most popular. Having collected data before and after the change, we are able to make some direct claims about the effect of the change in a quasi-experimental design, and we are able to analyse the point at which subjects can see the signatures of others in a natural experiment using a RD design. In Chapter 4, we report on a quasi-field experiment, conducted remotely via a custom-built interface that tests the influence of varying levels of social information on people's willingness to take part in collective action, and discuss a field experiment carried out with mySociety, a social enterprise that offers web support for those who wish to contact their political representatives. In Chapters 5, 6, and 7 we use data from a large-scale laboratory experiment where we simulate a social media environment to test the relative influence of social information and visibility, investigate differences according to personality, and appraise evidence of different thresholds as discussed above.

CLASSIC WORKS OF COLLECTIVE ACTION

In this book, we set out our theories of Internet-based mobilization and then examine and test different features of online environments on social media to uncover the mechanics of contemporary collective action. Are we proposing a new theory of collective action? The answer is no or largely no. This book is inspired by the classic books in social science, in particular Mancur Olson's *The Logic of Collective Action* (1965) and Russell Hardin's *Collective Action* (1982).[47] We broadly agree with the existing collective action framework developed by Olson in 1965 and his followers since that time. The fact that people act collectively on social media in no way changes the assumptions of public choice models, for example, that individuals are rational actors who maximize their utility by comparing the costs and benefits of any action. But social media do change the costs and benefits for individuals to participate politically.

We use a rational choice framework to reanalyse the decisions people make in these new conditions. In common with other scholars, such as Lupia and Sin, Bimber et al., and Bennett and Segerberg, we argue that important parts of the expected benefits and costs of collective action need to be reexamined and reworked for online contexts.[48] Our theoretical model focuses on the cost-benefit equation for individual people as they consider whether or not to undertake a participatory act aimed at provision of public goods. For example, one of the experiments reported here shows that visible social information about the behaviour of others increases the efficiency of a mobilization and so reduces the aggregate costs of participation. Likewise, visibility, by shaming certain types of individuals to contribute to the public good mobilization, decreases the monitoring costs that Olson considered important, increasing the viability of large groups. Effective use of social influence of this kind can reduce the need for leaders to apply selective incentives (which can be expensive) and reduce the need for well-resourced leaders to apply them.

Diverting from this school of thought, however, we think that the work of Olson can be applied to the problem with a more subtle and varied conception of individual psychology in order to understand how the effect of social influence in the form of social information and visibility might be based on different personality types, which is explored in Chapter 6. As we investigate in Chapter 7, personality may be the clue to someone's threshold, allowing us to gain understanding of how thresholds are distributed in a population. Drawing on work both from within and outside of political science, we meld a rational choice Olsonian model with a political psychological model emphasizing personality and context.[49]

MODERN-DAY COLLECTIVE ACTION CLASSICS

There are a number of works relevant to the relationship between collective action and social media that have already started to stand the test of time as modern-day classics, some from outside political science. Information technology in general and, more recently, the Internet in particular have long been identified as tools that have the potential to transform collective action and radically empower citizens in relation to the state or corporations. But it was in the early 2000s when some political scientists turned their attention to the Internet, reevaluating Olson's theories of collective action in the light of recent developments. Bimber, and Lupia and Sin reconsidered the logic of participation in the light of widespread use of the Internet, arguing that it affects opportunities and incentives that are relevant to collective action, advantaging some collective endeavours and endangering others.[50] These were surprising findings because the overwhelming conclusion of most of those who followed was that Internet-based technologies mainly reinforced earlier participation patterns, with those that had habitually participated participating more, and inequalities in participation becoming greater.[51] Later research, however, has started to evidence the 'new mobilization' thesis, showing that the Internet may be facilitating the mobilization of new individuals and groups of individuals who have traditionally not participated.[52]

The phenomenon of online mobilization, participation, and protest has received most attention from scholars operating outside political science. The law professor Yochai Benkler's *The Wealth of Networks* was a groundbreaking intellectual paean to the potential of peer production, which inspired a whole generation of scholarship on the Internet.[53] His book articulated for the first time how Internet-based platforms were allowing individuals to produce content, collaborate, and add value in a whole range of contexts, leading to an empowerment of citizens with potentially transformative effects for both the economy and society. Shirky's *Here Comes Everybody* was also a powerful impetus to the idea that in online contexts people could 'organize without organizations', although the focus of his book is on networks, groups, and what he calls 'pseudo-organizations', rather than the individual decision-making processes we deal with here, and is based on a mixture of individual anecdotes and economic theory, rather than empirical evidence or research.[54]

Some recent works do focus explicitly on collective action online. For example, Chadwick's *Internet Politics: States, Citizens, and New Communication Technologies* is a highly useful review of Internet-based political activity in general, with a chapter on 'Interest Groups and Social Movements' reviewing the literature at the time on collective action, but not providing the research-based analysis that this book puts forward, nor does it really employ the collective action approach that we use.[55] Chadwick's more recent work, *The Hybrid Media System: Politics and Power*, examines what he terms the political information cycle, exploring US election campaigning and the norms of operation for political organization, mobilization, and influencing the news agenda followed by organizational phenomena such as WikiLeaks.[56]

A prescient and seminal work investigating the relationship between information technology and politics was Bimber's *Information and American Democracy*, which introduced the idea of postbureaucratic pluralism as an organizational response to information abundance, where the organization of collective action requires fewer resources and informal association becomes more important, a discussion we engage with in Chapter 8.[57] Bimber's more recent work, *Collective Action in Organizations*, shares with ours the assumption that digital media are a vital and changing element of the context in which individuals decide to participate in collective action, but takes a different unit of analysis.[58] Although that book discusses extensively the phenomenon of organizing without organizations, the focus is to 'bring the relevance of formal organization back into contemporary collective action' (as its title suggests), arguing that digital media enable formal organizations to offer much broader opportunities for people to establish their own participatory styles.

Another programme of work with high relevance to ours is that of Lance Bennett, culminating in his 2013 book (with Segerberg), *The Logic of Connective Action: Digital Media and the Personalization of Contentious Politics*, and summarized in earlier articles.[59] In his most recent work, Bennett focuses on the Occupy movement and the extent to which it has developed without formal organizations at its core, but rather with self-organized networks of individuals with digital media platforms as organizing agents. The work reports valuable empirical qualitative research into why movements such as Occupy seem to succeed in gaining the critical mass of support to enable them to grow and sustain themselves over significant periods of time. However, in common with Bimber et al. and much other research in this burgeoning field, it focuses on successful mobilizations, rather than looking at the generic phenomenon of Internet-based mobilizations.[60] It cannot, therefore, and does not try to identify what is distinctive about those that succeed in contrast to the vast majority that fail as we do here.

Some of the work we draw on comes from even further afield; engineering, computer science and physics. From the earliest days of the Internet, physicists and engineers turned their attention to its network structure and how information diffuses and spreads in Internet-based networks, and some of these scholars have played a role in developing the field of computational social science, as noted above. The physicist turned sociologist Duncan J. Watts has played a key role in developing the 'science of networks'[61] as a way of understanding the role that network structure plays in determining system behaviour. In *Six Degrees* he replicated the earlier work of Stanley Milgram in order to demonstrate that Internet-based communication represents a 'small world network', characterized by high local clustering and short global separation, where each individual participant is on average only 'six degrees' or less away from every other, as in Milgram's analysis of offline communication networks.[62] Watts and other researchers in the growing field of computational social science have continued to explore patterns of information and behaviour diffusion and spread across Internet-based networks.[63] This work is drawn upon here, as is the extensive work on network diffusion carried out by James Fowler and his research team.[64]

WHAT THIS BOOK IS NOT ABOUT

This is a book about individual people and the influences that Internet-based information environments exert on them, and how such influences affect their behaviour. It is not a book about organizations, although, of course, people work within constraints set by organizations, like a petition site for example, and these constraints need to be taken into account.

This book is not arguing that the political system has been completely reinvented as a result of the Internet and social media. We are not arguing, for example, that institutions, organizations, or hierarchies are disappearing just because people use social media as that would not be a credible argument. They remain important influences on individual behaviour, but in the analysis presented here we have not analysed these influences.

This is not a book about people who do not use the Internet. We start from the assumption that most contemporary collective action has an online element and some action takes place entirely online. Most forms of collective action and political participation are moving in this direction. According to the World Bank (as shown in Figure 1.1), by 2014 Internet use had reached over three-quarters of the population in North America and Europe, significant proportions of East Asia and the Pacific, Latin America and the Caribbean, and the Middle East and North Africa, and nearly 20 percent of sub-Saharan Africa. Obviously, large portions of these populations still do not have access to the possibilities for collective action that we analyse here, although it could be argued that many of these are exposed to Internet influences, through friends, family, colleagues, traditional media sources, and street-based demonstration and protest.[65] But having identified social media use as an important element of contemporary collective action and noting that Internet penetration continues to grow rapidly (particularly in Africa and Asia), we consider our analysis of the dynamics of Internet-based political behaviour that can be applied to the 34 percent of the world's population that do use the Internet as a representative phenomenon, and one that will be a valuable pointer to future political behaviour.

This book does not aim to explore normative political theory about what kind of democratic interaction helps us lead the good life or make moral choices. We are interested in the theories and models of empirical political science. Neither do we look at deliberation or discourse here. The Internet in general and social media in particular have been much touted as venues for democratic expression, the new public sphere to replace Habermasian coffeehouses.[66] We do not examine these claims here, but note that the transformative potential of the Internet has yet to be demonstrated in these studies.[67] Implicitly, the approach we offer is an alternative to deliberation: rather than social media changing beliefs and values, they can harness existing values and behaviour, and coordinate them more efficiently to achieve collective goals. Social media revive the debate about the pluralist potential of democratic and public institutions in a way in which they can coordinate a large number of fixed preferences and give weight to more intensely held preferences. Of course this could be complementary with the encouragement of a more deliberative process, but it could more plausibly operate independently.

We do not look a great deal at the end point of collective action, that is, the actions of the state and policy change. Neither do we look at the interactions between citizens and the state, nor at the Internet-based activities of government itself, in terms of digital or 'e-'government. That is another subject, and one upon which one of the authors has already written extensively.[68] We do, however, consider possible governmental responses to new forms of collective action in the final chapter.

WHAT THIS BOOK *IS* ABOUT

Our aim is to analyse the effect that information provided by or presented to other people has on any one individual, and how cumulative tiny acts of political participation—'micro-donations' of money, time, and effort—scale up to form (or do not form) a mobilization. These are very small amounts of time, effort, or money contributed by individuals, which are insignificant on their own but when added together across hundreds of thousands of people make up very large sums. With these resources, the many small acts that citizens perform from day to day have large consequences when added together. Moreover, the theory of collective action tells us that the total of these actions is more than the sum of these parts, because of the tipping points and dynamic processes we discuss. We are particularly interested in the impact of social information and visibility and how these forms of social influence encourage feedback between potential participants and generate the impulse to undertake collective action. The impact of these influences is differential, depending on the personality and dispositions among individuals, which creates the possibility of leadership and activates people who can overcome the high start-up costs of engaging politically.

We are interested in developing a new understanding of the workings of political systems, and where the Internet and social media render existing institutions unfit for purpose. Our key aim is to develop a model of contemporary collective action appropriate for such turbulent times. We draw together the experimental and big data evidence from the following chapters, providing the reader with a methodological toolkit for understanding collective action in the twenty-first century.

We want to know what model of democracy appears to be emerging in the era of online collective action. Of all the *isms* of normative political theory, we argue in Chapter 8 that pluralism emerges as the model of democracy with most to gain from the political trends and patterns we have observed in this book. But this is not the ordered, organized vision of the early pluralists such as Robert Dahl, based on interest groups as the basic building block of society. Rather it is a chaotic, turbulent pluralism, characterized by collectives of individuals contributing micro-donations of resources, the majority of which fail but a minority of which succeed in securing political change. As in the past it may be a minority that trigger or drive forward successful revolutions or mobilizations for policy change, but the process from expression and dissemination of dissatisfaction and dissent to rebellion, revolt, or action on the streets is made quicker and more immediate because of real-time feedback among a huge majority of followers. This phenomenon poses challenges to governments in terms of forming a legitimate response. But it also offers possibilities in terms of using the data that social media provide—the kind of big data that we use in this book—to understand the needs, preferences, and behaviour of citizens and build them into policy making.

Understanding the dynamics of collective action in chaotic pluralism and the ways in which states can respond will be a vital task of political science in the future. We believe that the current period provides a unique time to understand the turbulence of contemporary politics, as we transition from a world dominated by paper, broadcast media, and face-to-face communications to a world where the Internet is the ubiquitous medium through which communication and coordination take place. This transitional period, the first two decades of the twenty-first century, when we can directly observe and reflect upon changes in political practice, provides the best chance of understanding the dynamics of the new political world.

CHAPTER 2
TINY ACTS OF POLITICAL PARTICIPATION

In this chapter we examine the ever closer relationship among collective action, the Internet, and social media. We aim to understand the way in which people participate politically using social media. Our argument is that social media are a permanent feature of the 'political weather'—the context within which political events take place. Increasingly every action and interaction has the possibility of involving very large numbers of citizens often acting independently from actors in traditional political or media institutions.

We identify two main periods of change in which digital technologies have influenced the way that people spend their daily lives and decide whether or not to participate in political activities. During the period when use of the Internet started to become widespread, from the end of the twentieth century to around 2005, it was collective action organizations (such as interest groups) that seemed to gain most from Internet-based political communication and interaction. The second period came with the widespread adoption of social media, which offered new ways in which individuals could generate content and participate politically without going through organizations. Citizens can now easily obtain political information, communicate with their peers, and disseminate views, issues, images, and information without belonging to anything.

Social media have extended the range of activities that are open to people wishing to participate politically so that even those without a strong interest in politics may find themselves contributing micro-donations of time and effort to political causes. These tiny political acts can scale up to large-scale mobilizations around collective goods. When people decide whether or not to undertake such acts, they are exposed through social media to new or different forms of social influence. We identify the key features of this changed information environment that are most likely to influence people's collective behaviour in the years to come.

BEFORE SOCIAL MEDIA: POLITICS AS USUAL

From the beginning of the century, the Internet has been identified as a potentially important influence on collective action. As we showed in Chapter 1, a number of scholars have considered how widespread use of the Internet affects political participation,[1] arguing that it changes the opportunities and incentives that are relevant to collective action, advantaging some collective endeavours and endangering others.[2]

These works demonstrate how the main influence of the Internet on collective action in those early days was mediated by organized interest groups. Internet-mediated interaction reduces the costs of large-scale coordination and organization so that costs remain largely constant for many sizes of group, with potential benefits for all kinds of associations large or small. Internet technologies were adopted by large, established interest groups (international charities, for example, such as Oxfam or the Red Cross) both for their own internal operations and in their interactions with members or supporters. Just as earlier media technologies such as radio and television were used more effectively by those groups large enough to be able to bear the costs,[3] the size of these established organizations meant that they were able to employ specialist information technology staff, invest in expensive information systems, and make the most of emerging Internet technologies to extend their political influence,[4] for example by producing professional-looking websites that were optimized for search engines and came near the top of search results.

Small interest groups (such as locally based community groups or clubs) also had much to gain from the use of Internet technologies, particularly in terms of increasing their visibility. Researchers specializing in political parties observed that smaller, newer political parties find it easier to exploit Internet technologies, particularly where they have little access to mainstream media (as in the United Kingdom).[5] John and Margetts found that an extremist party like the British National Party was adept at using the Internet to connect to members and attract supporters.[6] In the United States, Bimber's 2003 study showed that the infrastructure of information technology could for small organizations with few resources largely substitute for money and staff, 'permitting modestly or poorly endowed groups to behave as if they had greater resources'. For example, the Million Mom March, a rally against gun control held in Washington DC, in 2000, which was allegedly attended by about 750,000 people and matched by smaller rallies across the United States, used technology to build a viable network-based organization with very little funding.[7] However in those early days of Internet use, with burgeoning numbers of new users with unsophisticated search skills, it could be hard for small, new groups or parties to keep pace with larger ones, especially in terms of being able to develop professional websites, swiftly update site content and design, maintain search engine rankings, or provide functionality such as online donation facilities.[8] Of course, small, new interest groups could publicize issues, disseminate information, and coordinate activities across a far larger geographical range (including across national boundaries) than ever before, but in a zero-sum competition for political attention they struggled to compete against the large, well-established interest groups.

Internet-based interaction also brought new types of organization into the interest group ecology, organizations that would not have been viable without the Internet. In the United States in the early 2000s, a 'new generation of political advocacy groups'[9] entered the political area, characterized by low-cost, high-speed virtual mobilization and organization. One of the first was MoveOn, an Internet-based advocacy group that quickly grew in terms of members (five million by 2010), but maintained only thirty-eight staff members and no office space.[10] Established advocacy groups in the United States found it difficult to adopt Internet-based technologies to mimic the success of innovative groups like MoveOn, but a number of global advocacy groups emerged at this time, based entirely on Internet-based platforms, helped by publicly available code, and in some cases, following the perceived success of MoveOn.org.[11] Avaaz, for example, started as an international civic organization promoting activism (such as online campaigns and petitions to world leaders) on a number of issues, particularly climate change and human rights, with a stated mission to 'ensure that the views and values of the world's people inform global decision making' (Avaaz.org), claiming more than forty million members by 2014, representing every country in the world. The online NGO Kiva (founded in 2005) was the 'world's first person-to-person micro-lending website', offering potential entrepreneurs in developing countries the chance to enter their profile on the site. Potential donors visit the site, browse profiles, and choose someone to make a loan to; in so doing, they can receive email journal updates and track repayments. By 2008, Kiva's 270,000 lenders, who hand over money in $25 increments, had funded 40,000 borrowers in forty countries, totalling $27 million in funding.[12] Such a coordination task, involving the matching of individual lenders and borrowers, is hard to imagine offline without spiralling transaction costs.

Another set of Internet-based collectives that exist mostly or entirely online emerging earlier had a more radical and anarchistic nature, growing out of the controversial and often misunderstood 'hacktivist' movement. The term 'hacktivism' mixes 'hack' (the act of penetrating and altering the computer-based applications of other organizations) and 'activism' and was first used in the 1990s by the cDc, 'Cult of the Dead Cow', a collective that campaigned for access to information as a basic human right. While the term 'hack' is now often linked to illicit computer-based activity, as it originated in hacking circles a hack is more widely defined as the use of technology in 'an original, unorthodox and inventive way',[13] and hacktivism is based on the idea of using technology to perform acts of protest and civil disobedience in online settings: 'activism gone electronic' aimed at enacting positive social change.[14] The most famous hacktivist group from this early period of the Internet was probably the Electrohippies Collective, which mounted denial of service attacks (where hackers bombard a target machine with huge numbers of requests in a short space of time, overloading its capacity to the extent that other users cannot access the machine) as part of anti-globalization protests against world trade talks in Seattle in 1999 and in Doha in 2001.

Aligned to but extending beyond the hacktivist movement was a new strand of activist campaigning for new types of public or commons goods based on the Internet itself. Advocates of 'cyberlibertarianism' followed the US poet and lyricist John Perry Barlow in proclaiming the Internet (or 'cyberspace') as a new 'electronic frontier' requiring its own 'Declaration of Independence': 'imagine a continent so vast that it may have no end to its dimensions, imagine a new world with more resources than all our future greed might exhaust, more opportunities than there will ever be, entrepreneurs enough to exploit, and a peculiar kind of real estate that expands with development'.[15] Ever since a stream of activism has bubbled away around issues relating to the utopian or dystopian future offered by the Internet, including freedom of expression, net neutrality, freedom from copyright restrictions, and resistance to Internet censorship.

The early days of Internet-mediated interaction brought potential advantages for both large and small interest groups and facilitated the emergence of a range of new groups based on organizational innovations. In this way, the Internet changed the ecology of interest groups, with technological expertise and innovation taking on new importance in shaping a group's fate. The Internet extended the range of interest groups with which citizens could engage, and set up a fierce competition for citizens' attention. But most individual Internet users experienced online political participation and action as a fairly one-sided affair until the mid-2000s. They could search for political information (largely provided by political institutions and organizations), join political groups, and donate money to charities or groups; yet the ability to share information with their peers or to know what other people were doing politically in a way that was unmediated by an organization was not widespread. They could communicate with each other, but largely through email, which does not lend itself to widespread dissemination and relies on knowing an email address or belonging to an email group or list. In this context, it is easy to see why so much academic work at that time focused on the theme of 'politics-as-usual',[16] arguing that the Internet would intensify the participation only of people who are already involved in politics with individuals doing (or not doing) online what they used to do (or not do) offline.[17] As a result of this intensification of political action, inequalities in democratic participation would become greater. These scholars argued that although more fluid types of organizational membership had emerged, which allowed some groups to mobilize individuals and to raise money without suffering from the classic Olsonian free-rider problems of too-large groups, in general the types of individuals who joined them came from the same socioeconomic groups as those who had traditionally participated politically.[18]

'HERE COMES EVERYBODY'— THE RISE OF SOCIAL MEDIA

From the end of the 1990s arrived a raft of Internet-based innovations that really offered a different way of experiencing the Internet and challenged the claim that the Internet meant politics as usual. These innovations allowed ordinary users of the Internet to generate content themselves, instead of merely accessing available information provided by the professionally maintained websites of organizations. Although they started to emerge from 1998, it was not until the middle of the following decade that usage of these applications, known by this time collectively as 'Web 2.0', reached critical mass and the implications for collective action became apparent. This development started with weblog or blog hosting services (Open Diary, LiveJournal, Blogger): websites that were easy for non-technical individuals to set up and update, for example to put forward an opinion, start a discussion, or record a diary. By allowing ordinary users to easily generate content online, blogs opened up new possibilities for individuals with political or collective aims to publish and disseminate information and to interact with interested parties, through blog-based discussion and comment that was indexed and searchable. In the early days of blogs, research showed that the percentage of Internet users actually using blogs for sharing information and opinions was small, that the percentage writing them was even smaller, and that the majority of Americans did not even know what a blog was.[19] Increasingly, as predicted by Shirky, a small number of large blogs received the overwhelming majority of readership, attention, and hyperlinks from other Internet sources, in a power-law-like way,[20] and the political blogosphere in particular became populated by journalists crossing over from the mainstream media, with politicians joining in later. However, for the first time blogs offered ordinary people—or at least a self-selecting group of them—the opportunity to disseminate political information and comment in the same way as traditional media sources and at least have a chance of reaching huge numbers of people in what Shirky called the mass amateurization of journalism.[21] Blogs remain particularly popular in Russia, where the blogging platform LiveJournal (which incorporates some features from other social networking platforms, such as friends and newsfeeds) played an important role in the protests after parliamentary and presidential elections in 2011.[22]

As the political blogosphere grew and became integrated into political life, another Internet-based development brought a new approach to the promulgation of political information and knowledge. In 2001 Wikipedia, a web-based free content encyclopaedia, written collaboratively by largely anonymous Internet volunteers and owned by the Wikimedia Corporation, a not-for-profit organization, was established. By 2014 Wikipedia had nearly half a billion unique visitors monthly, making it one of the top ten (behind Facebook, Google, and YouTube) most visited sites in the world with about a hundred thousand active contributors in 287 languages working on over thirty-two million articles.[23] Wikipedia is important in collective action terms for a number of reasons. For its time it was a new kind of public good, collectively produced, and the most studied and cited example of the potential for online crowdsourcing and peer production.[24] If those who contribute share Wikipedia's stated aim to 'empower and engage people around the world to collect and develop educational content under a free license or in the public domain', then their contributions may be understood as collective action. Indeed the self-selected 'Wikipedia community', who meet at an annual Wikimania event and campaign for the continuation of the world's first 'free encyclopaedia that anyone can edit', also join other campaigns for free information goods, as in 2011 when the Italian-language Wikipedia community became the first to black out the site for three days in protest at the DDL intercettazioni (wiretapping bill). The English-language Wikipedia site supported a campaign against legislation in the United States that would have allowed the government to require Internet service providers to block websites in 2012 by blacking out the entire site for twenty-four hours, displaying only a message of protest and the words '*Imagine a world without free knowledge*'. Most contributors are acting to provide a collective good even if they get some private benefit from submitting the content, with only a few providing information purely for private benefit. Benkler extolled enthusiastically the virtues of peer production of public goods, based on the willingness of large numbers of people to contribute time and resources without either material incentives or organizational hierarchy.[25]

From 2002 a host of social networking sites appeared that facilitated the building of social networks or social relations between
people through the maintenance of a personal profile and a means
of communicating and disseminating information. Friendster, a
site that allowed users to contact other members and to share content and media output, was set up in 2002. It was the first social
networking site to acquire over a million users. It was closely followed by Cyworld in South Korea the same year, MySpace in 2003,
and a burgeoning range of other platforms, including Facebook,
Google's Orkut, which became very popular in India and Brazil,
and Mixi in Japan. Tuenti, in Spain, appeared in 2006. LinkedIn, a
social networking site geared for people in professional occupa-
tions, was launched in 2003 and reported three hundred million
users in more than two hundred countries by 2014, around one-
third in the United States. It ranks thirteenth in the Alexa Internet
list of hundred most popular websites. In addition, many sites that
sell goods and services, such as Amazon, eBay, and Alibaba (the
leading Chinese marketplace), and travel sites such as TripAdvisor,
increasingly incorporated an interactive feedback component where
individuals post and read comments and rank the performance and
trustworthiness of sellers.

Other social media developments include photo- and video-
sharing sites, in particular the photo-sharing site Flickr from 2004
and from 2005 the video-sharing site YouTube, which allows individuals to upload, share, and watch videos. By 2012, YouTube
was the third most visited website on the Internet, behind Google
and Facebook (Alexa). The site claims to receive more than one
billion unique users each month, with one hundred hours of video
uploaded every minute.[26] Users can set up their own channels, and
the most popular 'YouTubers' have many millions of subscribers
and sponsorship deals with advertisers, such as PewDiePie, whose
channel features jokes, profanity, and commentary on video games,
with thirty-five million subscribers by 2015 after two years at
the top of the list of most subscribed channels.[27] YouTube took
off politically during the 2008 US presidential election campaign

(branded the first 'YouTube election'), particularly thanks to Barak Obama, whose own official channel at BarackObama.com received over 250 million views by 2014 and for whom a host of videos were uploaded by external supporters (such as the notorious Obama Girl videos, which with over 120 million views were described as one of the top ten Internet memes of all time by *Newsweek*). As a place where videos may be easily uploaded and shared, YouTube has played an important role in all kinds of political events, the most grotesque of which were the beheadings of Western journalists by the radical terrorist group known as Islamic State in 2014, although within hours YouTube had removed the video and deleted the account that had posted it.

Figure 2.1 gives an indication of the increasingly large numbers involved and the speed at which topics gain attention on YouTube. In the 2009 Iranian election protests, only four years after YouTube was launched, Nedā Āghā-Soltān, who was shot dead on 20 June 2009, became the public face of the protests when videos of her death were uploaded, reaching nearly a million views in a few days. A video of US President Barak Obama unknowingly singing 'Call Me Maybe', in a 'mash up' that interpolates sections from his speeches into a popular song, reached forty million views in the summer of 2011. Obama's contest with Mitt Romney in the YouTube comic series Epic Rap Battles of History, which pits famous figures against each other in mock rap battles, was watched by over ten million viewers within a few days, reaching over a hundred million by February 2015. Eric Garner, who died on 17 July 2014 in Staten Island, New York, after a police officer put him in a chokehold, was featured in a video, titled 'I Can't Breathe' (his last words), which reached nearly 300,000 views in the first days after his death and 900,000 after another burst of protest activity when the police officer who caused his death was indicted in December. A glance at Figure 2.1 shows that cumulative views of these videos show a similar pattern, with extremely rapid growth in the first days or even hours of uploading, a pattern of growth we investigate in detail in Chapter 3.

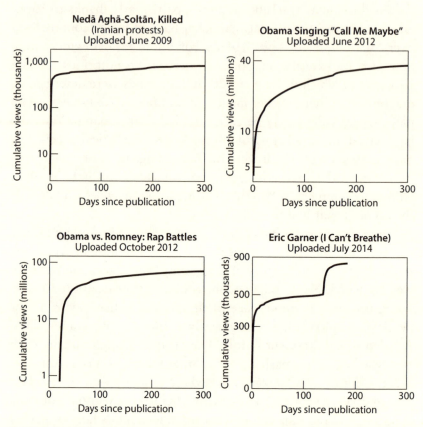

FIGURE 2.1 Cumulative number of views in the first three hundred days from upload for four YouTube videos

By 2008, Facebook had emerged as the leading social networking site, with 600 million people using it each month, rising to 1.35 billion by the end of 2014 (www.statista.com), having largely replaced regional platforms like Cyworld, Mixi, and Orkut. From 2010, Pinterest, Tumblr, and Google+ emerged to challenge Facebook, although Google+, even with 549 million users by 2013, has struggled to battle this kind of critical mass. These applications have been joined by newer variants such as Vine, WeChat, Snapchat, and Line. Instagram had gained 300 million monthly active users by 2014, only two years after launching. The photo messaging application Snapchat also gained huge popularity among young people from 2012, partly perhaps due to its promise to delete all data after transmission, with 700 million photos and videos a day being sent by May 2014. These sites make it possible to connect people who share interests across political, economic, and geographical borders, and as such even in countries with lower rates of Internet penetration, social networking sites have become a popular arena for political activity. Facebook in particular was credited by the media with a prominent role in the Egyptian revolution of 2011, with Egypt ranked twenty-first globally in Facebook usage with twelve million subscribed users of the site by 2012.[28] A large-scale survey of ten thousand respondents across Arab nations in 2012 showed Facebook as the third most popular news source, behind the Arab television networks Al Jazeera and Al Arabiya.[29]

Twitter, since its founding in 2006, has proved itself an important venue for political activity in recent years. The micro-blogging site allows its users to post a comment of 140 characters to their followers, who may (or may not) retweet it to their own followers. Twitter ranks in the top ten most popular sites,[30] and by 2014 there were 284 million active users.[31] Like other Internet platforms the number of followers each user has is highly skewed. While the most popular users are music or movie celebrities (notably Justin Bieber and Lady Gaga, with 58 million and 43 million followers, respectively, in December 2014), Barack Obama far surpassed other politicians in having 51 million followers by the same time, and new entrants to the political scene rapidly amassed a following, such the UK comedian turned political activist and campaigner Russell Brand, with 9 million followers by 2014. Twitter was credited with a particularly prominent role in protests against allegedly rigged elections in Iran in 2009 and the Tunisian revolution of 2011, and with the buildup of social capital more generally.[32]

The success of Twitter's micro-blogging format has been replicated in other countries, such as by Sina Weibo, launched in China in 2009, which now has a similar market penetration, in use by well over 30 percent of Chinese Internet users, with 368 million users and 100 million messages every day. But Sina Weibo imposes rigorous self-censorship at the behest of the Chinese government, and statements on politically sensitive topics containing black-listed keywords or links, which might have potential for generating collective political activity,[33] are prevented from being posted or quickly removed. Twitter works well with political action as it is easy to gain (and identify) followers and the communications are quick and easy, due in part to the character limit (and the ability for links to other content to be shortened and included) and also the ability for tweets to be published from mobile phones. Campaigns can send out short messages, for example coordinating where to meet or whom to email, but can also send longer reports to followers by linking to videos, images, and longer texts. Of course, our focus here is collective action in pursuit of public goods, which may be perceived as positive, but some forms of collective action can be negative, for example as happened in the riots in England in August 2011 when mobile messaging programmes and social media were used to communicate between rioters and to avoid the much slower and less tech-savvy police. But showing the other side of the collective action story, social media were used to organize a spontaneous cleanup straight after the riots (#cleanup). All the above are rapidly growing spaces where people can easily generate their own content and share it with friends, acquaintances, friends of friends, and strangers, bringing the facility to disseminate information, images, opinion, and comments into the mainstream, rather than being the property of a specialist elite as in the early days of the Internet.

Large proportions of the populations of countries with high levels of Internet penetration are using social media. In the United States, 75 percent of the population had at least one social media profile in 2014 and nearly a third of adults over sixty-five use Facebook. Similarly, 76 percent of all UK citizens used social networking sites, 72 percent of Mexicans, 66 percent of Japanese, around half of Russians and Brazilians, and a quarter of people in countries in the Middle East.[34] Among young people, these figures are even higher, with over 90 percent of UK, Spanish, and Italian Internet users between eighteen and twenty-nine using social networking sites and 89 percent of US Internet users in this age range.[35] Overall, estimates suggest that there were 1.8 billion users of online social networks by 2014, predicted to rise to 2.4 billion by 2018 (www .statista.com). Not only is a large portion of citizens using social media, but they are spending increasing proportions of their time there. In 2015, in the United Kingdom social media users spend on average 2.2 hours a day on social media, while in the United States this figure is 2.7 hours and in both Brazil and Mexico an astonishing 3.8 hours.[36]

All these social media platforms started to be used much more heavily from the mid-2000s as mobile phones increasingly provided access to the Internet and native smartphone apps made them even more readily accessible. At this point, social media became available to populations who did not have regular access to Internet-connected computers. Mobile phone subscriptions in the Arab world, for example, nearly matched the region's population by the end of 2011, at 346 million,[37] and increasingly the majority of these were Internet-enabled with access to the whole gamut of social media. Nearly half of all mobile users in the United Kingdom (with a very high penetration of mobiles) use social media applications on their phone. A report into 'non-use of the Internet' in 2012 revealed that many of those who claimed not to use the Internet in UK surveys of Internet use actually did use Facebook and other social media applications, but did not recognize this as Internet use,[38] meaning that many Internet usage figures underestimate actual levels.

One of the leading commentators on the Internet and social movements, Clay Shirky, encapsulated the ways in which social media had brought citizens into political organization with the title of his book *Here Comes Everybody*.[39] He emphasized the new capacity to 'organize without organizations', highlighting the role of technological networks in individual sharing, discussion, collaboration, and ultimately collective action, although at the time empirical evidence for the development was sparse and even Shirky admitted that this kind of collective action step was 'mainly in the future'.

THE DEATH OF MEMBERSHIP AND
THE RISE OF THE INDIVIDUAL

Social media focus on individuals, rather than organizations. They allow individuals to expand and shape their own social networks and to tailor the information environment in which people operate, in terms of the information they are exposed to on a daily basis. Social media allow Internet users to personalize their own experience online and thereby reinforce personalization of digital activity: 'whether through texts, tweets, social network sharing or posting YouTube mashups, the communication process itself often involves further personalization through the spreading of digital connections among friends or trusted others'.[40] By choosing which social media to use and which users to follow or friend, people create their own distinctive information environment and shape the social signals to which they are exposed on a daily basis, which influences any decisions they make as to whether or when to participate politically.

Most importantly, the decision about whether to undertake a tiny act of participation is much less lumpy than the decision whether to join an interest group or political party. The social media age then has advantaged individuals over organizations in terms of reducing the costs of participation. For organizations, the costs of co-ordination have dropped massively. However, there is also new competition for coordination, with the social media platforms themselves. Individuals who wish to raise an issue or participate in a campaign or debate can easily do so without belonging to anything, or even coming into contact with a political organization. Even if they do, the notion of 'belonging' to contemporary interest groups is a far looser concept than traditional membership, as discussed below. And on the Internet, where 'information is free' (echoing Wikipedia's mission statement), regular Internet users are resistant to the idea of paying for content.

This shift in the concept of membership is being reinforced by a generalized decline in membership of organizations in the offline world. Membership of political parties has long been in decline over most of the world.[41] What political scientists have termed 'partisan dealignment'[42] started in earnest about twenty-five years ago, culminating in what some have termed the 'rise of the apartisan American',[43] that is, a US citizen who is interested in politics and active but who does not want to align herself with a political party, and also the 'Cyber Party', a new ideal type of political party characterized by a far looser relationship with supporters than was normal for earlier ideal party types.[44] Traditional notions of membership of interest groups have also declined, although there is variation across countries, with the steepest fall in the United States,[45] and a more stable pattern over time in Europe,[46] with some recent declines.[47]

Newer organizations seeking to foster political engagement based on social media epitomize this shift from membership to far weaker patterns of allegiance, with a very different conception of membership to that of traditional interest groups. The civic activism organization Avaaz, for example, now calls itself a 'campaigning community' and shows the real-time number of 'members' (forty million at the end of 2014) on its front page at www.avaaz.org. These are people who have made any kind of contribution to one of its petitioning, emailing, donating, petition signing, or lobbying campaigns, however small (basically, anyone who has interacted with their website). Likewise, the successful UK campaigning organization 38 Degrees claimed over 2.5 million members by 2015, a member being anyone who has signed a petition or undertaken any other action from their website, blog, Facebook page, or Twitter handle. The organization polls their 'members' on what new campaigns they should undertake, and claims success in stopping the UK government's policy to privatize forests; blocking various building projects such as a mega-dairy in Lincolnshire; and convincing the

UK government to sign the EU directive on human trafficking. The 'Save Our Forests' campaign involved a petition that garnered half a million signatures and the crowdfunding of a national opinion poll. From 2008, the loosely formed hacktivist collective Anonymous has undertaken a range of online protests and email hacks and distributed denial of service attacks, for example against the Assad regime in Syria with its OpSyria campaign.[48] Anonymous was named by *Time* magazine in 2012 as one of the most influential groups in the world. Anonymous reflects its anarchist origins by taking the notion of membership to a new level of ambiguity: 'it is impossible to "join" Anonymous, as there is no leadership, no ranking, and no single means of communication: Anonymous is spread over many mediums and languages, with membership being achieved simply by wishing to join'.[49]

MICRO-DONATIONS OF POLITICS

The growing proportion of time spent by individuals on social media reshapes the context in which people decide whether or not to participate politically. Nearly all these media were developed for private use, for sharing content of private or semiprivate value. But they all have the potential to host a wide range of political activities: sharing and receiving news, information, and views; expressing opinions; discussing issues; coordinating activities; matching individuals across political, geographical, and economic boundaries; and disseminating political information and expertise.

There is every sign that the swelling ranks of social media users are indeed using social media sites for these political activities. In the United States, data show that in 2013, 39 percent of American adults took part in some sort of political activity (such as liking, sharing, or reposting content related to political issues) in the context of a social networking site, rising among younger people (eighteen to twenty-four) to two-thirds, which equates to nearly three-quarters of those young adults who use social networking sites.[50] Such figures challenge the widely held perception of political disengagement among young people, and show that the youngest American adults are more likely to engage in political behaviours on social networking sites than any other venue. They also suggest that political activity on such sites is likely to lead to further engagement, as 43 percent of users say they have decided to learn more about an issue because of something they saw on a social networking site, especially among the youngest age group.[51] In Arab countries the proportions are also high; shortly after the events of the Arab Spring, more than 60 percent of users of social networking sites (around one-third of the citizens in Lebanon, Tunisia, and Egypt) said that they use the sites to share views about politics and 70 percent use them for community issues.[52]

In addition to general social media sites, there are now a range of Internet-based platforms dedicated to political activity, which may be regarded as social media in that they allow users to generate content through some kind of participatory act such as generating an email to a political leader or signing a petition. The newer civic activism groups discussed above such as Avaaz and MoveOn encourage users to contribute a range of micro-donations of political resources quickly and easily, such as joining an email campaign or online protest, signing a petition, or contributing money. Also worthy of note are the growing number of electronic petition sites operated by both governments and non-governmental organizations (including Avaaz), discussed in Chapter 3, which are used by a significant proportion of citizens in many liberal democracies. Internet-based platforms for charitable giving have also become popular, such as JustGiving, a platform that allows individuals to set up their own donation pages for specific causes, often linked to some sponsored activity, which they then circulate to their own social networks.

The range of participatory acts is extended further through sites geared at encouraging citizens to seek redress or make contact with political institutions, such as those run by the social enterprise mySociety. Since the mid-2000s they have operated a number of sites that make it easy for citizens to undertake a number of collective activities, such as write to their political representatives (writetothem.com), find out what their representatives are doing (theyworkforyou.com), and complain about local infrastructure problems to their local council (fixmystreet.com). Similar sites run in many other European countries, while in the United States the equivalent SeeClickFix.com claims to have fixed over 1.2 million non-emergency issues for US citizens, and the application is now being adopted by cities across the world, including in India.

With so much political activity around on social media, there is some evidence that Internet skills are joining the traditional resources of time, income, and civic skills,[53] in predicting whether people will participate politically.[54] Norris, in an analysis of nineteen countries, used the European Social Survey to analyse the relationship between Internet use and political activism, finding that regular Internet users are significantly more politically active across all twenty-one indicators of activism captured in the survey;[55] it was not possible to establish any causal effect, but use of the Internet continued to be significantly related to political activism even when controlling for prior social or attitudinal characteristics of Internet users such as age, education, and civic duty. After these factors, use of the Internet proved the next strongest predictor of activism, more important than other indicators such as social and political trust or use of any news media. Recent research from Spain has demonstrated an association between general Internet use and political participation, with the authors arguing that by reducing participation costs, use of the Internet diminishes the role of political motivation in participation, leading frequent and skilled Internet users to participate in politics even without political motivation.[56]

All the social media and campaigning platforms described above play a role in extending the ladder of political participation that was described in Chapter 1. That is, they introduce new 'micro-acts' of participation, such as updating a status on Facebook, sending a tweet or retweet, signing of an electronic petition, sharing a political news item, posting a comment on a blog or discussion thread, making a micro-donation of funds to a political cause or campaign, uploading or sharing a political video on YouTube, and so on. All these are tiny acts of participation that for most people were not available until the advent of social media. Taken individually they may seem insignificant, but as we shall see later, they can scale up to large-scale mobilizations and campaigns for policy change.

The ease of micro-donation reduces the cost, in terms of time, effort, or money, of political participation. This cost is actually made up of two components. First, there is the actual expenditure of time, effort, or money (in expressing an opinion publicly, making a financial donation, or signing a petition, for example, to which can be added the risk of reputational damage if the participant cannot act anonymously). Second, there are transaction costs of the operation (which might include for these three examples transport costs to the venue, writing and posting a cheque, and acquiring information about the petition). We have seen that social media not only reduce the costs of participation, but also lower the transaction costs both in absolute terms and as a proportion of the participation costs. Take a poster by the canal side that asks passersby to contribute to a campaign to save Britain's canals by sending a text message, which will automatically trigger a donation of £3. Here the transaction costs, even for such a small donation, are very small, especially in comparison to sending the donation by post: the time to send the text message is probably less than locating the cheque book and addressing an envelope, and the cost to send the text message is usually less than a postage stamp and possibly free in a bundle. In addition, the electronic transaction can happen immediately and avoid the mental effort to remember the details on the poster. Without such a mechanism, the transaction costs of sending the £3 by post would have been much higher as a proportion of the donation; enough, indeed, to discourage the donation unless the prospective donor was willing to contribute more. Thus the mechanism for making the transaction facilitates a new sort of micro-donation, or tiny act of political participation. This lowering of transaction costs is accelerating all the time, even tending towards zero as potential participants receive requests for micro-donations of political resources in the course of their normal lives both online and offline. The start of this trend was highlighted in the 2007 Obama primary election campaign, in which Obama raised more than $35 million in individual contributions, 40 percent of which were $25 or less.[57]

SCALING UP

On its own, each individual micro-donation of time, effort, or money does nothing for the political cause that it is intended to support. One signature alone on a petition renders it worthless, a tweet that only one person sees is nothing more than pixels, a video that no one views will change nothing. But via interactions on social media, through downloading, sharing, viewing, following, retweeting, and so on, tiny acts of participation can scale up to make a major contribution to a political mobilization.

We show here four examples of this scaling up, in the form of attention paid to four campaigns or mobilizations that took place between 2012 and 2014. The first was in October 2012, after the Pakistani schoolgirl Malala Yousafzai, a campaigner for the education of schoolgirls and a blogger on the BBC Urdu website, was shot by Taliban militants on her way back from school. Malala became one of the most famous teenagers in the world, showered with accolades including most famously the Nobel Peace Prize in 2014. Her resilience and actions are widely regarded as leading to the ratification of Pakistan's first Right to Education Bill in 2013, after a petition sponsored by UN Special Envoy Gordon Brown was launched in her name, receiving more than one million signatures. Figure 2.2 shows the daily page views on the English version of the Wikipedia entry for Malala and the tweets mentioning 'Malala' from August 2012 to April 2013. Both show huge spikes in interest followed by periods of relative stasis. The largest spike occurs nearly immediately after she was shot, and further spikes are prompted by new events, such as being named as runner-up to *Time* magazine's Person of the Year in December 2012 (an event that generates considerably more interest on Twitter than on Wikipedia).[58] An even larger spike (not pictured) occurred when Malala was awarded the Nobel Peace Prize.

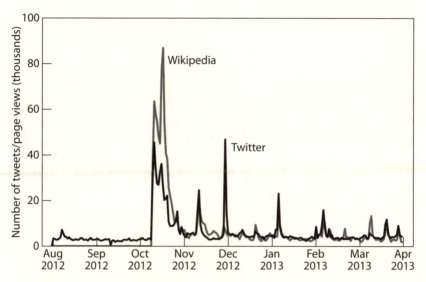

FIGURE 2.2 Daily page views of the Malala Yousafzai page on the English edition of Wikipedia and daily mentions of 'Malala' on Twitter

The second example is a campaign by several organizations to 'Save Our Bees', culminating in the successful passing of EU legislation banning for a period of two years three neonicotinoid pesticides that were tentatively linked with risks for bees. Figure 2.3 shows a steady increase, with the largest spike in tweets occurring on 29 April 2013, when the EU legislation was passed. Simultaneous efforts in the United States were less successful in achieving a change of policy.

In the third case, in 2013 the feminist activist Caroline Criado-Perez started a petition on change.org calling for the Bank of England to reconsider the decision to replace Elizabeth Fry with Winston Churchill on the five-pound note, which left no women, other than the queen, featured on UK bank notes. A combination of the petition, signed by thirty-five thousand petitioners with crowdfunded financial support, led the governor of the Bank of England to announce a change of plan in July 2013, with the eventual agreement that the image of Jane Austen would appear on the ten-pound note from 2017. The success of the campaign also resulted in threats and harassment of Criado-Perez, which in turn

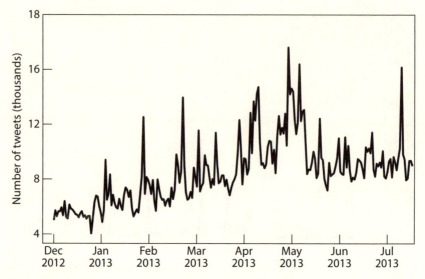

FIGURE 2.3 Graph of the number of tweets mentioning 'bees' from December 2012 to July 2013

led to substantial public pressure for Twitter to make it easier to report hate speech followed by changes to the platform to ease the reporting of such tweets. Figure 2.4 shows the massive spike of interest, a pattern different from that of the Save Our Bees campaign, this time with a large leap in attention after the bank governor announced the change of plan.

The activities on Twitter around these three campaigns are shown together in Figure 2.5 to illustrate the key role that large numbers of ordinary people, with modest followings, play in the scaling up of mobilizations or campaigns. As noted above, Twitter users vary hugely in the number of followers that they accumulate: the celebrity Justin Bieber has 58 million, whereas the median number of Twitter followers was 61 in 2013, and that only if those who had been inactive for 30 days were excluded.[59] In general, users on Twitter consume a personalized stream or timeline of content based on the users they choose to follow, so content authored by a given user generally reaches only the users who have chosen to follow that user, but can reach wider circulation through retweets.

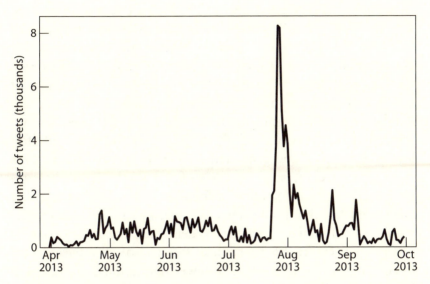

FIGURE 2.4 Graph of the number of tweets about the Women on Banknotes campaign from April to September 2013
Note: Selected tweets mentioned one of the main accounts advocating for the campaign, linked to the campaign's petition on change.org, or mentioned male/female/man/woman and banknote(s)/Bank of England in the same tweet.

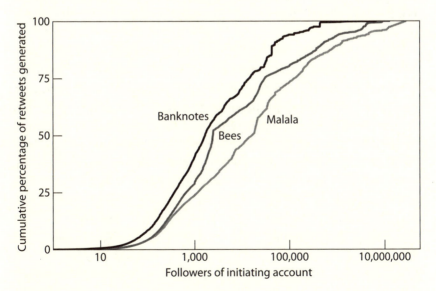

FIGURE 2.5 Cumulative number of retweets of messages originally authored by users with different numbers of followers

When users retweet a message on Twitter, they forward that message to all of their followers, enlarging the number of people who will have the tweet in their timeline. Within the three campaigns described above, most tweets (85 percent of those related to each topic) generated no retweets at all. Considering the 15 percent of tweets that generate at least one retweet, users with the largest number of followers generate the most retweets per tweet. For instance, Justin Bieber tweeted about Malala to his 28,960,137 followers at the time and generated 24,558 retweets. While Bieber's tweet generated the most retweets of any single tweet, these retweets still account for only 2.6 percent of total retweeting that mentioned Malala. In all three campaigns, users with far smaller numbers of followers collectively generated the most retweets, as shown in Figure 2.5. Over three-quarters of all retweets were of content created by users with fewer than a hundred thousand followers in all three campaigns and over half of all retweets in the Bees and Banknotes campaigns were of content created by users with only a few thousand followers. For Malala, there were 956,885 retweets of 218,449 unique messages. For Women on Banknotes, there were 64,403 retweets of 20,759 unique messages. For Save Our Bees, there were 1,052,477 retweets of 323,110 unique messages.

Fourth and finally, we show how a mobilization played out across two social media platforms: Facebook and Twitter. As noted in Chapter 1, 2014 brought a wave of protest and demonstration against racist policing in the United States, after the deaths of two African American citizens by white police officers. Eric Garner died in New York on 17 July 2014 after a police officer put him in a chokehold. On 9 August 2014 Michael Brown was fatally shot by a police officer in Ferguson, Missouri (a suburb of St. Louis). There was considerable unrest with protests and riots in Ferguson from August through December 2014. The protest activity increased again after 24 November 2014, when the grand jury announced that the officer who shot Michael Brown would not be indicted (charged with any crime), and shortly thereafter on 3 December, when a grand jury in New York similarly decided not to indict

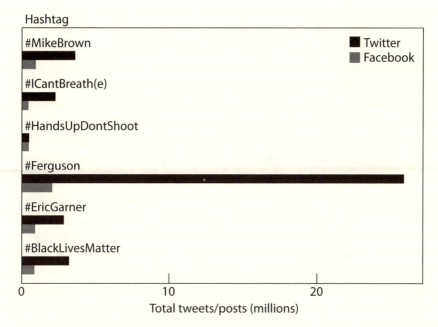

FIGURE 2.6 Total volumes for posts on Twitter and Facebook from 17 July 2014 to 31 January 2015

the officers involved in the death of Eric Garner. Large-scale protests took place in New York City, San Francisco, Boston, Chicago, Washington DC, Baltimore, Minneapolis, and Atlanta in early December 2014.

In response to the deaths of Eric Garner and Michael Brown, and even more so in response to the decisions of the grand juries to not press charges, citizens started using several hashtags to comment on the developments: #Ferguson, #MikeBrown, and #HandsUpDontShoot for the death of Michael Brown, and #EricGarner and #ICantBreathe for the death of Eric Garner, while #BlackLivesMatter was used to raise attention to the more general issue of the disproportionate number of African American men dying in police custody, bringing together online activities from both these and previous deaths. Each hashtag has been used a substantial number of times on both Twitter and Facebook: Figure 2.6

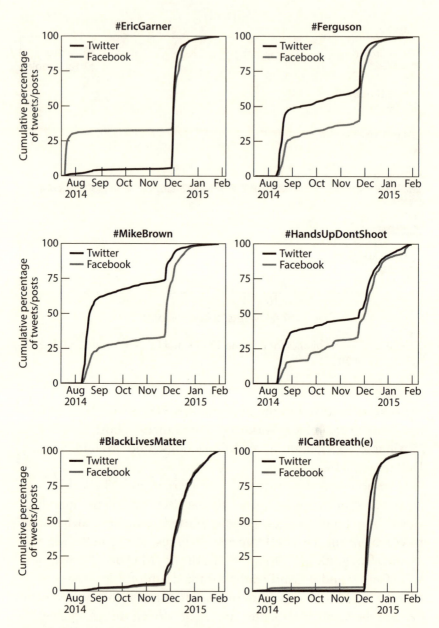

FIGURE 2.7 Cumulative uses of hashtags related to the deaths of Eric Garner and Michael Brown on Twitter and Facebook from 17 July 2014 to 31 January 2015

shows the total number of uses of each hashtag in both original posts and tweets as well as in shares and retweets. The most used hashtag, #Ferguson, occurred approximately twenty-six million times on Twitter and two million times on Facebook between August 2014 and January 2015. Volumes for both platforms are estimated from a 10 percent sample of all public posts. The volume data for Facebook further include private reshares of public posts.

The cumulative growth of all these hashtags on both Facebook and Twitter is shown in Figure 2.7, indicating large and sharp rises in attention at the time of death, and the time of indictment. Most of the graphs show that Twitter activity slightly precedes activity on Facebook, although activity on both platforms exhibits a very similar pattern (the one exception being the death of Eric Garner, which seems to have gone almost unnoticed initially on Twitter), with a sharp rise at each new event. This is a pattern that we observe and analyse extensively in Chapter 3, where we analyse mobilizations around petitions. The data were collected from 17 July 2014 to 31 January 2015 and include only public content. The Twitter data are based on a random 10 percent sample, while here the Facebook data include all public posts and public shares.

These visualizations illustrate the different patterns of mobilization that can take place on social media, and one of the tasks of this book is to understand the dynamics by which they rise (and fall). The following subsection considers the influence of the information environment on the individual participation patterns that scale up in this way.

HOW SOCIAL MEDIA EXERT SOCIAL INFLUENCE

In the short time since bursting onto the scene, social media have continued to evolve as they have competed for people's attention and as individuals and organizations have continued to find innovative ways to develop new applications and uses. For today's Internet users, social media provide an increasingly heterogeneous information environment within which people operate, a continually flowing stream of information about issues, actions, opinions, and the behaviour of others. As people move from searching for information, individuals, and organizations in online environments, to spending increasing quantities of time on social networking sites in which they have already preselected their information sources and informants, they start to exist in what some commentators have called a 'time-based worldstream'[60] or 'stream of consciousness'[61] or (with more negative connotations) 'echo chamber'.[62] In these lifestreams, where search models, operating systems, and even computer devices become secondary to the information environment that social media provide, 'the goal is not to be a passive consumer of information or to simply tune in when the time is right, but rather to live in a world where information is everywhere. To be peripherally aware of information as it flows by, grabbing it at the right moment when it is most relevant and valuable, entertaining or insightful. Living with, in, and around information. . . . The idea is that you are living in a stream: adding to it, consuming it, redirecting it'.[63] Political information and activity form a tiny proportion of most people's information streams: any political issue must join the fight for limited attention and engagement, including time, money, and other resources. Individuals must choose from the many available possibilities when directing their (limited) political attention.

In the social media age then, individual citizens considering whether to undertake small acts of participation by making microdonations of time and effort are likely to undertake such a decision in a predominantly online environment and are susceptible to the influences presented to them by their participation in social media. They are increasingly unlikely to be susceptible to the offline influences of institutions or organizations to which they have a strong allegiance, through membership or some other significant and longstanding attachment. Their decision to participate with one small act is extremely low-cost, and therefore vulnerable to small shifts in their information environment, whereas in the pre-social-media era the decision to belong to a political party or interest group organization was much more significant and time-consuming, more likely to be shaped by social norms and pressure from peers or family and less vulnerable to small changes in political information.

There are three key ways in which we might expect this changed information environment to influence the participatory behaviour of individuals. First, the networks that develop through their participation in one or more social media platforms shape the social influences from people that they know, know of, or would like to know, termed here 'network structure effects'. Second, by participating in social media, individuals are exposed to social information: information about the participatory behaviour of others, the number of people who have signed a petition, voted, or participated in a campaign, for example. Third, social media present them with an opportunity to publicize their actions to the outside world, through sharing information, for example, or making their name visible on some participatory platform. Each of these features of individuals' personalized experience of social media has the capacity to influence their decisions whether and when to participate in a mobilization or collective action. The potential influence of network structure effects, social information, and visibility is discussed below. These influences will vary across social media platforms, so once individuals have made the decision to use one, the platforms themselves will further shape their information environment. These variations between platforms are therefore also very important.

NETWORK EFFECTS—WEAK TIES, STRONG TIES

Networks have always formed an important part of the context in which people operate politically,[64] providing pathways to facilitate the spread of information (and other resources) and exerting social influence on the decisions of individuals. Earlier Internet-based technologies had limited network structure effects. An individual or organization either had a public presence online or not and was found generally by looking for the individual or organization directly by name with search engines or through links and email. Internet users then might make contact through email with the organization. Although there were network structure effects, they could be analysed only at a high level of abstraction.[65] The advent of social networking sites made a far more substantive difference to the extent to which people were likely to be influenced by or share information with other people they know, 'automating and accelerating the social signals that pulse through the human network on a daily basis'.[66]

The founder of the sociology of networks, Mark Granovetter, made a distinction between the different types of influence that social networks provide which has influenced the way networks have been perceived ever since.[67] He argued that weak social ties were analytically distinct from strong ties, but were crucially important in spreading information across networks. He argued that the 'personal experience of individuals is closely bound up with larger-scale aspects of social structure, well beyond the purview or control of particular individuals',[68] and that this finding revealed the paradox that, contrary to the sociological thinking of the time, 'weak ties' are 'indispensable to individuals' opportunities and to their integration into communities; strong ties, breeding local cohesion, lead to overall fragmentation'.[69] This observation has been extremely influential in our understanding of online social networks, which lend themselves so well to the accumulation of weak ties. For example, in the 2010 US presidential election, the political scientist James Fowler collaborated with Facebook in a massive experiment (with sixty-one million subjects) to test the influence of Facebook on people's decision whether or not to vote. About sixty million users (98 percent of their sample) received a message with social information at the top of their news feeds showing the profile pictures of up to six randomly selected Facebook friends who had clicked the 'I voted' button, as well as an 'informational message' encouraging them to vote, providing a link to information on polling stations and a counter of Facebook users who had clicked the 'I voted' button. Two control groups of 1 percent each received either nothing or the informational message about the election as a whole. The researchers then compared the groups' online behaviour and matched six million users with voting records. The results showed that those who saw the social message were 2 percent more likely to click the 'I voted button' and 0.3 percent more likely to seek information about a polling place than those who just got the information and 0.4 percent more likely to vote.[70] It did not make any difference whether the six friends shown were close friends or not, suggesting that even the weak ties between acquaintances could also send social signals strong enough to influence political behaviour.

In contrast, some of Granovetter's followers have used his model to argue that mobilizations based on social media platforms could never attain political success. As we discussed earlier, Malcolm Gladwell in his 2010 *New Yorker* article argued that without the strong ties that characterized the civil rights movement, mobilizations relying on social media could never attain the same sort of importance—which was rather ill-timed given the events of the Arab Spring, which soon followed. Although there has been much empirical evidence to set against this argument, the view that weak ties are somehow inferior in their capacity to engender political change has been extremely pervasive, forming part of the politics-as-pain principle introduced in Chapter 1.

Different social media platforms vary in the type of network structure effects they produce. Facebook, for instance, started on college campuses with the goal of representing real-world friendships with most content being shared privately among friends or friends of friends and requires users to mutually accept each other's friendship for a link to form (a symmetric or undirected network). In contrast, Twitter started with most messages being public, gaining notoriety with weak-tie conference co-attendees sharing messages on the platform during South by Southwest Interactive 2007. Twitter generally allows users to follow any user without requiring that user to approve the tie (forming an asymmetric or directed network). Old-fashioned email is still being used in large-scale mail-outs, which can be personalized (as in email from Barak Obama or 38 Degrees), but do not introduce peer-to-peer connections. Politically oriented social media platforms such as Avaaz or petition websites do not necessarily put individuals or peers in touch with each other at all, so network structure effects will rely on the dissemination of these activities on generic social media sites, for example through the sharing of a petition on Facebook, or the tweeting or retweeting of a petition to followers, or the forwarding of mass emails about the petition sent by the campaigning organization. These design differences engender different network structures and different diffusion patterns. Centola, for example, has shown that network structure has a significant effect on the dynamics of behavioural diffusion, with behaviour spreading farther and faster across clustered-lattice networks than across control random networks with the same degree distribution; that is, the reinforcement from locally clustered ties can be highly efficient for promoting behavioural diffusion.[71] His study looked at the diffusion of health behaviours, but could equally well apply to the diffusion of political behaviour, particularly given the institutional constraints to geographically scattered policy influence.

We do not address network structure effects in this book: the kind of information received from online social networking platforms, such as the retweet of a retweet of a tweet or the sharing of a YouTube video from the friend of a friend, often comes from such a distant part of an individual's personal network that the effects are reduced to the information provided in the shared content. So we do not explore the mechanisms by which information diffuses or spreads across networks, although we do present some secondary research on this topic. Rather, we view the weak tie influences that emerge from social media as just one more piece in the jigsaw of contemporary collective action, an aggregate 'social other' that people interpret without reference to the specific users from whence the information comes, as discussed in the next section.

Recent research from computational social science tends to support this view, such as the programme of research led by Duncan

Watts, a key figure in the study of online social networks and the small worlds phenomenon,[72] discussed in Chapter 1. Goel and Watts investigated generic patterns of Internet-based diffusion across communications platforms, networked games, and micro-blogging services, each involving distinct types of content and modes of sharing, including the diffusion of Twitter news stories and a third-party Facebook application asking about people's political views.[73] They found strikingly similar patterns across all the domains they looked at: multistep diffusion was rare across all the online domains, and the vast majority of adoptions occurred within one degree of a seed node. Even for those initiatives that do achieve a large number of participants, the vast majority are only a small distance away from the originator on the network.[74] In follow-up work unpublished at the time of writing, Goel at al. found that the spread of petitions is comparatively more viral than that of videos, pictures, and news on Twitter, which they speculate as resulting from the lack of large broadcast channels for petitions. This fits with our preliminary analysis of the network of users who tweeted links to the petitions on the UK government site, which showed that the most central accounts belong to individual users not representing any organization. Although different organizations may be important for any one petition, there is no single organization that is central with many petitions, which reflects the diversity of inputs and underlying pluralism. Even so, Goel et al. found that 'median structural virality remains surprisingly low and also surprisingly invariant with respect to [diffusion/cascade] size' for petitions, images, and videos.[75] Likewise, Suri and Watts investigated the relationship between the structure of social networks and aggregate levels of cooperative behaviour,[76] a relationship hypothesized to be positive through contagion, based on the phenomenon of conditional cooperation (discussed below).[77] They do not find evidence of positive contagion in the sense of multistep propagation along a sequence of ties in a static network. Their explanation of this result suggests that network structure is a far less clear determinant of collective action behaviour than previously hypothesized.

A CORNUCOPIA OF SOCIAL INFORMATION

Another way in which social media shape the context of collective action is by providing real-time information about whether and when other people are participating. As outlined in Chapter 1 and discussed in Chapter 4, we use the term 'social information' to indicate information about what others intend to do, are doing, or have done. Potential participants take this information (or, lacking this information, their perception of what it might be) into account when they are deciding whether to participate. When such participation takes place online, there is a far greater possibility of the potential participants receiving real-time feedback information about how many other people have participated, something that someone who signs a petition in the street or throws money into a charity collector's bucket is unlikely to receive.

If you sign a paper-based petition in the street, you don't know how many other people have signed it. You are reliant on proxy signals, such as the number of signatures on the particular sheet you yourself are signing or the numbers of people queuing to sign it; the assurances of the person with the clipboard who tells you it is going really well; or some kind of gut feeling that other people will sign. When you sign an electronic petition, chances are you will be provided with real-time information about how many others have already signed it. You may well also be provided with a real-time chart showing how many more signatures are required to attain some sort of success, such as to receive the attention of policy makers, or the remaining time until the petition closes. On social media, when you decide whether or not to sign a petition, donate money to a political cause, or participate in an email campaign, the chances are that you will know how many other people have already done so.

We know that social information is an important influence on social behaviour. Through experimental work on conditional co-operation, economists have shown the importance of information about the contributions of others on any person's willingness to cooperate. This work has shown that people are more likely to contribute to a campaign if they are provided with information that other people are also doing so, and that increasing the numbers of other participants enhances this effect.[78] In sociology and political science, a number of experimental studies have shown the importance of social information on people's willingness to contribute to public goods by undertaking activities such as recycling,[79] and voting.[80] Social information also provides a crucial signal of viability for a mobilization, that is, evidence of whether or not it has reached or will reach 'critical mass'.[81]

As noted above, there is a sense in which network structure effects also act as social information. As network ties become increasingly diffuse as a result of the inclusion of many weak ties, it can be argued that they become more like other sorts of information signals about people's behaviour, such as the number of people who have signed a petition or voted, rather than providing the stronger social pressure that 'strong ties' would engender.

VISIBILITY

Just as social media make individuals aware of what other people are doing, they also have the potential to make other people aware of what the user herself is doing. If a user tweets on Twitter, posts a status or comments on someone else's status on Facebook, signs an electronic petition that shows the names of signatories, or posts a video on YouTube and disseminates it on other social media, that user is increasing her public profile and making herself visible to a wider audience. Andy Warhol's 'fifteen minutes of fame' may not be any easier to attain today, but the chances of getting a photograph or video viewed by over a million people are almost infinitely higher now than they used to be in the pre-Internet era. In the context of collective action, if a user undertakes some participatory act, it is more likely to be visible to others and therefore to influence them in their own participatory decision making, as we investigate in Chapter 5.

The flipside of visibility is anonymity, and Internet-based plat-forms vary in the extent to which they provide visibility or anonymity. The most famous cartoon from the early days of the Internet showed a dog typing at a computer screen with the caption 'On the Internet, nobody knows you're a dog'.[82] This theme has been taken up at various points since, notably in a play by Alan Perkins, *Nobody Knows I'm a Dog*, about the lives of six people who find refuge in the anonymity of the Internet. For political action, the extent to which a platform provides visibility or anonymity can be crucially important, and the potential influence of this characteristic varies widely with context. Various experiments have tested the effect of visibility on political participation in liberal democracies, showing that people are more likely to make charitable donations when visible,[83] and more likely to vote when other people know whether they vote or not.[84] In other contexts however, anonymity may be crucial to whether people feel safe to participate in political action. In the revolutions against authoritarian regimes that constituted the Arab Spring of 2011, for example, early protestors who aligned themselves with online protest groups (such as the Facebook page 'We Are All Khaled Said' in Egypt) early on faced risks that most would not have been willing to undertake. Those joining later could hide in the swelling numbers of people who clicked 'like' on the page—over five hundred thousand by the time the regime opted to turn off the Internet at the height of the protest—sending a crucial signal of viability to those who came later. But for the earliest joiners, the potential costs of showing themselves to be supportive of the protest could have been tragically high.

Indeed, in the era of social media, it can be argued that the ability to remain anonymous is severely and even dangerously circumscribed on the Internet. In his book *Delete*, Viktor Mayer-Schönberger argues that Internet-based platforms are endangering society's ability to forget because of the traces of activity that often remain on computer systems.[85] In Mayer-Schönberger's world of everlasting digital memory, no one will be able to forget that you are—or at one time were—a dog. Such arguments have led to the prospect of policy change at the European level: expiration dates on personal data, after which time they would be removed unless explicit consent were given for them to remain.

As with social information, social media platforms vary in the extent to which they offer visibility or anonymity, and the extent to which they allow your previous contributions to expire or be erased. On most platforms, visibility is vital to operation; people post things on Facebook because they want their friends to see them, tweet because they want their followers to know about something, upload a video to YouTube because they want it to be viewed, and edit an article on Wikipedia (in part, at least) because they want in some way their view of a subject to be widely accepted. But all these platforms have restrictions that will shape any kind of political activity that takes place. On Facebook, most people want only their friends to see most things, meaning that people must befriend someone and have that person approve the friendship if they want to be notified of status changes, whereas on Twitter, a user wishing to follow someone generally requires no approval and is faced with a looser and more public arrangement.

Civic engagement sites also vary in the extent to which they offer visibility or anonymity. The No. 10 Downing Street petition platform that operated from 2006 to 2010, for example, published the names of the most recent five hundred signatories, but the redesigned platform introduced in 2011 shows only the name of the petition initiator. The German petition platform requires the name of all signatories to be public, while the US petition site allows petition signers to list just their zip codes and initials. Some charitable giving platforms, such as JustGiving, offer the option of anonymity for contributors, whereas others do not. Some groups have emerged based entirely on the premise of anonymity, such as the loosely formed Anonymous, discussed above.

BRINGING ORGANIZATIONS BACK IN?

We have argued here that social media individualize the information environment for collective action, highlighting three forms of social influence: network structure effects, social information about the participation of others, and visibility of one's own actions. In so doing, we have given ourselves a different focus from other work in this field. Academic work on Internet-mediated participation has emphasized the importance of bringing back organizations into the collective action sphere. Bimber and Bimber et al. explored the possibilities for what they call organizationless collective action and introduced the idea of 'postbureaucratic' or 'accelerated' pluralism,[86] but returned to the idea that we will not see 'an end of the organization in civic life, but rather its transformation'.[87] Bimber et al.'s 2012 work *Collective Action in Organizations* aims to 'bring the relevance of formal organization back into contemporary collective action', arguing that digital media enable formal organizations to offer much broader opportunities for people to establish their own participatory styles. David Karpf's *The MoveOn Effect* argues that rather than 'organizing without organizations', the new media environment has given rise to 'organizing through different organizations', and that it is on organizational innovation that we should focus.[88] Both works differ from this book by taking successful collective action organizations as the unit of analysis.

In contrast, a long-running programme of research conducted by Bennett and Segerberg has explored the 'personalization of collective action'.[89] Their focus of analysis is the networks of individuals and organizations that make up contemporary protest movements, and they develop a new model of the 'connective' action with networks at the core.[90] They define three ideal types of contemporary mobilization, of which one is based on the traditional logic of collective action with formal organizations at its core—that is, large organizations seeking to overcome the tendency for members to free ride by providing leadership and individualized goods and services to members. The other two either are based on self-organized networks of individuals with digital media platforms as organizing agents, or are hybrid forms composed of both informal organizational actors and individuals. Their work shares with this book a focus on individuals, but their focus on the network as a unit of analysis and an organizational form in itself moves away from our focus on individual motivations to participate.[91]

THE POLITICAL WEATHER

We have seen that a decade of exploding social media use has brought important changes to the information environment in which citizens decide whether or not to participate politically. Most importantly, it has facilitated new tiny acts of participation, micro-donations of resources such as time or effort, which were not available before. Both the costs of participation and transaction costs continue to decrease, rendering political participation ever more susceptible to the influences that abound on social media. As rising numbers of citizens spend increasing amounts of time in an information environment that provides them with a continuous stream of consciousness, they are susceptible to different types of social influence on their decision to participate: network structure effects, social information, and visibility. These influences vary across platforms and the contexts in which individuals operate (such as their physical location), which in turn will influence their choice of platform and the way in which they use it. Social media, then, are a permanent, evolving feature of the political weather, in terms of the interconnected system of communication about political events that affects everyone. While the political weather has always been turbulent, subject to changes and frequent squalls, social media draw people into political events in much more surprising and sometimes dramatic ways, from YouTube elections to Twitter storms.

CHAPTER 3
TURBULENCE

Social media are a source of instability and turbulence in political life. They make possible new forms of political participation, micro-donations of political time and effort that, by the very ease with which they may be undertaken as part of everyday life, draw swathes of new people into the political process. These almost cost-less acts can scale up to large-scale mobilizations. But because they cost so little, people considering whether to undertake them are likely to be highly susceptible to the influences that social media provide, relative to other influences. They will be at least partially immune to many of the influences that have been shown to sway people's decision to undertake higher cost acts such as voting, attending a meeting, or participating in a demonstration, such as the weather, lack of time, or transport costs. Online platforms exhibit what other people are doing in real time and make other people aware of what they themselves are doing, creating feedback loops and chain reactions that draw in more people, whose actions in turn are likely to influence others. It seems reasonable to claim that mobilizations formed in this way are vulnerable to the impulses from which they start, which can push them over into critical mass, or cause them to fade and die almost as soon as they appear, making them hard to understand or predict.

As well as creating an environment of instability and uncertainty, social media can also provide the tools with which to understand political mobilization. As citizens increasingly experience and participate in political activities in digital settings, they leave a digital trace of what they have done, which may be collected to generate large datasets. These are large-scale, real-time transactional data of online behaviour, sometimes referred to as big data. This chapter presents some of these data as they relate to collective action. As we discussed in Chapter 1, the recent availability of these kind of data is enabling a shift in social science research, with a move away from the reliance on sample-based survey data (what some people think they did or will do) to transactional data (what people have actually done), often based on whole populations rather than samples. This new source of information offers real potential to understand how people respond to different online platforms. Through the development of computational social science' approaches (or social data science), it is possible to analyse the shape of mobilizations over time and to identify the fat-tailed or extreme distributions that tend to characterize human activities in general and particularly Internet-based activity.

In this chapter we test the hypothesis that social media bring instability to political participation. We use data from social media to understand that instability and apply some of the methods used by Salganik et al. to explore inequality and unpredictability in cultural markets for a more political context.[1] We analyse data pertaining to Internet-based mobilizations around petitions, generated from three electronic petition platforms in the United Kingdom and the United States: the petition section of the No. 10 Downing Street website (from 2009 to 2011); the current UK petition site, which was developed by the UK Cabinet Office in 2011; and the US petition platform We the People, operated on the main White House website (whitehouse.gov) from 2011. We analyse the growth of petitions and the distinctive characteristics of the mobilization curves of successful and unsuccessful petitions on these three platforms.

First, we provide some background on petitioning as a form of collective action and outline the distinctive features of the three petition platforms we examine here. Second, we outline how we generated data from these platforms. Third, we discuss two key findings from the data: that most petitions fail to take flight and, for the few that do, the number of people who sign the petition on its first day is crucial to ensure it gets airborne. We develop a model of attention decay to understand this rapid decline in signature growth and the overall shape of the mobilizations, finding that they are characterized by short periods of rapid change and long times of stasis, leading to a leptokurtic distribution (i.e., a large number of small changes and a small number of large changes) of the frequency of daily changes, suggesting that online collective activity could contribute to a punctuated pattern of policy change, as defined by Baumgartner and Jones.[2] Using a natural experiment from a design change to the UK petitions platform and a range of big data generated from social media and Google analytics, we find that social information exaggerates the success of popular petitions, that this effect is reinforced through social media, and that small changes to the design of the platform can have unanticipated consequences, and we identify a group of aimless petitioners who come to the site looking for petitions to sign. These various sources of instability make it likely that online mobilization around petitions emerges as a driver of turbulence in political systems.

PETITIONING AS TINY ACTS OF POLITICAL PARTICIPATION

Signing petitions has long been one the more popular political activities, leading the field for participatory acts outside voting, and with other social benefits ascribed to it such as the reinforcement of civic mindedness,[3] in addition to its potential to bring about policy change. Petitions have a long history, including petitions to sovereigns in medieval times, and petitioning was a popular activity in the United States in the nineteenth century.[4] Petitioning online is one of a growing portfolio of Internet-based democratic innovations.[5] Both governments and NGOs, such as Avaaz and 38 Degrees, have made widespread use of petitions, for which they have received accolades for their democratic contribution by academic commentators.[6] Online petitions that are created and signed on digital platforms are now rapidly replacing paper-based petitions, so although the term 'e-petitions' was widely used in the early days of Internet-based petitioning, we use the generic term for the rest of the chapter.

Petitioning epitomizes the tiny acts of political participation via social media that were discussed in the previous chapter. Although there are start-up costs in getting to know the platform for people who initiate petitions, organizers can find supporters easily, rather than having to canvass them door-to-door or approach people in the street. For those wishing to sign petitions, the search costs are far lower: they may sign a petition instantly on receipt of an email or post on a social networking site, or visit one of the large number of petition platforms and look for a petition to sign, rather than having to wait until they encounter a petition organizer or deliberately look for petition signing activity. Once they have signed a petition, they can share it on almost any social media site with

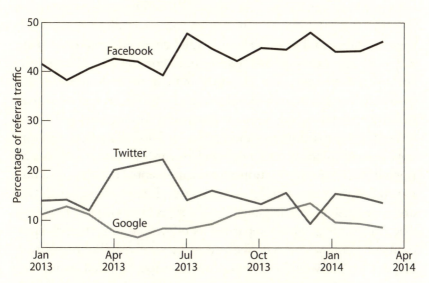

FIGURE 3.1 Sources of traffic to the UK Cabinet Office petition site
Source: Google Analytics data provided by the Government Digital Service.

their close ties, their close friends and family, and any number of weaker ties, such as acquaintances met on the Internet, who in turn may disseminate it further. There is clear evidence that petitioners are using social media in this way. Figure 3.1, which is derived from Google analytics data shared with the authors by the UK Government Digital Service, shows that over half of visitors to the UK government petitions site come from Facebook or Twitter, with 45 percent coming from Facebook alone. In this way, petitions are created, disseminated, circulated, and presented online. Although policy makers may discuss responses in offline contexts, their responses are also generated and sent online.

GOVERNMENTS ENTER THE PETITIONS MARKET

The first online petitions platform in the United Kingdom was launched on the No. 10 Downing Street website in November 2006, created by the social enterprise mySociety. Over the course of its lifetime until 4 April 2011, the No. 10 site received more than eight million signatures from over five million unique email addresses.[7] Both the No. 10 site and its successor allowed anyone to view petitions, and any user with a valid email address could create a new petition or sign an existing one. For the No. 10 site, prospective petitioners were told that if their petition achieved five hundred signatures, they would receive an official response from the government. There were no other official measures of success, although one petition on road pricing in 2007 did succeed in raising over one million signatures, which research identifies as a possible tipping point for mobilizations; that is, if potential participants know that more than one million people have already participated, they are more likely to participate themselves (as discussed in Chapter 4). The petition was widely regarded as influential in getting the government's policy reversed. With regard to the visibility of petitioners, this site showed the names of the first five hundred signatories; by default petitions closed twelve months after they first launched.

This No. 10 site was shut down by the incoming Liberal-Conservative coalition government in March 2011. The Cabinet Office launched a new petitions site in August that year, initially on the direct.gov portal (which eventually became the new www.gov.uk portal in the autumn, which has a different format). The new petitions site shows only the name of the petition creator. The site also provides new measures of success of a petition; the point at which the respondents get an official response from government was initially unclear from the site, but the government later clarified that petitions with over ten thousand signatures would receive a response. More importantly, in the early days of the coalition, Prime Minister David Cameron promised that petitions obtaining more than a hundred thousand signatures would generate a parliamentary debate on the issue. In 2012, a change was made to the site to show trending petitions on the homepage—a list of the six most popular petitions in terms of signatures within the past hour, with updates every hour.

The US petition platform We the People is hosted on the main White House website (whitehouse.gov) and allows any citizen to create or sign a petition to ask the Obama administration to take action on a range of issues. The platform operates under a different arrangement, with higher bars to entry than in the United Kingdom and a shorter deadline for all petitions. The entry costs are higher, because petitioners must gain 150 signatures in order for their petition to be publicly searchable on the whitehouse.gov site. They are provided with an automatic email that they can forward to their immediate contacts to get started. After a petition is created, it has only thirty days to gain a hundred thousand signatures, the requirement for a White House response. Although the site does not show the trending petitions on the homepage like the current UK government site, it is easy for any user coming to the site to search for a petition, and then click through to the most popular petitions. In the first year since its launch on 22 September 2011, the platform generated 3.4 million signatures from 2.8 million users. The popularity of the facility was illustrated in its first week, when eight thousand petitions were created, racking up more than 600,000 signatures from 375,000 users.[8]

Other governments have also launched petitions platforms, of which the German one has received the most extensive analysis by political scientists.[9] The UK petition platforms have received rather less attention in recent political science research, with the exception of Wright's and our own work.[10] The US petitions platform is relatively new, having been launched in September 2011, and has not received academic attention to date.

GENERATING DATA FROM PETITION PLATFORMS

In the past, petitions left little record other than the pages of signatories and the record about how they were received by those in power. Although such documents may be scanned and analysed to understand some aspects of petition-signing behaviour,[11] they contain no information about petitions that failed. Online petitions are different as they leave a digital imprint—the entire transaction history for both successful and unsuccessful mobilizations around petitions. Data like these represent a big shift for social science research into political behaviour, which has traditionally relied on survey, turnout, or census data. They also present a challenge, in that they do not come with demographics attached, nor do we generally know where people have come from (to any one interaction) or where they are going, and it is difficult to match online activities across different platforms. These data however, make it possible to examine the different patterns of growth in mobilization curves and identify the distinctive characteristics of those mobilizations that succeed and those that fail. Such an analysis, using data that have rarely before been available to political science researchers, tells us something about the nature of collective action itself in a digital world.

To generate the data we analyse and discuss here, we accessed both the UK and US petition platforms over long time periods.

TABLE 3.1 List of the most successful petitions in the UK Cabinet Office and US White House petition sites as of January 2015

UK	Petition title	Signatures
1	Stop the badger cull	304,254
2	SOPHIES CHOICE, smear test lowered to 16	327,483
3	Convicted London rioters should loose all benefits	258,276
4	"Drop the Health Bill"	179,466
5	Reconsider West Coast Mainline franchise decision	174,578
6	Stop Holiday companies charging extra in school holidays	170,929
7	Full disclosure of all government documents relating to 1989 Hillsborough disaster	156,218
8	Return VAT on Air Ambulance fuel payments	154,662
9	Stop mass immigration from Bulgarian and Romanians in 2014, when EU restrictions on immigration are relaxed	153,827
10	Put Babar Ahmad on trial in the UK	149,470
US	**Petition title**	**Signatures**
1	Legally recognize Westboro Baptist Church as a hate group	367,180
2	Deport Justin Bieber and revoke his green card	273,968
3	Democracy crisis in Malaysia: foreign workers were employed for fraud voting in Malaysian General Election	223,913
4	Declare Muslim Brotherhood organization as a terrorist group	213,146
5	Immediately address the issue of gun control through the introduction of legislation in Congress	197,073
6	Support Hong Kong Democracy and Prevent A Second Tiananmen Massacre in Hong Kong	197,001
7	Pardon Edward Snowden	163,602
8	Mike Brown Law. Requires all state, county, and local police to wear a camera	154,747
9	Invest and deport Jasmine Sun who was the main suspect of a famous Thallium poison murder case (victim:Zhu Lin) in China	151,250
10	Stop expanding trade with Vietnam at the expense of human rights	150,945

Source: UK and US petition data.

Note: Titles (including use of capital letters and language errors) are shown as in the actual petitions.

We utilized an automated script to access the UK government's first petition website (petitions.number10.gov.uk) daily from 2 February 2009 until 4 April 2011, when the site closed and no further signatures could be added. Each day, the number of overall signatures to date on each active petition was recorded. In addition, we collected the name, text, launch date, and category of the petition. Overall, 8,326 unique petitions were tracked, representing all publicly available petitions active at any point during the collection period. Initial analysis of these data after the site closed revealed the importance of the first day in the future success of a petition,[12] and suggested that more frequent scraping of the data could deliver a more fine-grained analysis. For this reason, when the new petitions site was launched in August 2011, we set the automatic script to scrape it every hour, recording the same details as for the previous site and leading to a dataset of data points for all the petitions (19,789) submitted to the new site between 5 August 2011 and 22 February 2013. We started collecting data in the same manner for the US petition site, but the US administration later started releasing database dumps of all the anonymous activity on the site that made further scraping unnecessary. In Table 3.1 the titles of the most successful petitions during the data collection period on the direct.gov portal and the US petition website are listed.

MOST PETITIONS FAIL QUICKLY

To identify patterns in how petitions grow, the percentage change in new signatures was calculated each day for the first site. Most petitions showed a long period of inactivity prior to their deadline date. In order to consider only the period during which petitions were still actually growing, the data were truncated after a petition's final signature, removing any final period of 'zero signature per day' growth prior to the petition's deadline. First, we explored the data collected from the first petitions site on the No. 10 Downing Street website, which produced a set of 8,326 unique petitions. The most immediate finding of interest was that 94 percent of them failed to obtain even the modest five hundred signatures required to elicit an official response, the only measurable success indicator for the earlier site.

Nearly all the petitions that succeeded in obtaining five hundred signatures did so quickly, taking a mean time of 8.4 days to reach the threshold, but a median time of only 2 days. In fact, 230 of the 533 successful petitions succeeded in obtaining five hundred signatures on the day they were launched. Only a few petitions took a much longer time to reach the five hundred signature mark: thirty-one petitions (6 percent) succeeded after taking more than thirty days, and only five petitions in our dataset reached the five hundred signature mark after being active more than four months. A logit regression revealed that the proportion of signatures received by a petition on its first day is the most important factor explaining its success, and a linear regression showed that it was also the most important factor in explaining the total number of signatures received by a petition during its lifetime.[13] All other factors tested—the topic of the petition, the day of the week on which the petition was launched (or simply whether it was a weekday or a weekend)—had no significant effect on the growth of a petition once controlling for the number of signatures it received on its first day.

The identification of the first day as crucial for the success of a petition led us to reexamine our data collection techniques as we took the data harvesting and analysis forward with the new site that opened in the summer of 2011. That is, the mobilization on this first day was so rapid that daily scraping of the site could not provide a fine-grained analysis of potential tipping points. Therefore, as noted above, when we collected data from the new site we obtained 19,789 petitions up to February 2013. For these data, Figure 3.2 shows those petitions that attained the first level of success (that is, the ten thousand signatures required for an official response) and those that attained the second level, the hundred thousand signatures required to generate a parliamentary debate.

Once again, it is immediately clear that the vast majority of petitions failed to achieve any measure of success. Only 5 percent of petitions obtained five hundred signatures, which we calculated

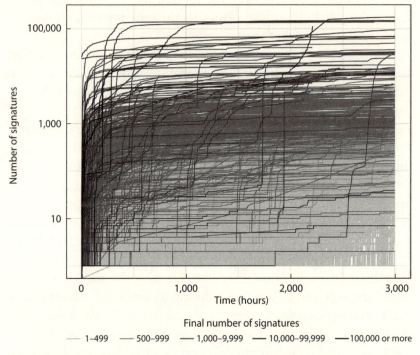

FIGURE 3.2 Petition growth on the UK Cabinet Office petition site, 2011–13
Note: The graph represents 19,789 petitions, created between 5 August 2011 and 22 February 2013. A logarithmic scale is used on the y-axis. The shading indicates the total number of signatures received by each petition at the end of the data collection period. The darkest colour shows the level required for a debate.

to compare with the threshold set for the first dataset, and only 4 percent received one thousand. Only 0.7 percent attained the ten thousand signatures required to receive an official response, and 0.1 percent attained the hundred thousand required for a parliamentary debate. As we saw with the first dataset, the first day was crucial to achieving any kind of success. Any petition receiving a hundred thousand signatures after three months needed to have obtained three thousand within the first ten hours on average.

The US petitions paint a different picture, in the sense that petitions must pass the 150-signature bar before being eligible to appear on the site, so clearly our data contain no petitions with very few signatures. Of those that remain, then, 89 percent have more than five hundred signatures, suggesting that those that have passed the first bar have enough momentum to proceed. But only 15 percent reach more than ten thousand and only 0.7 percent reach more than one hundred thousand, the official measure of success. The US petitions are shown in Figure 3.3 and demonstrate a much higher density of petitions in the middle range, with a similar number of high successes as for the current UK site, and none of its failures.

To compare the pattern of petition signatures in the two countries, we removed all the petitions with fewer than 150 signatures from the UK data and calculated the Gini coefficient (a measure

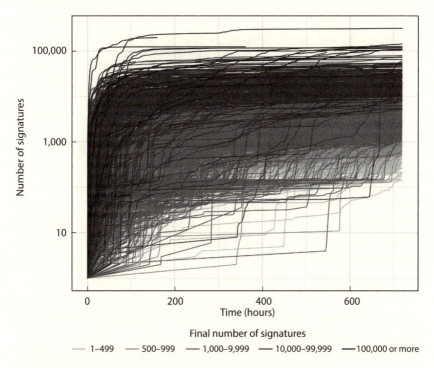

FIGURE 3.3 Petition growth on the US petition site, 2011–13

Note: The graph represents 19,789 petitions, created between 5 August 2011 and 22 February 2013. A logarithmic scale is used on the y-axis. The shading indicates the total number of signatures received by each petition at the end of the data collection period.

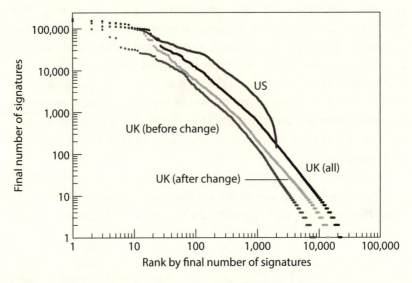

FIGURE 3.4 Comparing the signature distributions of US and UK petitions
Note: The total number of signatures given to each petition is plotted against the rank of the petition among all of them after sorting according to the total number of signatures. The US petitions curve has a slower decrease, indicating that there are more midrange petitions in the US compared to the UK samples.

of inequality in a distribution) for the two datasets. The Gini coefficient or Gini index for the UK petitions was 0.82, while that for the US distribution was much lower, at 0.70. Basically, by barring the entry of all petitions until they get 150 signatures and imposing a strict deadline on petition life (one month), we have shown that there is less variation between petitions in the US case. Figure 3.4 shows this graphically.

HOW COLLECTIVE ATTENTION FADES

The results from all three datasets show just how few petitions actually attain success by any measure. For the earlier data from the No. 10 Downing Street site, the five-hundred-signature mark seems at first consideration a very low threshold that should easily be passed. However, by far the majority of petitions (94 percent in this time period) failed to attain even this modest number of signatures, illustrating that in online environments, the low costs of initiating a collective action portend large numbers of unsuccessful mobilizations—though of course we need to be careful making a comparison with the past as we often do not know how many small unsuccessful petitions there were in the period when petitions were done on paper. Petitions are most active when they are first launched, and most petitions (presumably in the lack of support) make no impact after a couple of months despite one-year deadlines on both UK petition sites. Our second UK dataset tells the same story, suggesting that this finding may be generalized to other mobilizations, rather than representing some characteristics of the original No. 10 Downing Street platform. The finding that most mobilizations of this kind fail to take off in any sense chimes well with recent research into the spread or diffusion of initiatives across online networks. As discussed in Chapter 2, Goel et al. analysed the diffusion patterns arising in various online domains, ranging from networked games to micro-blogging services, finding that the vast majority of adoption cascades, whereby attention rises and crosses over to many networks and venues, are small, and are described by a handful of simple 'tree structures' that usually terminate within one degree of an initial adopting 'seed'.[14] Even for the few large cascades that they observed, the bulk of adoptions often take place within one connection of a few dominant individuals. Although we have not yet made an attempt to model the network activity behind the petitions studied here, it seems likely that they would reveal a similar pattern.

The pattern of early, rapid growth that we observe consistently across the successful petitions is contrary to what we might expect from formal theoretical analysis of collective action. That is, the function commonly used to describe collective action, mobilization more generally, and other social phenomena such as technology diffusion is an S-shaped curve,[15] with a gradual start and buildup, eventually tipping over into critical mass. As with the mobilizations against racist policing in the United States on Twitter and Facebook shown in Chapter 2, we see little sign of this pattern here for those petitions that clearly do attain critical mass.

We attempt to capture the characteristic of early rapid growth and decay revealed by the data with a model of collective attention decay, drawing on Wu and Huberman on the novelty of new items in Digg.com, the link-sharing platform.[16] In their model, they calculate a novelty parameter relating to the freshness of news items on the platform, but in a more general framework the decay in attention could have reasons other than novelty, for example due to a failure of viral spread. In our model, N agents at time t bring $N\mu$ new agents into the next step on average, with μ being a multiplication factor; in our case, this would mean that every signature brings μ new signatures in the next hour, leading to an exponential growth of rate μ in the number of signatures. This model works quite well at the beginning but decays very quickly as new signatures come at a much lower rate. Therefore we let the multiplication factor decay by introducing a second factor $r(t)$, which atrophies in a way that is intrinsic to each medium; each signature at time t, on average, brings $\mu r(t)$ new signatures in the next hour. To correct for the early saturation observed in the empirical results, we enter an outreach parameter that can change over time and dampen the fast initial growth. To calculate that empirically, we average over the logarithm of the number of signatures in hourly bins, starting from the launching time, and then calculate the hourly increment at time t and normalize it by the logarithm of the number of signatures up to time t as follows:

$$r(t) = \frac{E[log(N(t))] - E[log(N(t-1))]}{E[log(N(t))]} \qquad (3.1)$$

In other words, the outreach factor measures the relative growth of the logarithm of number of signatures within an hour, averaged over the whole sample. This parameter is shown as a function of adjusted time (time from the launch of each petition) in Figure 3.5. This shows that collective attention on petitions decays very fast indeed and that after twenty-four hours a petition's fate is virtually sealed.

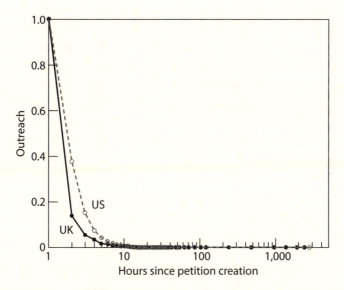

FIGURE 3.5 Time evolution of collective attention paid to petitions
Note: The figure shows how the collective attention to the petitions measured as 'outreach factor' based on Equation 3.1 decays in time for the Cabinet Office and the US petition websites. The x-axis uses a logarithmic scale.

PETITIONS AS A SOURCE OF TURBULENCE

Having identified the crucial importance of the early stages of a petition, we went on to examine other factors that affect the shape of mobilization curves. A possible hypothesis may be derived from previous research on agenda setting in political systems. The best-known model of how policy attention develops in a liberal democracy is punctuated equilibrium, developed by the American academics Frank Baumgartner and Bryan Jones (whose work was discussed earlier in this book) and then tested in the Policy Agendas Project (www.policyagendas.org), a research programme on US politics and institutions, and also replicated in the Comparative Policy Agendas Project (www.comparativeagendas.org).

The model implies that policy attention to any issue will be characterized by long periods of stasis during which little change occurs. When issues do eventually hit the policy agenda, it is usually because of positive feedback causing all eyes (including the media, public opinion, interest groups, and politicians concerned) to turn to the issue, resulting in money being spent, institutions being created, and policy change occurring.[17] As a result of these processes, political attention punctuates. The punctuated equilibrium model occurs in many contexts and venues, and has been illustrated by a range of empirical data across policy areas and within different dimensions of attention, such as public opinion, budgetary change, and congressional attention,[18] and in various countries, including the United Kingdom.[19] Baumgartner and Jones do not discuss Internet-related activity to any great degree; however, we might hypothesize that the pattern of mobilizations around a petition would proceed in a similar way. For example, a petition that has languished for months (e.g., repressive laws about child protection) might suddenly become massively popular if something external happens, such as the murder of a child, and then is taken up politically. In this way, Internet mobilizations contribute to or even accelerate the same sort of issue expansion that has been observed many times over in agenda-setting research, such as with focusing events that are associated with a change in attitudes and attention. Such a model would predict that the distribution of daily changes in attention would be leptokurtic, that is, with a small number of large changes in the 'tails' of the distribution and a large number of much smaller ones in the central 'hump'. The model would not be normal with random distribution of changes around a median point.

Such a finding could not show any causal effect, as only the activity of petitioners is being analysed here (though tipping points could suggest the broadcast media are important, although it is extremely unlikely that this could take place before substantive amounts of signatures had amassed). It could, however, point towards a role for online mobilization in policy change analogous to that of the media in the agenda-setting analysis, which are ascribed a lurching effect, due to the capacity of the media to parallel process only a small number of issues; at the point at which a punctuation occurs, media attention will tip over from specialist outlets into the mainstream media.

Leptokurtic distributions have a more acute peak close to the median and longer tails than normal distributions. Several tests in combination help to demonstrate that a distribution is leptokurtic.[20] One is a test to show whether or not the distribution is normal. The most rigorous test is the Shapiro-Wilk test, which checks whether the points could possibly be drawn randomly from a normal distribution.[21] Leptokurtic distributions should reject the Shapiro-Wilk null hypothesis of normality. The Kolmogorov-Smirnov test establishes whether a set of frequencies is normally distributed by focusing on the skewness and kurtosis (i.e., the degree to which the bands of frequencies cluster at the central and extreme points) of a distribution;[22] this null hypothesis should be rejected if a distribution is leptokurtic and therefore non-normal. Visualizing the histogram and plotting a log-log plot, which should be nearly a straight line if changes are leptokurtic, provides further evidence of a leptokurtic distribution.

We looked for evidence of leptokurtic distributions in our data harvested from the first UK petitions platform on the No. 10 website, and the results are shown in Figure 3.6. The figure shows the percentage change in new signatures at intervals of 5 percent, adjusted so that the mean growth of each petition lies at zero. While we can see that most daily change is small, petition growth is punctuated by a few large changes. The distribution of growth strongly rejects the Shapiro-Wilk null hypothesis of normality with a w statistic of 0.17, translating to a p-value less than .000001, and also rejects the Kolmogorov-Smirnov test for a normal distribution ($p < .0001$). The distribution has a kurtosis score of 1,445 (very leptokurtic) and a skewness of 30.53. When we applied the same tests to the population of petitions that were successful in achieving five hundred signatures (that is, when excluding the unsuccessful ones), we found a similar leptokurtic distribution (Shapiro-Wilk w statistic of 0.10, $p < .000001$).

As we would expect from the earlier section of this chapter, which identified the importance of the first day for the later success

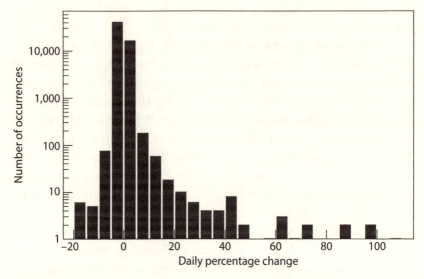

FIGURE 3.6 Log of daily percentage change in number of signatures, centred around each petition's mean
Note: Any final periods before the closing dates during which petitions gained no more signatures were removed from the data (i.e., the tallest bars do not include these 'zero change' days).

of a petition, the largest daily changes happened at the start of petitions' life cycles. Looking at the distribution of the days on which changes occurred, we see that (for example) all daily changes of more than 80 percent occurred in the first 5 days, and greater than 40 percent in the first 8 days, and even for all changes over 40 percent, the median day is 1, the mean is 2.2, and the third quartile is 1. Petitions tended to grow shortly after their launch and then stop growing. This active period of growth for petitions had a mean length of 57 days and a median length of 27 days.

We can see therefore that mobilizations around petitions have a leptokurtic distribution, with short bursts and long periods of stasis. This finding suggests that in online environments, collective action could play a role in a punctuated equilibrium model of policy change. That is, the norm in terms of policy attention is for issues to remain largely dormant or in stasis, with a generally low level of attention. Some issues (by far the minority) that attract attention quickly gain a critical mass of activists and start to vie for policy attention, joining the range of other institutional influences in helping to punctuate the equilibrium. Such an argument would not include the claim that the mechanism by which collective action acts to bring about instability would be the same as the role played by the media, which performs a distinctive lurching function in Jones and Baumgartner's analysis. In the context studied here, the social media boost would tend to predate media attention, although they could also have a reinforcing effect once a petition did receive media attention.

HOW TWEETS SPUR ON PETITIONS

As shown above, many petitioners arrive at the petitions site via social media, but to what extent does activity on social media fuel petition signing? To investigate the relationship between petition signing and tweeting about petitions, we employ data derived from collecting tweets for two months within the time period in which we collected the UK petition data. For the 481 petitions that were active between April and May 2013, we have 327,430 signatures and 35,540 tweets. We found a fairly clear correlation between these two in terms of attention (the correlation coefficient between the logarithms of the number of signatures to each petition and number of tweets mentioning that petition is 70); the larger the number of signatures, the larger the number of tweets. Of course such data give no indication of causality as it could be that more tweets produce more signatures, or the other way around.

To check the causality, for each petition we created two time series: the number of daily signatures and the number of daily tweets. We carried out a time-shifted cross-correlation analysis, by shifting the tweets time-series by τ days (τ could be positive or negative, resulting in a shifting forwards or backwards in time), and calculated the cross-correlation of the shifted series of tweets to

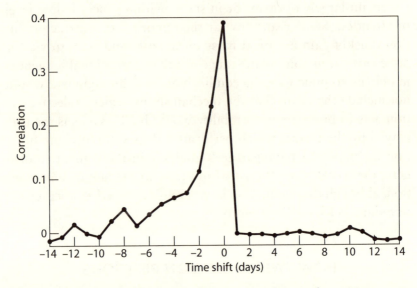

FIGURE 3.7 Comparing the timing of signatures and tweets for petitions
Note: The plot shows the value of the time-shifted cross-correlation C against the amount of time shift τ. C decays much slower for negative values of τ, indicating the priority of tweets to signatures in time and possible causalities.

the non-shifted time series of the signatures for each petition. Then we averaged over the whole sample to calculate the correlation, C. Figure 3.7 shows C plotted against τ. The largest value of C happens at $\tau = 0$, meaning that most of the fluctuations in both number of signatures and tweets happened on the same day. However, C drops rapidly for $\tau > 0$ (the tweets series shifted forwards) whereas it drops more slowly for $\tau < 0$ (tweets shifted backwards), meaning that fluctuations in the number of tweets take place before corresponding fluctuations of the number of signatures, suggesting that the tweets are driving signatures and not the other way around. A content analysis of the tweets undertaken by the authors points to the same conclusion, with frequent use of imperative terms and words like 'please' and 'sign' suggesting the use of twitter for requesting participation rather than simply broadcasting the success of the petition.

SOCIAL INFORMATION AS A SOURCE OF INSTABILITY

We have shown that most petitions fail, but that those that succeed do so quickly, and that social media seem to reinforce this process. We now turn to other influences on individuals' decisions to sign petitions. We would expect the strong effect of petitions tending to succeed quickly or not at all to be influenced by the design of the petition website; that is, the outreach factor we have introduced above will vary across platforms, according to the social information that is differentially presented to users about the popularity of petitions. For users starting at the homepage of the earlier No. 10 Downing Street site, it was possible to view petitions overall or within a specific category and to sort petitions by the number of signatures or the date added. It was therefore easiest to look at petitions with the largest or smallest number of signatures and the oldest or newest petitions. On the current Cabinet Office site, petitions can be sorted by signature or closing date, or viewed by government department, but not by topic. On the US We the People site, visitors have always been able to view the most popular petitions, sorted in descending order. In addition, we may expect different behaviours from users who either start from the homepage (who may engage with the available information cues by looking only at the newest or most popular petitions, contributing to the effects we have observed), or who follow links to a specific petition shared via email and social media, which may result in the user encountering different information cues.

These alternative effects on a user's behaviour due to the differing information environment they encounter can be tested using an experimental approach. As we have already noted, in April 2012, the UK Cabinet Office introduced a change to the petitions site that altered the information environment of prospective petitioners, by introducing a 'trending petitions' facility on the homepage, providing potential signatories with a new kind of social information about which petitions were successful and how many other people had signed. We assume that such a change is exogenous to

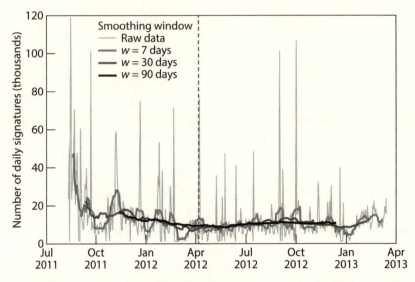

FIGURE 3.8 Aggregate number of daily signatures on the UK Cabinet Office petition platform before and after introduction of the trending petitions facility
Note: Dashed line shows the point of introduction of the trending petitions facility. Data have been smoothed with time windows of widths *w*.

political participation itself, so the time directly before and after the change is as if random. The fact that we captured data from this site both before and after this change provides us with a natural experiment (avoiding 'bundling' problems)[23] whereby we can test the effect of this change using a variety of methods, including interrupted series and regression discontinuity design.

First of all we tested the hypothesis that the trending facility would increase the overall number of signatures on the site, by attracting visitors to the most popular petitions. We calculated the daily number of signatures to all petitions for a period of twenty-two months, including ten months before the change and twelve months after it (Figure 3.8). We calculated an autoregressive moving-average time series under the null hypothesis that the introduction of trending petitions had no effect on the daily number of signatures, with the smoothing time windows of width $w = 7$, 30, and 90 days. We found that the change had no significant effect and fail to reject the null hypothesis (Figure 3.8). We can say, therefore, that the introduction of the trending facility on the website had no significant effect at the aggregated level and did not result in higher levels of petition signing overall.

If the introduction of the trending petitions facility did not affect the overall number of signatures on the site, did it change the distribution of signatures across petitions? Do the most popular petitions that appear in the trending box become more popular than they would have been had the facility not been introduced? We attempted to answer this question by calculating the Gini coefficient (the measure of inequality in a distribution) for all signatures on all active petitions during a short period, to see whether the distribution had become more unequal. We tested the distribution of signatures over petitions for windows of four days, calculating the Gini coefficient of the distribution within the time window. We then averaged for a period of three months before the change and

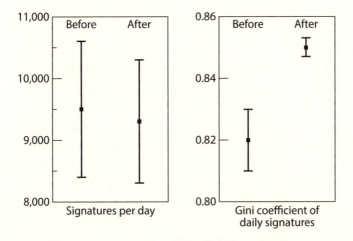

FIGURE 3.9 The effect of a change in design on daily signatures
Note: Left panel: The average number of daily signatures over a three-month period was 9,500 before the addition of the trending petitions facility and 9,300 after the addition, a non-significant difference (*p*-value = .2). Right panel: After the trending petitions facility was introduced, the Gini coefficient increased significantly from 0.82 to 0.85 (*p*-value = .002).

three months after, and calculated the standard deviations among the four-day windows within each of those two periods. The result of this analysis is shown in Figure 3.9, right panel. It shows clearly that after the trending petitions facility was introduced, the Gini coefficient increased significantly, meaning that there was a different shape to the petition after the change in design (error bars are calculated based on the standard deviation between the Gini coefficients calculated in each time window). The increase in the Gini coefficient indicates that signatures were significantly more concentrated on a small number of petitions after the design change than they were before.

We see that the addition of a trending petitions facility means that trending petitions receive more signatures. Given the fact that the overall number of signatures has not changed significantly, those that do not appear in the trending box receive fewer; that is, the information-rich get richer, and the information-poor get poorer. Such a result provides evidence of the heavy-tailed distributions (sometimes referred to as 'power laws') that crop up so often in Internet-based distributions, where social information is available about which online initiatives are popular.

SMALL DESIGN CHANGES HAVE UNINTENDED CONSEQUENCES

We now investigate which petitions benefit most from the 'rich getting richer' effect by investigating to what extent petitions in different positions on the homepage were affected. Here there are aspects of the presentation of social information that vary by chance, which have to do with the ordering of when people see how many other people have signed. The UK petition platform shows on its homepage the top six petitions receiving the most signatures in the past hour, with an option to click to see a further six petitions. If there is an impact of social information, there should be a greater impact of petitions at position 6 compared to petitions at position 7, but for all other purposes the differences between those signatures are assumed to be random. The change in the Gini coefficient indicates that the distribution of signatures across petitions has changed. Presumably the trending petitions have captured more signatures at the expense of non-trending petitions. This hypothesis can be tested directly with a regression discontinuity (RD) design, which is where a regression on the outcome using observations around the cut point can estimate the impact of the variable of interest.[24]

At this point, it is worth saying something in more detail about the design of the petitions site. Trending petitions appear on the homepage in a two-column ranked-ordered list. The petition with the most signatures in the past hour is in the top-left corner of the grid (position 1), while the petition with the second most signatures in the past hour is in the top-right corner of the grid (position 2). Position 3 is in the left column of the second row, position 4 is in the right column of the second row, and so on. The top trending petitions are shown in a two-column, three-row grid with the option to click a link to expose petitions in positions 7 to 12. Each user may sign a petition only once, and users do not know how many others will sign the same petition or another petition. It is therefore not possible for one user to directly control the position at which a petition trends on the homepage (or if it trends at all). The important difference in outcomes is between the ranks, and we can compare the signatures petitions in adjacent positions receive while trending on the homepage.

Our analysis differs from a classic RD design in three ways. First, the number of signatures a petition receives is a discrete variable, so we use the generalization of the RD design for discrete values used in Narayanan et al.[25] Second, the position of a petition is determined by the number of signatures in the hour prior to trending, whereas we measure the number of signatures in the hour while trending. We cannot assume complete independence between these values. Finally, we observe trending petitions only once an hour while the list is updated continuously in real time.

Figure 3.10 shows the difference in the number of signatures petitions in adjacent positions receive while trending. Petitions in

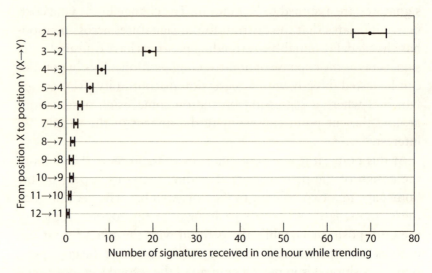

FIGURE 3.10 Comparisons of raw signatures in adjacent positions
Note: The graph shows 95 percent confidence intervals in the difference in the raw number of signatures petitions trending in adjacent positions receive while trending.

position 1, for instance, receive sixty-six to seventy-four more signatures in the hour while trending than petitions trending in position 2. This effect diminishes rapidly for lower positions.

This analysis, however, does not take into account the differences of individual petitions. To control for these differences, we calculate the mean number of signatures for each petition over a number of hours before it trends. Figure 3.11 shows a comparison of the differences from these means for adjacent positions. The means for the figure are calculated over a window of eighteen hours prior to each petition trending. The results are stable for values larger than this.

Within the limitations detailed above, our analysis shows that the trending petitions facility does concentrate attention and signatures on the first few ranked petitions. We find that the petition trending in the first position receives 3.8 to 11.3 more signatures above its mean than the petition trending in the second position. Similarly, a move from position 4 to position 3 is associated with 0.2 to 2.1 more signatures above the petition's eighteen-hour mean.

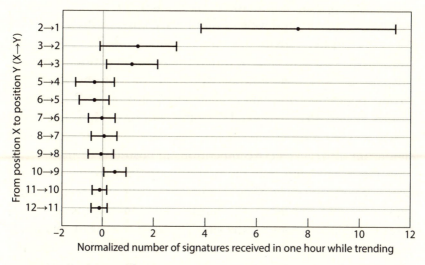

FIGURE 3.11 Comparisons of difference from eighteen-hour means in adjacent positions

Note: The graph shows 95 percent confidence intervals in the difference between petitions trending in adjacent positions simultaneously, but first subtracts from each petition its mean number of signatures for the eighteen hours prior to trending in order to control for individual variation of petitions.

The effect quickly dissipates for petitions in lower-ranked positions. So, while the trending facility does concentrate signatures, it does so only for petitions in the first few positions. Strangely, we see significant effects for moving from position 2 to position 1 and from position 4 to position 3, but not for moving from position 2 to position 1. We suspect the two-column layout is responsible for this oddity given the findings of eye-tracking studies with web search results in the field of human-computer interaction.[26] Users of search engines usually fixate on the results in the top position and then skim down the left side of the page (at least for users with left-to-right languages). This tendency to skim down the left side of the page means petitions in the left column (positions 1, 3, and 5) may stand out more than petitions in the right column (positions 2, 4, and 6) and likely explains why a move from position 3 to position 2 has no significant effect at a 95 percent confidence level.

Overall, our results provide a unique test for the provision of social information, and we find that the trending petition information concentrates attention to the top few ranked petitions. We expected to find a significant difference between petitions in positions 6 and 7, because position 6 appears in the bottom right of the trending petition information while viewing position 7 requires a further click to 'see additional trending petitions'. However, attention is so concentrated on the first few positions that we find no significant difference between petitions in positions 6 and 7.

So we have found that the addition of the trending petitions facility causes the most popular trending petitions to receive more signatures, and that these signatures come at the expense of signatures to other petitions on the site. The implications of this result are somewhat surprising. It suggests that some people come to the homepage of the petitions website looking for petitions to sign, or that they come to a specific petition on the site and then move on to the homepage looking for other petitions that interest them. These people have a zero-sum attention capacity: they will sign a certain number of petitions, but this number does not appear to have varied before and after the trending facility was introduced; so, if a particular petition attracts their attention, they will sign that one at the exclusion of another that they otherwise might have signed. It is worth noting that the petitions site lets users sign petitions only one at a time, and users must reenter their details (name, postcode, email address) separately for each petition they wish to sign. This evidence that people are coming to petition sites just to 'find something to sign' (rather than coming to sign a petition on a specific issue) suggests a general desire for political engagement— the 'aimless surfing' identified by Borge and Cardenal—without a firm view as to what the engagement should be about.[27] This group is not completely composed of aimless surfers however, because they know what they want to do, that is, to sign a petition. We might call this group 'aimless petitioners', people who want to do a 'little bit of politics' and sign a petition, but are not yet sure what about. We investigate their behaviour in more depth in the next section.

FOLLOWING THE 'AIMLESS PETITIONERS'

In the previous sections, we identified a significant change in the Gini coefficient of signatures per petition, but of a small magnitude (changing from 0.82 to 0.85). The largest possible change in magnitude, however, is limited by the number of visitors to the site exposed to the trending information, which is only on the homepage. In this section, we use site analytics data to understand what percentage of visitors is exposed to the trending information on the homepage. This allows us to compute that the largest possible shift in the Gini coefficient is only 0.04, and thus the 0.03 magnitude shift we observed indicates that a large portion of users exposed to the trending information are affected by it. These are the 'aimless petitioners' identified in the previous section.

We cannot match the analytics data (which relate to user visits to the site) with the petitions data (which relate to petition signatories), and in any case do not have the analytics data for the time that the platform was changed (our analytics data are limited to the period of December 2012 to April 2014), but we can use them to examine the behaviour of users of the site who visit the homepage, and therefore see the trending information. To further understand user behaviour on the petitions website, and specifically to characterize the 'aimless petitioners', we analysed the behaviour flow of the users through the site, in order to investigate how many users see the trending petitions information on the homepage and from where those users come.[28]

As noted in Figure 3.1, nearly half of the traffic to the petitions site now comes from Facebook, but these visitors tend to arrive at the site on a page relating to a specific petition. Overall, only about 3.5 percent of all the visits to the website start at the homepage displaying the trending petitions information. If we look at the traffic sources of this 3.5 percent, we observe a very different pattern compared to the overall visits; only 6 percent of this 3.5 percent is sourced from Facebook (equally from mobile and desktop), while Twitter is only responsible for 2 percent of this direct traffic to the front page. About 44 percent of the visits starting at the homepage originated from Google, and 30 percent of them were direct visits (by users who had typed the web address of the petition site directly into their browsers, bookmarked the page, or clicked a link in an email). That many users starting at the homepage come from Google is not surprising, considering that the first search result in Google for the keyword 'petition' directs to this page (at least for users in the United Kingdom).

These observations contribute to a picture of aimless petitioners: they either just go to the website directly or look for the petition website in Google, without aiming at a certain petition. Apart from this group who visit the homepage and trending petition information directly, almost 10 percent of all the first clicks within the website (that is, by users who arrived at a page other than the homepage on the site) lead users to the homepage (with the trending petition information). This is followed by 7 percent, 8 percent, and 9 percent of second, third, and fourth interactions of the users with the website. Eventually, a consistent number of site visits at each stage directs to the trending petition information on the homepage. This also includes the users who sign a petition and then visit the homepage. Overall, this led to 2.35 million visits to the homepage (1.40 million unique visitors) out of the 63.6 million page views on the site overall (47.1 million unique page visits) during the period of traffic analysis. There were about 5.9 million visit sessions with at least one interaction with the site content (there were 21.8 million sessions in total, out of which 15.9 million ended without the user clicking on anything), and about 20 percent of all these sessions passed through the homepage at least once during the first ten clicks.

Using these numbers it is possible to estimate the theoretical maximum amount of change in the Gini coefficient of the signatures distribution that we would expect to see due to the social influence. We denote this change Δg, and based on a rough estimation it is straightforward to show that it cannot be larger than 0.04 even if all the visitors who had ever seen the trending petitions were to be affected and signed the top-ranking petitions instead of any other petition that they would have signed otherwise. The amount of actual change in the Gini coefficient that we observed in the signature data is 0.03, indicating that the effects of the local treatment is very strong, although due to the relatively small size of the treatment group (visitors who see the homepage) the overall effect on petitions as a whole is not extremely large (about 3 percent). The maximum value for Δg is limited not only by the relatively small size of the treatment group $(\frac{\Delta N}{N})$, but also by the large starting value of the Gini coefficient even before the introduction of the trending petition information. Since the Gini coefficient was already large even before the trending information was introduced $(g_0 = 0.82)$, it is rather unlikely to increase a large amount. If g_0 had been smaller before the change in the design, then the effect of the design change could have been even stronger. These results suggest that of the 1.4 million visitors to the homepage during this four-month time period, a significant proportion, around 80 percent, are influenced by the trending information on the site and opt to sign one of the most popular trending petitions. Some of this group may be visitors who had heard about a particular petition and used the trending information to find it quickly, but the high numbers of petitions available on the site at any point suggest that these would be a small proportion. So we can assume that the majority of those who are influenced by the trending information are indeed aimless petitioners, are open to mobilization, and are seeking to be mobilized.

INSTABILITY, AIMLESSNESS, AND UNPREDICTABILITY

We have found a number of sources of instability and turbulence in the process of mobilization around petitions. First, we have found that for petitions, growth tends not to occur, meaning that most mobilizations that are initiated fail. But where success happens, it proceeds in rapid bursts followed by periods of stasis. That is, in terms of this relatively popular collective activity of petition initiation and signing, a vast number of petitions are initiated; most of them fail, and attention tends to die away very quickly indeed. But those that succeed do so rapidly and dramatically, and it would be hard to predict which will succeed. In this way, we argue, online collective action of this kind acts as a source of instability and turbulence on the political environment. As petition platforms become increasingly popular, run not just by national governments but also by civic activism sites at both national and international levels such as the hugely successful petition platform change.org, we can expect the kind of turbulence we observed here to be a common feature of political life. This turbulence is reinforced on social media, where petitioners appeal to other users to sign petitions that they themselves have signed. In the case of Twitter at least, we have found evidence to suggest that these micro-donations on social media do indeed bring other petitioners to sign and spur on the accumulation of signatures for successful petitions.

We have investigated social information as a possible source of this turbulence. Platform designs that show social information about the most popular petitions help them to receive more signatures than one would expect just by virtue of their popularity, and in this zero-sum race for collective attention, those for which there is less evidence of popularity receive fewer signatures than their popularity would indicate, even though their actual signature levels may be very close to those that are shown as trending. In this way we have found the same kind of effects that Salganik et al. observed for cultural markets, where experimental subjects were shown varying information about the popularity of songs and were asked to rank them.[29] Subjects were more likely to rate highly those songs for which there was evidence of popularity, meaning that the information injected a source of instability into cultural markets: 'our results support the hypothesis that social influence, which here is restricted only to information regarding the choices of others, contributes both to inequality and unpredictability in cultural markets'.[30] It seems likely that this finding could be generalized to other forms of online collective action, as these kinds of popularity indicators are present in some form by default on most social media. Twitter, for example, displays unique words, phrases, and hashtags that are popular in recent tweets on the main screen of the user, and the 'Top Tweet' facility means that the most re-tweeted tweets produced by the accounts that a user follows are shown at the top of her Twitter feed. On Facebook, any post will show information about the number of likes, shares, and comments it has received, and popular items are shown at the top of the user's screen; YouTube shows the number of views, likes, and comments for each video, as well as the most popular videos, and so on. All this social information about popularity is likely to have the same kind of reinforcement effect on collective action via social media, reinforcing the popularity of some activities, and detracting from that of others, and increasing the level of instability in political markets for public attention.

The developers of the UK petitions platform did not anticipate that the trending information would significantly influence petition-signing behaviour. In contrast, we have found here that it did indeed have an effect, showing the importance of testing the impact of changes to platform design either in advance or in a natural experiment of this kind. Social information has proved itself influential on how people behave in digital settings, so it is reasonable to assume that if it is changed, then the change will affect behaviour. Our findings with respect to petition positioning on the screen show how quite small design decisions can have a large effect on behaviour, and in this case one that is not encouraging rational behaviour, as people sign petitions based on their positioning on the screen, rather than their popularity. Such findings show the importance of continually monitoring the effect of design alternatives.

For one group, social information seems to have a particularly strong effect. Although the effect size of the natural experiment for the complete population of petition signers was small, we identified a group of 'aimless petitioners', who deliberately sought out the homepage of the petitions platform where the information was displayed, knowing that they wanted to sign a petition but uncertain as to which one. For this group, the effect of the information was strong. The finding that some people are keen to participate politically in a generalized (rather than an issue specific) way might be taken as encouraging at a time when so much political commentary bemoans both the time that certain groups (particularly young people) spend online on social media, and growing political disengagement among these groups. We have some modest evidence here that in fact, significant numbers of people are looking for political causes as they go about their lives online. However, their existence also points to a further source of instability in political life, given that they represent a significant group who will be primarily influenced by social information such as peaks in popularity, and may well be influenced by rapidly accelerating trends appearing in social media regardless of issue salience or importance.

We have identified a number of drivers for turbulence in petition signing: the accelerating effect of social information and its reinforcement through social media, the rapid decay of collective attention, the unintended consequences of small design changes, and evidence of aimless petitioners who are particularly influenced by evidence of popularity, or unpopularity. These various sources of instability combine to produce a leptokurtic distribution of daily change in petition signing, with rapid bursts at the start of successful petitions, and long periods of stasis. This finding is no surprise, given the tendency for this type of fat-tailed distribution to emerge in so many areas of Internet-based activity. If online collective action is characterized by punctuations, then such activity could inject more instability into political systems that already have a punctuated pattern of policy making, observed so often in agenda-setting research.[31] In the theory of punctuated equilibrium, the media play a key role in encouraging decision makers to shift attention from one issue to another: there is feedback between public opinion and other agenda-setting venues. But the online mobilizations that we have studied here often come about independently of the conventional media, gaining media attention only when they obtain significantly high levels of support. For example, the UK petition on road pricing, which was successful in playing a role in policy change, received a great deal of media attention on reaching one million signatories. Of course, it can work the other way round, whereby attention in the conventional media, such as stories about child abuse or the preservation of sites of natural beauty (e.g., forests), can influence actions taken online. What is important is that these two venues are influencing each other in ways that magnify attention to issues and create large shifts in attention. Research that develops our understanding of the mechanics of this turbulence will be important for scholars and policy makers alike as collective action continues to move into online settings. If mobilizations follow a pattern of very low levels of attention punctuated by occasional spurts that grow rapidly into full-scale mobilizations that merge with other elements of the political system to push policy change on to the agenda and the institutional landscape, then we can expect to see increasing turbulence in contemporary politics, adding to the instability that Baumgartner and Jones and their co-investigators have uncovered so extensively in previous research.[32]

This chapter has demonstrated the potential for this type of big or large-scale data in political science research. The data we report here were automatically and non-obtrusively scraped to provide a dataset of real-time transactional data of a kind that have rarely before been available to political scientists. Of course, the data we have gathered are not so large in absolute terms and would be considered puny in some natural science disciplines. The point here is that our data represent the whole population of petition signing activity for the two countries in the periods we have studied, rather than a sample thereof, and they are real-time transactional data, rather than a survey of what people think they did or think they might do. The methods we have used here to harvest and analyse the data require skills and expertise and conceptual approaches that span academic disciplines. As large-scale data like these begin to be used more extensively for this kind of research, the ability to work across disciplines in this way will become increasingly important. Big data generated from social media also present possibilities for natural experiments, for example when a change to an online platform is introduced and data are collected before and after the change in order to understand its effects. Research of this kind can be shared with policy makers and inform the design of petition platforms into the future.[33]

We have identified instability and turbulence in online collective action, and in particular have identified social information about the participation of others as having a reinforcing effect on this turbulence. The natural experiment we describe here presented itself as one way of getting around the inability to make a causal inference in data of this kind. In the chapters that follow, we move on to further experimental work to delve further into the effects of this kind of social information on the propensity of people to participate in mobilizations, analysing the direct effect of different information environments on participation.

CHAPTER 4

HOW SOCIAL INFORMATION CHANGES THE WORLD

Information about what other people are doing is everywhere on social media. On Facebook users can see the most intimate details of what their friends are up to, who liked or shared what, when, and where, and simultaneously, on another part of the screen, find out what is most popular on Facebook across the nation or across the world. For any person users decide to follow on Twitter, they will know also how many other people have made the same choice; for any piece of information they view, they will know also how many times it has been shared; and at the same time, they will be made aware of what is trending on Twitter in real time. On YouTube, they will see how many people have watched any video they care to view and also the most popular videos on the YouTube platform as a whole, or in any category they select. Platforms vary in the way in which they alert people to what others are doing and the amount of such information they provide. YouTube, Facebook, and Twitter abound with it, while more private messaging systems like Snapchat and WhatsApp have less. But all provide some kind of social information about the actions of other people.

What effect on behaviour does all this social information have? In previous chapters, social information has been diagnosed as a form of influence exerted by social media on people deciding whether to participate. When citizens are invited to take part in a small way in some kind of political campaign or mobilization by friends, campaigning organizations, or some remote part of online social networks, these requests are accompanied by some kind of social information, and this information will influence their decision making. In the last chapter, we started to investigate the effect of one particular kind of social information, trending information, on people's propensity to sign petitions. We used a natural experiment and aggregate data to establish that petitions included in a 'trending' list receive disproportionately more signatures than those that are not, making popular petitions even more popular and unpopular petitions more unpopular, reinforcing inequality in the competition for public attention. Here we develop our analysis of social information effects at the individual level, investigating how social information acts upon individual subjects in an experimental setting.

We borrow the term 'social information' from social psychology, where 'social information processing' refers to the study of the informational and social environments within which individual behaviours occur and to which they adapt.[1] Social information may be presented in a variety of ways: as an aggregate count of participants, as the total amount contributed to a cause, or as some indication of relative popularity.[2] Potential participants construe this information as representing the behaviour of a 'generalized other' or social aggregate and take it into account when they are deciding whether to participate.[3] Social information may crowd out contributions (by making it appear that enough have been made already) or crowd them in by making them feel as if they also should be contributing, with evidence pointing to the latter as a result of conformity, social norms, or reciprocity.[4] Social information can also operate by affecting the perceived viability of a political mobilization, thereby impacting upon the perceived benefits of joining and altering the incentives of individuals to participate.

As discussed in Chapter 2, in online environments there is a far greater possibility of the potential participants receiving real-time feedback about how many other people have participated in any kind of activity, however small, in terms of how many have signed, participated in, donated to, supported, shared, liked, or downloaded something. Before social media became so ubiquitous, such information was likely to be available only when undertaking a high-cost act of political participation, such as joining a political party or attending a demonstration. Even then, the accuracy of the information was often questionable, with political parties always inclined to overstate their membership numbers and organizers of demonstrations often arguing with other bodies (such as the police) about how many demonstrators were involved. In a 2003 London demonstration against the Iraq War, police estimated protesters at three-quarters of a million, while the organizers claimed two million.[5]

In this chapter we start to probe the mobilization patterns analysed in Chapter 3. Can the provision of social information and its effect on individual decision making at different points in time explain the shape of the mobilization curves? We present two experiments designed to tackle this question, by investigating social information effects on the propensity of people to engage with political representatives and to support global issues relating to public goods. First, however, we review previous work on social information and collective action, identifying four lines of argument on social information effects from across the social science disciplines of political science, economics, communication, psychology, and sociology. Second, we discuss some of the strengths and flaws of previous experimental work in this field, and review more generally the experimental method. Third, we outline and report the results of our first experiment, an online field trial to test the effects of social information on people's propensity to write to their representatives on the social enterprise website writetothem.org. Fourth, we discuss our second experimental design, a quasi-field experiment where participants were asked to support global political issues under varying levels of social information. Finally, we discuss the implications of these experiments for political participation on social media more generally.

HOW SOCIAL INFORMATION PROMOTES
COLLECTIVE ACTION

What do we know already about the impact of social information on political participation? There is a body of work on collective action in political economy, sociology, and psychology, where theorists and empirical researchers have considered the informational context of participatory decision making. We consider below four distinct arguments regarding the effects of social information that have been identified in previous work: social pressure, conditional cooperation, tipping points, and bandwagon effects. Research that uses these perspectives identifies different causal mechanisms to explain how citizens react to social information.

One argument about how social information can exert social pressure on individuals' decisions about whether to participate can be linked to Olson's classic work *The Logic of Collective Action*, in which he argues that individuals take into account information about the potential size of the group when they consider whether to participate.[6] If they perceive the group to be small, they consider it worthwhile to contribute; but in a large latent group no member will be significantly affected by the actions of another, so no one will have an incentive to contribute. Although Olson does not discuss social information explicitly, he does consider the effect of social pressure to incentivize group members to participate in small groups, but discards it for larger groups: 'In general social pressure and social incentives operate only in groups of smaller size, in groups so small that the members can have face-to-face contact with one another'.[7] As discussed in Chapter 1, there is a body of work discussing how the widespread use of the Internet could affect Olson's thesis, particularly by reducing the costs of coordination, which makes large groups more viable.[8] Lupia and Sin point to a possible effect of the Internet's capacity to provide social information as a form of coercion,[9] highlighting a footnote in *The Logic of Collective Action*: 'If the members of a latent group are somehow continuously bombarded with propaganda about the worthiness of the attempt to satisfy the common interest in question, they may perhaps in time develop social pressures not entirely unlike those that can be generated in a face-to-face group, and these social pressures may help the latent group to obtain the collective good'.[10] Writing in the pre-Internet era, Olson argued that such social pressures would be prohibitively expensive for groups to exert, but decades later 'evolving technologies reduce substantially the costs of communicating with large audiences'.[11] We join Lupia and Sin in viewing this hypothesis as worthy of testing, which we perform below.

Economists studying the effect of information about the contributions of others on people's willingness to undertake pro-social behaviour, in particular making charitable donations, have labelled it 'conditional cooperation' (that is, cooperation dependent on evidence of the contribution of others). Such work has shown that social information increases charitable giving and willingness to participate in public goods provision and that this effect increases with larger numbers of additional participants.[12] It has also been shown that people are likely to increase their contribution (by donating more money, for example) if they know that other people are increasing the size of their commitment.[13] This work provides robust evidence of social information effects, and we follow these researchers in using experiments to vary randomly the existence and level of social information provided to participants. But the experiment presented here diverges from this work in a number of ways. First, most of the work undertaken thus far on conditional cooperation looks at charitable donations, rather than an explicitly political context as we do here. Second, work on conditional cooperation has tended to focus on the influence of social information on contribution amount, rather than participation per se. Psychological research shows that 'decisions about whether to act and about how much to act, although positively correlated, may be caused by different psychological motivations',[14] indicating that the specific question of how social information affects people's decision whether or not to act politically is worthy of further investigation.

Other claims about social information effects can be drawn from sociological work on critical mass and tipping points. The sociologists Marwell and Oliver claim (in contrast to Olson) that larger groups find it easier to form, as their size ensures a critical mass of activists who organize around public goods and any indication of large group size will act as a sign of viability and increase the rate of mobilization.[15] They claim that the costs of collective action do not vary with group size because they are the same regardless of the number of potential contributors, so it is irrelevant how many others there are over and above the critical mass, removing the free-riding problem: 'It is not whether it is possible to mobilize everyone who would be willing to be mobilized. . . . Rather, the issue is whether there is some social mechanism that connects enough people who have the appropriate interests and resources so that they can act'.[16] In this view, evidence of a critical mass sends a vital signal to potential participants about the viability of the group, and social information of this kind could act as a tipping point, making a movement self-sustaining and bringing a rapid increase in participation. As discussed in Chapter 1, both Schelling and Granovetter used threshold models to develop the concepts of critical mass and tipping points and to explain why some mobilizations succeed and some do not.[17]

The fourth argument supporting the idea of a dynamic relationship between collective action and social information is based on the bandwagon effect, a label given to a situation where the information about majority opinion will cause individuals to rally to that opinion. In the same way, some authors have argued that individuals who perceive themselves to be in the minority will feel pressure either to express the majority opinion or to remain silent, in what has been termed the 'spiral of silence',[18] which would act to reinforce the bandwagon effect. Conversely, an underdog effect is held to exist if low levels of social information cause some people to support a minority view.[19] Studies of the bandwagon effect are usually carried out on voting behaviour—where opinion polls provide the social information—and have also been applied to public opinion on key policy issues,[20] reflecting the concern of such research with opinion formation. Researchers of the bandwagon effect are interested in whether potential participants change their views in response to knowing the views of others, rather than people's willingness to participate at all, as in the research reported here. However, given that the effects of social information on these different parts of the decision-making process can be difficult to distinguish, we use the bandwagon idea to provide an alternative hypothesis for the effect social information might have. Empirical support for the bandwagon effect is sparse,[21] and where an effect has been identified it seems to apply only to social information about trends rather than to current levels of support. Nadeau et al. find only an absolute effect of information about trends with no numbers.[22] Marsh also shows that information about 'static' public opinion (that is, absolute percentages of support) has no effect on people's willingness to participate, although information about dynamic public opinion trends (e.g., that support is rising, as in trending information) has an effect on support.[23] A meta-analysis of survey studies from spiral of silence research finds little support for the theory.[24]

Previous research thereby provides four alternative arguments about the possible effects of social information on collective action: social pressure, critical mass, conditional cooperation, and the bandwagon effect. We test how social information provided online affects political participation by fostering conditional cooperation,[25] by applying social pressure,[26] by sending a signal of viability or critical mass,[27] or by generating a bandwagon effect.[28] We focus on anonymous information about other people rather than on effects deriving from individuals' social and personal networks. Our expectation is that social information about the preferences of others will affect the decision whether to incur costs in the pursuit of collective action, with the influence varying according to the levels of participation. Previous work provides us with alternative expectations about the effect of different levels of social information. That is, work on conditional cooperation, critical mass, the bandwagon effect, and Lupia and Sin's revision of Olson's social pressure argument leads us to predict that a high number of social information would have a positive effect, either because it is an indicator that other people are cooperating and therefore encourages reciprocity or compliance with social norms; because it exerts social pressure; because it acts as a signal of viability, indicating the likelihood of attaining critical mass; or because it indicates majority opinion and exerts a bandwagon effect. Where social information is low, Olson would argue that evidence of a small number of petitioners could encourage individuals to incur the costs of signing up, while the other views would claim that low levels of social information would have a negative effect, in the early stages of a petition for example.

Within this generalised pattern, the different arguments discussed above would lead us to expect different effects from social information at the higher end. For conditional cooperation, we expect social information to have a greater effect for reports about high numbers of other participants. However, experimental work has indicated that the differential effects would not be very large. Frey and Meier found, for example, that for two treatment groups given information about a relatively high percentage of contributors to a charitable campaign (64 percent) or a relatively low percentage (46 percent), participation rates varied by only 2.3 percent, which was not a statistically significant difference.[29] For arguments about social pressure, with the hypothesis that indications of large numbers of participants could exert the same type of social pressure as Olson observed for small groups, there is little available evidence to inform our expectation of the relative weights of such pressure; large numbers might have the same effect as small numbers, meaning that the effect of social information would be relatively consistent, or could dip for middling numbers. For bandwagon effects, we expect that there would be a continuously positive effect of information about the participation of others, which would increase in a cumulative way, yielding an exponential curve if the percentage of people participating were plotted against the percentage expected to participate.

EXPERIMENTING WITH SOCIAL INFORMATION

Experimental methodologies are the perfect way to investigate the effect of social information. As discussed in Chapter 1, by randomly varying the information provided to subjects and observing the resulting effect on their behaviour, we can obtain unbiased estimates of how different kinds of information affect participation. Provided they have been implemented without threats to internal validity, experiments can provide a causal inference of the effect of one variable on another.

Experiments have already been used to test some elements of the four groups of arguments outlined above, first to test the social pressure claim, particularly to investigate people's willingness to undertake environmentally conscious behaviour, but also for charitable donations and voting turnout. In Goldstein et al.'s widely reported experiment with the recycling of towels in hotels, a treatment group received a message to say that 75 percent of guests had recycled their towels.[30] This group was 26 percent more likely to recycle than those who saw the basic pro-environmental message about not laundering towels unnecessarily. Where participants were given more local information, which was feedback information on the past recycling behaviour of guests who had used the same room, the difference with the control group was even greater. Schultz conducted a randomized controlled trial examining the impact on recycling behaviour of providing written feedback on individual and neighbourhood recycling behaviour, finding statistically significant increases from baseline in the frequency of participation and total amount of recycled material.[31] The most influential treatments were door hangers informing households of the average amount of material collected from householders and the percentage participating in recycling in their immediate locality. Similarly, Gerber, Green and Larimer ran a large-scale field experiment to show the positive effect of social pressure on voter turnout, by telling subjects which of their neighbours had voted,[32] which has been followed up by a series of papers and tests.[33] For conditional co-operation, economists have used laboratory experiments involving public goods and cooperation games,[34] and, more recently, field experiments in which subjects are provided with varying levels of information about the participation of others.[35]

There is much less experimental research investigating either critical mass or bandwagon effects. Marwell and Oliver give a largely theoretical argument for the existence of critical mass and do not attempt to put a numerical value on it, either in terms of absolute numbers or percentages, nor do they test its existence empirically. However, empirical support for the bandwagon effect does come from an experiment, suggesting that there is an effect of around 5 to 7 percent;[36] when subjects were told that opinion was growing for an issue, they were 5 to 7 percent more likely to support this issue themselves compared with a control group. The meta-analysis of spiral of silence research mentioned above found the field to be dominated by survey-based studies, but noted that 'experimental studies are perhaps better suited' to answer the type of questions asked.[37]

In the next section, we present the first of our two experiments aimed at answering these kind of questions by testing the effect of social information on people's participatory behaviour. We examine how social information influences people's propensity to engage with politicians by contacting them with a concern or regarding a policy issue.

AN EXPERIMENT ON CITIZEN ENGAGEMENT WITH POLITICIANS

The potential influence of social information extends to the whole range of political behaviours. One common citizen action is to make contact with their politicians, which can be for a variety of reasons: to express a viewpoint on a policy issue, to complain about something in the jurisdiction, to express a view about the quality of a public service from a recent experience, or to make a representation about a wider policy issue that the respondent cares about. Websites and social media make the process much easier than before, as previously it was harder to find out who was one's local elected representative. It may have been possible in the past to have phoned the local council to ask for the information; or perhaps a leaflet had been dropped off and the citizen had kept it; or maybe the details were found in a telephone book. It is likely that many people who thought about writing to their representative did not follow through because of the associated costs, unless they were very angry. Now such information is readily available online.

As introduced in Chapter 2, the nonprofit organization mySociety has a number of web applications that aim to make it easier for citizens to contact or engage with representatives. For politicians in the United Kingdom, the associated website is WriteToThem. Respondents fill in their postcode and the screen lists their representatives, such as the local MP, member of European Parliament, and local government councillors. The website indicates the activities these representatives are responsible for. It is possible to click on a name, and the website generates a form starting with, for example, 'Dear Emily Thornberry . . .', an MP for Islington (where one of the authors lives), then some blank space for completing the letter. All the respondent has to do is fill out some personal details, then click on the 'Preview and Send' button, and the letter goes straight to the MP. Here is a case where an Internet-enabled application reduces the costs of participation.

The experiment utilizing WriteToThem was conducted from October to December 2013. It took advantage of a common phenomenon when people examine information and decide what to do next—only some follow through and make an enquiry through the website. The mySociety tools enabled us to vary randomly the information that the respondents saw on their screen. Respondents were randomly allocated to two groups. For the control group, the screen remained as before, with no social information; the intervention or treatment group was shown social information in the form of how many others had already written to the MP (see an example in Figure 4.1). Over the three-month period, this field

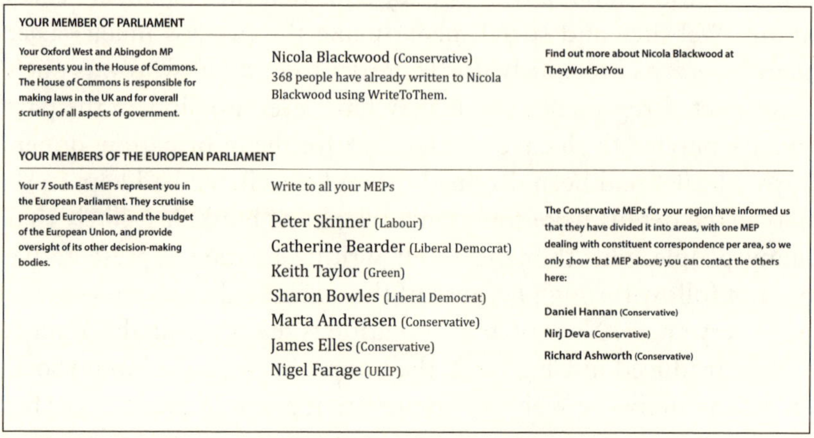

FIGURE 4.1 Screenshot of example of the intervention in the WriteToThem experiment. Courtesy of Tom Steinberg, director, mySociety.

experiment produced a sample of 18,818 people in the control and 11,818 in the treatment groups.

Our expectation is that overall, social information will not affect the numbers of people in the treatment group who write to MPs as different levels of social information will have different effects. That is, the information that many other people have written to an MP could increase the propensity to write for those users who saw information about that MP in comparison with the control group, while information that few other people have written could decrease that propensity, with the potential that the effect of high and low levels of social information will cancel each other out. Respondents experienced a lot of variation: at the lower end fifty-five subjects saw MPs to whom nobody had written, and at the top end fifty-one subjects saw an MP to whom 560 others had written (Gerald Kaufman, a former minister). The mean is 169 and the spread (standard deviation) is 83 (see Figure 4.2, a histogram of the numbers shown to the treatment group). The effect of positive social information should increase the numbers of people going forward, but we would expect this to be countered by the drag of people seeing low numbers who would be discouraged.

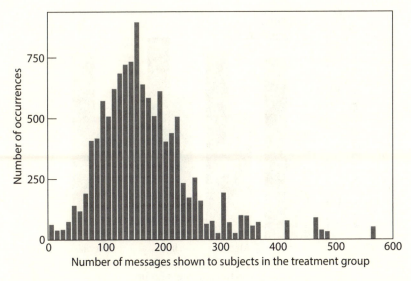

FIGURE 4.2 Variations in the social information given to users in the treatment group

Moving to the results, overall 39 percent of visitors who went to the message page for their MP went on to send a letter. Out of these, 32.6 percent in the control group sent a message, compared to 49.5 percent for those who saw social information, a significant difference ($z = 20.4$, $p < .001$). This is a substantive social information effect, and runs contrary to our expectations that social information would not make a significant difference until we controlled for the actual numbers shown. This finding is rendered the more remarkable by the fact that we might expect a third variable to be dampening the difference between the control and treatment groups. That is, some MPs have higher profiles than others, for example through ministerial roles or high media exposure. We might expect these high-profile MPs to receive more contacts from members of both the control and treatment groups anyway, regardless of whether social information is provided, and this 'third variable effect' could dampen the impact of social information by reducing differences between groups in a non-random way. We proceeded, therefore, to test the effect of varying levels of social information, which might control for the effect of this third variable.

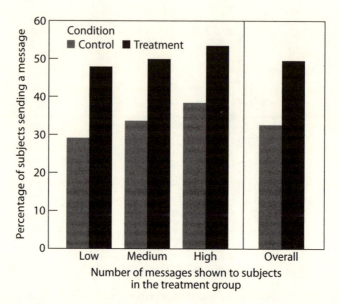

FIGURE 4.3 Percentage of messages sent to MPs grouped into low, medium, and high

Grouping the numbers shown associated with each MP into three bins of equal size (low, medium, and high), we find that citizens writing to MPs in the medium and high groups send a greater percentage of their messages than do citizens writing to MPs in the low group (Figure 4.3). Within the treatment group, however, the percentages of citizens going on to submit their letter do not differ significantly between the groups.[38] That is, while the overall effect of social information is substantive, a high level of social information has no greater effect than a low level. Again, the finding that all levels of social information had more or less similar effects is contrary to what we expected.

So social information seems to be affecting people's propensity to contact their representative, in a field experiment setting that provides us with external validity and allows us to generalize to other real-life contexts. Social information has a strong positive effect overall, but we have not identified any variations in effect from different levels of social information, something observed in some of the experiments discussed in the second section. There are three possible explanations for this finding, all of which derive from the field experiment setting. First, the effect of the third variable noted above, the profile of MPs, might also be having a mediating effect, in that it is affecting the social information (the independent variable) as well as the propensity for citizens to write to that MP (the dependent variable). A second possible explanation operating at the higher level of social information is provided by the small numbers of participants in the higher groups; only fifty-one participants saw social information numbering over five hundred (those who saw Gerald Kaufman), which reduces our ability to test for the effect of social information at this level, particularly as even this level might not be regarded by participants as especially high, in a constituency of over seventy-six thousand. A third explanation is provided by the distinctive context of contacting a representative in a UK setting, where this action is an official part of the citizen redress process. Constituents who are writing to complain about an issue relating specifically to themselves, in this sense a private rather than public good, are unlikely to be affected by the information that very few or no other citizens have contacted the representative, and in this way are immune to the social information effect.

We proceed therefore to our next experiment, using a more controlled environment that allowed us to design out some of these issues deriving from the field setting and to test for varying levels of social information with no third variable effect as provided by the profile of the representative. We could also ensure that there were sufficient numbers of participants receiving higher levels of social information and use a context, support for global political issues concerning public goods, where the mechanism for reacting to social information was likely to be similar across issues.

AN EXPERIMENT ON WILLINGNESS TO SUPPORT GLOBAL POLITICAL ISSUES

In order to test for the effect of different levels of social information, we designed a quasi-field experiment,[39] drawing on experiments that have tested for social information effects in non-political contexts, particularly those conducted by Goel et al. and Salganik et al.[40] As discussed in Chapter 3, Salganik et al. explored the effect on cultural markets of information about other people's preferences through an Internet-based field experiment that encouraged people to participate by providing them with free downloads of songs.[41] For political activity, however, such incentives are difficult to build into an Internet-based environment, so we adopted a quasi-field design, where we used subjects from our own subject database, but they participated remotely in their own homes using a custom-built interface, making the environment more 'natural' and allowing us to lower the incentives in comparison with the laboratory. In this way, we could (to some extent) control people's exposure to other forms of social information during the course of the experiment (which was strictly timed), but were able to recruit a far larger sample than would have been possible in a laboratory setting, thereby overcoming some of the external validity problems of laboratory experiments and some of the internal validity problems of field experiments.[42]

From our OxLab subject database we recruited a subject pool of 668 people who participated in the experiment remotely by considering six global issues successively through a custom-built web interface. They were invited (1) to express their willingness to sign a petition supporting the issue and (2) to donate a small amount of their participation fee to either supporting or fighting the issue. To express their willingness to sign a petition, subjects were required to provide their name, email, and address. This meant they had to incur some costs to support their statement even though they did not sign the petition. As a second step, we asked participants if they would like to donate twenty pence towards or against every issue, a sum that the experimenters matched in the final donation. We randomly allocated the subjects to a control group (of 173) and a treatment group (of 495).

All participants received the same six petitions with different levels of social information. In the control condition, participants received no information about how many people had already signed. For social information, we defined three categories; high, medium,

and low. We defined high numbers as over one million (having observed a distinctive effect for numbers over one million in the pilot
laboratory experiment), low numbers as below 100, and medium
numbers as between one million and one hundred, after observing
a weaker but still statistically significant effect of medium numbers
in the pilot. We randomized the social information (low, medium,
or high numbers of other signatories) across subjects for each petition, allowing us to control for the effect specific to particular
issues as well as for specific levels of social information.

In the treatment groups, subjects were shown two petitions in
each of the following categories:

- Petitions with very large numbers of signatories (S > 1 million)
- Petitions with medium numbers of signatories (100 < S <
  1 million)
- Petitions with very low numbers of signatories (S < 100)

We randomized the order in which participants saw the six petitions to eliminate systematic biases relating to ordering. Members
of the control group were shown the same petitions, with no social
information, again in random order.

The issues were all selected to be of international significance,
and petitions were drawn from across different geographical spaces
and points in time within the previous three years. The petitions
were shown in a generic format (to control for the reputation effect that different web platforms would bring), but the numbers of
signatories shown to the participants were taken from existing online petitions that had been created on these issues with different
numbers of signatories (low, medium, and high). In this way we
ensured that there was no deception in the experiment, because all
were a representation of a real online petition with numbers that
were current for that petition in some context.

The petitions were (with the high, medium, and low numbers
shown in parentheses) the following:

1. National governments should put pressure on the Chinese
   leadership to show restraint and respect for human rights

in response to protests in Tibet (high: 1,682,242, medium: 1,189, low: 76)

2. National governments should negotiate and adopt a treaty to ban the use of cluster bombs (high: 1,200,000, medium: 330,000, low: 7)

3. Governments should lobby the Japanese government to stop commercial whaling of the humpback whale (high: 1,082,808, medium: 57,299, low: 98)

4. Governments should support a stronger multinational force to protect the people of the Darfur region of Sudan (high: 1,001,012, medium: 5,978, low: 16)

5. World leaders should negotiate a global deal on climate change (high: 2,600,053, medium: 575,000, low: 53)

6. Governments should work to negotiate new trade rules— fair rules to make a real difference in the fight against poverty (high: 17,800,244, medium: 22,777, low: 25)

Subjects did not sign the (real) petitions in the experiment, but at the end of the experiment the interface directed them to a site where they could. The research team made the donations to the causes after the experiment. We incentivized the participants with a small payment (six to eight pounds), which varied according to the amount they chose to donate, which we paid with Amazon.co.uk vouchers. A pre-experiment questionnaire established the extent to which participants agreed (or not) with the issues in the petitions. We anonymized all subject information and did not collect addresses, in order to isolate the social information effects (visibility is investigated with a different experimental design in Chapters 5 and 6).

To calculate our results, we examined the variance across the 4,008 petitions completed by control and treatment groups, having stacked the data (showing one record for each person-petition). Overall, participants in the control group signed 61.5 percent of the petitions. When presented with low numbers, these participants signed slightly less often (0.9 percent less) than those in the control group, and when presented with medium numbers they signed slightly more (1.9 percent more). Neither of these results is statistically significant, however, so we do not find evidence to support

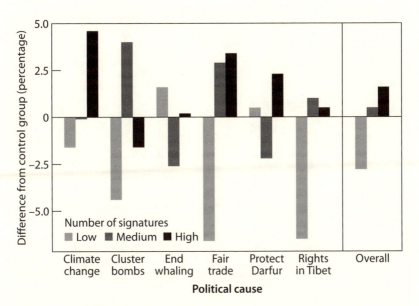

FIGURE 4.4 How different levels of social information affect signing behaviour
Note: Percentages of treatment group participants signing each petition, compared with the control group, shown as the baseline. Low, medium, and high refer to the social information provided.

our hypothesis that small numbers per se discourage participation. For those presented with high numbers, the treatment group signed 66.7 percent of the time, 5.2 percent more than the control group. This is a statistically significant difference (p = .015), confirming our first hypothesis that high numbers (in this case of one million or more) increase participation. Figure 4.4 shows the percentages of the treatment group signing each petition, compared with the control group, shown as the baseline. We found the effect of the high numbers treatment to be strongest for the petition on fair trade, which also had by far the highest number of signatories in this category (17.8 million), leading to a further hypothesis that the effect of high numbers varies according to the number of signatures in a linear way. But when we tested this hypothesis by using the logarithm of the number of signatures in a regression, we found no statistically significant effect.

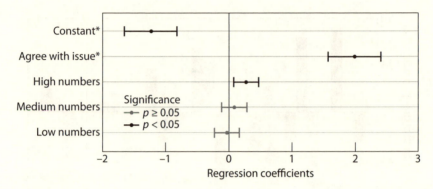

FIGURE 4.5 Logistic regressions showing the effect of varying levels of social information
Note: The figure combines three separate logistic regressions: one for high numbers, one for medium numbers, and one for low numbers. The two terms marked with asterisks (constant and agree with issue) are the averages from these three regressions. The remaining terms appeared in separate regressions but are shown on the same plot for readability.

To delve further into the relationship between social information and willingness to support an issue, we ran separate logistic regression models for subsets of the data comprising participants of one treatment together with the control group, using the high, medium, and low numbers as independent variables to represent social information.[43] It seemed likely that the effect of social information on an individual's likelihood to sign would vary according to the extent to which the person supports the issue at stake. So we looked at the variable indicating subjects' agreement with a given petition, which we had measured in a pre-experiment questionnaire. Initial support varied across the issues; for example, climate change (92 percent) and fair trade (91 percent) were by far the most popular issues, while protect Darfur (77 percent) and end whaling (79 percent) were the least popular and also had the highest numbers of undecided subjects (11 percent).

As expected, initial support for the issue has a strong positive effect on people's willingness to sign, so we controlled for this variable in all subsequent analysis. The summary of the three logistic regressions for different levels of social information is shown in Figure 4.5. For each variable, the point shows the size of the coefficient (measured on the x-axis) and the width of the line shows a 95 percent confidence interval for the coefficient. Only variables with confidence intervals that do not cross zero are significant at the 95 percent confidence level. Only for high numbers did we observe a consistent and statistically significant effect on the likelihood of signing, which confirms our prediction, and the results from the descriptive statistics shown in Figure 4.4.

We carried out a range of other tests, testing for results that would lend support to the bandwagon argument that the higher the number of signatures, the greater the social information effect, discussed earlier in the chapter. First, we investigated whether the numbers of signatories as an independent variable (rather than dummy variables for low, medium, and high numbers) yielded statistically significant results. However, using neither the number of signatories for each petition nor its natural logarithm transformation yielded statistically significant results.[44]

We also tested the effect of the ordering of petitions. Findings from social psychology and behavioural economics suggest that the order of presentation will affect respondents' decisions.[45] As participants were shown petitions with varying numbers of signatories in random order, we investigated whether—for instance— the fact of being prompted to consider an ostensibly unpopular petition just after a highly successful one could significantly alter a decision. Our tests did not substantiate such effects, but it remains a relevant hypothesis to examine in future research.

SOCIAL INFORMATION FUELS
POLITICAL PARTICIPATION

We have investigated the effects of various types of social information on the willingness of a person to participate in an online political mobilization, applying models of social pressure, conditional cooperation, tipping points and viability, and the bandwagon effect. Internet-based social information does not challenge the assumptions of these models but, as with previous research, is shown to make a statistically significant difference to the likelihood that a person will participate in politically motivated collective action, varying across context and level of social information. We see how the social pressure exerted in the setting of small groups that Olson described but considered prohibitively expensive for large groups can now have much more widespread application in the age of social media, when real-time information about other participants is readily available. Our findings lend support to Lupia and Sin's hypothesis that by facilitating communication with large audiences, the Internet and social media can replicate the social pressure applied in Olson's small groups to very large groups indeed.[46]

Our results from both experiments support the findings of previous work on social information effects for more political contexts. That is, when potential participants are provided with an indication of how many other people have participated, they are more likely to participate themselves, confirming previous findings on conditional cooperation in charitable giving for a more political context.[47] In the context of contacting representatives, as in the first experiment, this effect operated at all levels of social information. The field setting provided us with high external validity, but also introduced some dampening and moderating third variable effects, limited our range of social information applied to the treatment group, and, due to the different motivations for contacting representatives distinctive to the UK setting, made it difficult for us to investigate fully the effect of different levels of social information. In our second quasi-field experiment we were able to design away some of these issues, and in the context of supporting global policy issues, found evidence of social information effects only at the highest level. These effects seemed to be stronger than the effects on charitable giving observed by Frey and Meier,[48] perhaps the most directly comparable study to those undertaken thus far because it also looked at the rate of participation rather than the contribution amount. In this second experiment, the social information effect was observed only when the number of participants reached the figure of one million, suggesting the existence of a threshold below which social information does not influence the behaviour of potential participants in this context.

We also found evidence in the second experiment for some kind of critical mass or tipping point, when participation reaches a million people. This figure seems to be higher than Oliver and Marwell envisaged (but did not enumerate) as the critical mass for a large group, but then the level of commitment required to sign an online petition in an experimental setting is far lower than anything they discussed.[49] The importance of the one million figure and the mechanism by which it has an effect on behaviour remain open questions. The figures over a million were high in relation to the other social information provided to participants, but we did not ask subjects about expected levels of participation or whether they themselves considered these numbers to be high. We did not provide subjects with an estimate of the size of the latent group (that is, the potential number of people who might sign such a petition), so we could not expect them to estimate the figure as a percentage of potential participants, but one million is less than two percent of the UK adult population and insignificant in terms of the global population, more relevant to the international nature of these petition issues, so it seems unlikely that this was the mechanism at work. It could be just that one million is a large, significant, and memorable number, likely to attract media attention and act as a signal of viability for that reason. However, a further possibility could be that participants make some calculation of the absolute number of participants that a petition must attain to make a difference. One UK petition that has been shown to have a significant policy effect is a petition against road pricing, with 1.8 million signatories (noted in Chapter 3). In future experiments of this kind, this possible effect could be tested by saying to the participants beforehand, 'Research suggests that petitions that attain two million signatures do lead to policy change', which would give a much clearer indicator of viability.

Advocates of the bandwagon effect will find little comfort in the results from either experiment. Evidence of a uniform effect of social information (as in the first experiment) or crucial points where social information makes a difference, others where it does not, and others where it has a negative effect (as in the second experiment) goes against the bandwagon hypothesis, although the somewhat depressive effect of low numbers in the second experiment might lend some support to the 'spiral of silence' argument. As discussed above, researchers looking for bandwagon effects have tended to test the effect of dynamic information about trends rather than static information about actual numbers, meaning it is unclear where they would expect the bandwagon effect to start. Even if we were to hypothesise from our results that it impacts at one million, we would have expected to see a continuously increasing influence of social information after the crucial million was reached, which we did not. This finding corroborates our finding in Chapter 3 that it is the rank of a petition in the trending box shown on the government's petition website (that is, relative popularity) rather than the actual number of signatures shown against the petition that has an influence.

These results provide insights into the influence of one type of social information—the number of participants—but there is potential for further investigation into the influence of other types of social information, such as the number of participants still required for a successful outcome, progress towards a target set by a pressure group, or what potential participants are willing to pledge if other people also participate, as in some pledge bank platforms. Other types of social influence might involve information about the personalities and preferences of other participants, their sociodemographic statuses, or their experiences of past participation. Social media regularly support the provision of feedback information, including recommender systems, reputation systems, user feedback applications, blogs, video sharing sites, and discussion streams, such as Twitter. When used for political activities, these applications allow participants to see many other types of social information, including comments and feedback in real time or information about people with similar preferences.

These experiments also highlight the sensitivity of collective action to the way that social media platforms are designed, in terms of what social information they present. In the context of contacting representatives, as in our first experiment, it seems that social information, whatever the level, increases participation. There may be different mechanisms at work, according to the level of social information, which reduce susceptibility to social influence. But regardless of the mechanisms at work it seemed that social information had a positive effect at all times in this context, and platforms that provide social information will be more successful in raising participation than those that do not. In the rather different context of expressing support for global political issues, we saw how different levels of social information may have different effects. In designing this second experiment we found a large range of online petitions set up by non-governmental organizations and individuals, some of which provided no information at all about how many people had participated and some of which gave full information. Our findings suggest that the use of social media that provide information when numbers reach critical mass, for example where one million people have participated, but withhold such information when numbers are low, may be more successful. Similarly, it may make sense for those who do not want a mobilization to succeed to withhold numbers, which may be one reason why police organizations and official authorities generally play down estimates of the number of people involved in demonstrations and protests, as noted above.

A key finding is the evidence of tipping points in online mobilization, as identified in our second experiment. Tipping points lead to instability, a flipping from inactivity to activity, from inaction to a flood of action. If collective action intermediated by social media is characterized by tipping points, then it fuels the argument that Internet-based collective action is a source of instability, unpredictability, and turbulence in political systems, introduced in Chapter 3. Both chapters used experimental methods to establish the importance of social information in shaping the way that people participate online. In the next chapter we compare the way that this information influences people's political behaviour with the second form of social influence that we identified in Chapter 2 as an important feature of social media environments, that is, visibility of our actions by others.

CHAPTER 5

VISIBILITY VERSUS SOCIAL INFORMATION

In the summer of 2014, social media were peppered with video clips of people sitting in gardens and courtyards having buckets of iced water poured over their heads. Before they did so, they nominated three other people to undergo the same ordeal or donate an unspecified sum to a charity benefitting amyotrophic lateral sclerosis (ALS), a subtype of motor neurone disease, or do both. This was the Ice Bucket Challenge—celebrities and politicians took part, but so did civilians, in droves. There were 2.4 million tagged videos circulating on Facebook alone in August,[1] and more than 14 million videos overall,[2] while hits to the English Wikipedia's article on ALS grew from an average of 163,300 views to 2.89 million in August, with similar increases in other languages. The ALS association received over $100 million in additional donations, while the Motor Neurone Disease Association received an additional £7 million. Although a number of criticisms were made of the Ice Bucket Challenge, with claims of 'slacktivism' for those who did not donate and 'funding cannibalism' for those who did, in terms of the opportunity costs for other causes, it did represent a mobilization with social good aims, where large numbers of people used social media to raise awareness of and generate funds for the treatment of an important health issue.

The form of social influence at work here was visibility. For the thirty or so seconds of every video, participants were highly visible to their social networks and beyond, undertaking a charitable act. Conversely, the fact that they had not done so after being nominated would be visible at least to their own social networks. This is the strongest form of visibility discussed in Chapter 2, where people's names and faces are clearly associated with their actions. Social information, the other form of social influence exerted by social media that we identified in Chapter 2 and discussed in the last chapter, played less of a role. When deciding whether to take up the challenge, nominees would not know how many other people had done so, other than their nominator, their friends whose videos they had seen, and some high-profile celebrity Ice Bucket Challenges (perhaps those of George Bush, Bill Gates, and Donatella Versace, flanked by two shirtless assistants). So what sort of social influence works best for encouraging collective action? Having identified and examined social information effects in the last chapter, we now extend our analysis to include visibility, comparing these two forms of social influence on both individual participatory decisions and collective capacity to contribute to public goods. Visibility on social media comes in part from the ease with which individuals can exhibit themselves, share information, or express opinions that have at least a chance of being viewed by large numbers of people, stretching far beyond the individual's own social networks. Even people who are passive rather than active users of social media are more likely to be visible to others through the ease with which any kind of information about them can be found using search engines both inside social media sites and on the Internet more generally. As discussed in Chapter 2, visibility is likely to be a factor at work when individuals are deciding whether to contribute to collective action in a social media environment.

As for social information, previous research has shown visibility to be an important influence on individuals when they decide whether to participate, eliciting higher collective action responses. For example, Gerber et al. found that telling people that their neighbours will know whether they voted or not (as well as giving them social information about their neighbours' voting behaviour) increases the effect of a vote mobilization treatment,[3] a finding confirmed in other studies.[4] Likewise, as we demonstrated in the last chapter, providing potential participants with social information about how many other people are participating has been shown to increase other types of participation, although the extent of social influence depends upon the level of participation reported. Most existing research either treats these two social influences in isolation (that is, looks in depth at either visibility or social information) or follows a research design that makes it difficult to separate out the effects. Gerber et al., for example, gave voters social information at the same time as telling them that their voting behaviour would be visible.[5] Using an experimental design that tests for both social influences allows for a comparison of their relative impacts, as we do here.

In this chapter we first review previous work on visibility and collective action and lay out our expectations for the relative effects of social information and visibility. We then report a public goods laboratory experiment in which subjects were invited to contribute to a range of collective goods in randomly ordered rounds. These rounds were subject to three experimental conditions: visibility of individual contributions, social information about contributions within groups, and a control group where visibility was not applied, nor was social information received. By exposing experimental subjects to these conditions, we hope to simulate a social media environment and estimate the absolute and relative effects of both forms of social influence. We report the results and discuss the implications both for our understanding of social media influences on collective action and for the design of platforms geared at encouraging civic engagement and campaigning.

FAME AND SHAME: HOW VISIBILITY WORKS

Why should visibility influence participation? The explanation is based on the concept of social pressure whereby the fact of an action being observed can invoke two distinct mechanisms: shaming and prestige seeking. Indeed, social pressure may be defined as 'communications that play upon a basic human drive to win praise and avoid chastisement'.[6] Research using large-scale field experiments has shown that citizens will be more likely to vote when they are informed that their behaviour is public and that it can or will be monitored or publicized due to a desire to appear compliant to social norms.[7] 'Shame aversion' for failing to vote also boosts compliance levels significantly.[8] Research using the idea of 'image motivation' describes how citizens may be motivated by how others perceive their behaviour, seeking their approval. Ariely et al. elaborate two dimensions of image motivation: 'Actions that imply personal traits such as being pro-social, fair-minded, or caring yield a positive image, while actions that imply personal traits such as being unfair or greedy reduce a positive image or even result in a negative image'.[9] Their laboratory and field experiments demonstrated that if participants liked the prestige they got from having their contributions made public, they acted in a more pro-social manner.[10] Similarly, when donations are advertised in categories (e.g., gold, silver or bronze donors), people will more often give the minimum amount needed to appear in a higher category.[11] A field experiment seeking to test the effect of a pledge to donate books for charity found that listing participants' efforts increased the level of donations.[12]

Both harsh shaming tactics and soft applications of visibility seem to have comparable effects in the various experiments that have been carried out, mostly focusing on voter turnout.[13] Panagopoulos found a shaming intervention to increase voter turnout to be more effective than simply listing out the names, but also showed that simply thanking voters can improve turnout by implying that someone has observed whether they voted or not.[14] Panagopoulos divides such interventions into two categories:[15] negative social pressure, which activates shameful feelings,[16] and positive social pressure, such as positive feedback, reinforcement, or recognition, where the intention is to engender positive feelings.[17] Some of these studies explore the effect of positive social pressure on different demographic groups. The most recent finding appears to show a similar motivational effect on both higher propensity voters and those in groups with lower propensity for voting, such as Hispanics and African Americans.[18]

Overall these studies reveal that whichever mechanism is enacted, making the pro-social actions visible to others is likely to increase contributions, leading us to predict that in the laboratory experiment we report next, visibility will increase the amount that individuals contribute. The difference made by visibility on propensity to vote in the field experiments discussed above is significant. Gerber et al., who used both negative and positive social pressure, reported an increase in turnout of around 4 percent,[19] while Panagopoulos, using positive social pressure, reported increases in turnout of 2 to 3 percentage points on average compared to control conditions.[20]

In the previous chapter, we identified the effect of varying levels of social information on people's decisions whether to participate, finding evidence that high levels of social information make an individual more likely to participate, while low and medium levels do not. Likewise, in Chapter 3 we showed how evidence of relative popularity makes people more likely to sign petitions, at the expense of petitions for which there is no such evidence of popularity.

BEING SMART WITH SOCIAL INFLUENCE

What would we expect to find when we compare the effect of social information and visibility? The need to coordinate individual actions to provide collective goods means that the effect of social influence could vary depending on whether the unit of observation is the individual or the collective. At the individual level, the research outlined above would suggest that visibility has a greater effect, given the effect sizes observed in experiments that have explored the impact of visibility, compared to most of those observed for social information in Chapter 4.[21] Such an impact comes in part from the fact that we might expect a given level of visibility to have a more uniform effect across different points in a mobilization, while Chapters 3 and 4 suggest that the provision of social information will have different effects at different stages. For example, people may be negatively affected by low levels of participation in the early stages of a campaign to raise funds for a new scanner at their local hospital when it provides no signal of viability and they feel their resources will be wasted if the initiative is not going to get off the ground. Likewise, news that enough contributions have been made for the scanner to be provided could discourage participation, because people could feel their contribution was no longer needed. In contrast, information that the amount of funds raised was just below this point might give participation an extra boost as people feel their contribution will really make a difference.

In short, the provision of social information allows participants to use their resources of time, effort, and money more efficiently. Such causal processes may not be observable when contributory behaviour is viewed at the individual level. But at the collective level (and in the rounds in our experiment), under social information we would expect the threshold for success to be met more efficiently, given the incentives to act strategically, particularly when the provision point is nearly reached, or has already been reached and further contributions will not benefit the collective good. Under visibility, particularly when it acts through some kind of shaming mechanism, the total contribution amount may exceed the threshold or resources may be devoted to non-viable initiatives, leading to inefficiency. We would expect visibility to have a greater positive effect than social information on the amount that individuals contribute, while social information will have the same or greater positive effect as visibility on the likelihood of a round being funded in our experiment or a collective good being provided.

APPLYING SOCIAL PRESSURE IN THE LAB

To test our predictions we use data from a public goods game laboratory experiment undertaken by the authors, which also provides data for the two chapters that follow. Public goods games are a common method of experimental economics to model collective action problems. Subjects are provided with tokens that they contribute to a public pot, which is shared between participants at the end of the game, according to the payoff structure that forms part of the design. Subjects choose whether to cooperate by contributing tokens or whether to free-ride and maximize their own benefits. The information environment in which they do so can be manipulated as part of the experiment, while all other conditions are controlled in the laboratory; so, it is a good way to test the different forms of social influence that we are interested in here. However, laboratory experiments have limited external validity (that is, the difficulty of generalizing from a laboratory simulation to the outside world),[22] which we have attempted to mitigate through our research design, as detailed below.

The experiment took the form of a one-shot public goods game in which 186 subjects were invited to attend a series of sessions in the laboratory, with between 14 and 20 in each session. In each session, subjects were seated at a computer screen (see Figure 5.1, which shows the interface), provided with a number of local public goods scenarios (one at a time), and asked to contribute tokens to each good in a series of twenty-eight rounds, which they played anonymously in small groups (7–10). Participants were randomly reallocated into two groups at each round, so that subjects never interacted with exactly the same group and did not know which group they were in, so there was no opportunity for learning the behaviour patterns of other participants.

At each round, subjects were shown one of six different scenarios (Figure 5.1 shows an example), phrased as a request to fund a local initiative, namely a local campaign for bicycle lanes; a local fund-raising initiative to send aid to victims of an earthquake in Haiti; a health campaign to save the local accident and emergency department; a local campaign to provide free public Wi-Fi; a group effort to clear snow for elderly neighbours; a campaign for more street lights to be installed by the council; and a collective effort to organize a street party (full wording of the scenarios is shown in the Appendix). These scenarios were chosen to capture elements of collective action around different types of public goods (donating

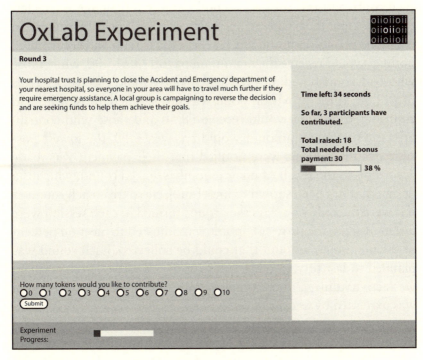

FIGURE 5.1 The experimental interface (social information treatment)

money to Haiti is a different kind of public good from campaigning for street lights, for example, because participants receive direct benefit from the latter but not the former). By using scenarios (in contrast to most experimental economics research),[23] we tried to approximate real-world situations while preserving the incentive structure of a public goods game.

Subjects were endowed with ten tokens at the start of each round and could donate an amount from zero to ten to the collective effort in each round. They were informed that a fixed bonus would be redistributed among all participants in the group if the provision point—corresponding to 60 percent of the maximum amount collectable for that round—was met (the Appendix shows the instructions to participants, including a table of payoffs for each contribution). Subjects could keep any remaining tokens left to them after they had made their contribution to a round. So when the provision point was reached, those who had contributed nothing would receive the maximum payoff of £15.00, while those who had contributed all their ten tokens would receive a payoff of £12.50. If the provision point was not reached, those who had contributed nothing would receive £8.50 and those who contributed the maximum amount would receive £6.00, the lowest possible payoff. Subjects were notified that their payment was made according to the result of one randomly selected round, which is a design that has been shown to impel subjects to treat each round as if it were the only one.[24] As the groups formed in each session were different sizes, the provision point was adjusted to meet 60 percent of the maximum amount that could be collected. Each round was planned to last fifty seconds; but to avoid deadline effects, if there was activity during the last five seconds of elapsed time, the round was extended by another five seconds.

Two treatments were implemented in addition to a control condition and all subjects would experience all conditions more than once in the course of their session. In control rounds, the subjects received no social information about the contributions of other subjects, and their own contributions were not visible to other subjects. Under the social information only treatment, subjects were shown real-time information on their computer screens about the total amount raised within their subgroup, and the number of individuals in their group who had already contributed (see Figure 5.1). This information was updated continually in real time throughout each round, as contributions were made; when the round was over, the information was set back to zero. Under the visibility only treatment, subjects were shown real-time information about the amount the individual participants in the room were giving on a screen at the front of the laboratory, showing the desk plan of the room (so contributions were highlighted on the screen as they were made). They were not told, however, which contributions were from participants in their own subgroup, which would have provided them with social information and contaminated our aim to keep the two treatments separate. Under this treatment therefore, all subjects knew that their contribution amounts would be visible to all other subjects as a number against their position in the laboratory and thereby identifiable to themselves. Taken together, these conditions ensured there was no possibility that reputations based on repeated interactions between the same individuals could develop. The combination of these two treatments resulted in the last treatment, a combination of the social information and visibility conditions.

After the experiment, the subjects completed a questionnaire (shown in the Appendix), which included various demographic questions and a short personality survey (to allow us to carry out the analysis presented in Chapter 6). Individual contributions were not returned if they were made in excess of the provision point (i.e., no rebate), nor if the threshold was not reached in the given round (no refund). As a consequence, this public goods game has two sets of Nash equilibria, that is, two states where all participants are making the best decision they can, taking into account the decision of the other players. The first equilibrium is inefficient (in terms of providing the good) and corresponds to the case in which no individual gives tokens and the group bonus is not paid out; the second equilibrium is when the provision point is exactly met and the public good is provided.[25] This experimental design allowed for both strategic and non-strategic behaviour, according to treatment. That is, under the control condition, we would not expect strategic behaviour as participants receive no information as to how likely the provision point is to be reached. Likewise, under the visibility treatment, although participants saw the donation amounts of other participants in real time, they had no way of knowing which subjects were in their particular subgroup for that round, so could not use this information to play strategically, although it may have had some conditional cooperation effects, in that they felt like contributing if they saw that other subjects were doing so.

Under the social information condition, in the early stages of the round, when no one or few had contributed within a group, there was no information available to any participants to make a strategic decision. In these contexts, an individual contribution provides information about that individual's personality and general propensity to give (discussed in Chapter 6). Under the social information condition in the later stages of the round, there was much more opportunity for strategic play, for example contributing tokens to push the total amount of contributions over the provision point or withholding contributions because the provision point had been reached. So later contributions are more likely to reflect strategic play, and we would expect that under the social information condition there would be more chance of reaching the efficient equilibrium.

VISIBILITY GETS PEOPLE GIVING

The overall effect of the two main treatments is compared in Figure 5.2, which shows the frequency distributions of individual contributions broken down by treatment conditions (across all scenarios). The y-axis displays the frequency of each possible contribution amount that subjects made across rounds (note that the lines are constructed to join up points indicating whole contributions; it was not possible to give a part contribution). The black line representing the control treatment has a tri-modal shape. A large proportion of subjects contribute either zero or ten tokens (although these are not necessarily their consistent strategy across rounds), and others provide what could be termed the 'fair' share (60 percent of their endowment), which corresponds to the amount each should contribute for the provision point to be reached at equal cost to all participants. Frequency of contributions under the social information condition is represented by the dark gray line, showing that a larger proportion of participants are inclined to free ride on the contributions of others, compared to the control treatment. When contributions become individually visible (light gray line), the largest proportion of individuals give the 'fair' amount of six tokens. This is almost twice as many as under the social information

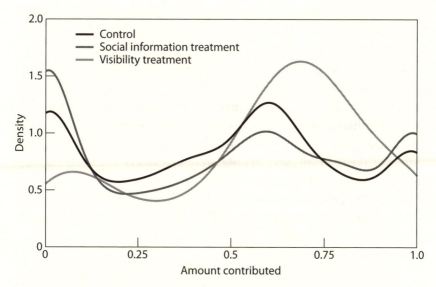

FIGURE 5.2 Frequency distribution of the normalized amount contributed by individuals across treatments

treatment. Likewise, far fewer individuals under this treatment were likely to free ride by contributing zero tokens.

Overall, these results show that visibility will increase the amount that individuals contribute. We confirmed this result by carrying out a left- and right-censored Tobit regression on a collapsed form of the experimental data (with standard errors clustered around individual subjects), in which each observation refers to one person-round. Preliminary analysis using the information from the questionnaire showed that the contribution amount increased with the importance ascribed by subjects to the particular issue, and decreased with the size of the group in which they participated, as we would expect,[26] and we used these as control variables in subsequent analyses. We excluded all rounds run under the social information treatment, which means that those held under both treatments are also excluded. The results showed clearly that visibility predicts individual contributions, with a clear significant effect ($p < .01$). Including variables for the scenarios increased the fit of models for the regressions (increasing the pseudo-R^2 by .005 for social information and .013 for visibility), but did not change the results at all, with the coefficients changing by less than 0.1 only and never gaining or losing significance.

In contrast, when we carried out the same regression analysis for social information, we found no overall effect of social information on individual contributions. In fact, under the social information treatment participants were more likely to free ride by contributing no tokens at all, and people were less likely to contribute six tokens than the control group (Figure 5.2). So visibility seems to have a greater effect on individuals' willingness to cooperate and contribute to the collective good than either social information or the control.

SOCIAL INFORMATION TRUMPS VISIBILITY IN THE ROUND

We then analysed the data at the round level, using 'funded', a binary variable that indicates whether the provision point was collectively met. Figure 5.3 shows the effects of treatment conditions on the likelihood of a round being funded. Looking at the aggregate effect for all scenarios at the right of the graph, we can see that both treatments have a very similar impact on the likelihood of a round's being funded. Logit regressions with 'funded' as the dependent variable (shown in Figure 5.4) confirm this finding: both visibility and social information are significant, with similar coefficients and levels of significance. In the regression analysis, we controlled for the differences in importance ascribed by subjects to the issues involved, by using subjects' responses to the post-experiment questionnaire, where they were asked to rate the scenarios for importance.

Figure 5.3 also shows variation in the likelihood of rounds being funded and treatment effects across the six scenarios used in the study. It shows that the scenarios relating to saving an accident and emergency department (under both treatments) and providing aid to earthquake victims in Haiti (social information treatment

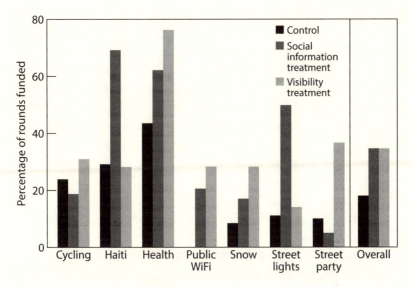

FIGURE 5.3 Effect of social information and visibility treatments on the likelihood of rounds being funded, shown across scenarios and for all rounds

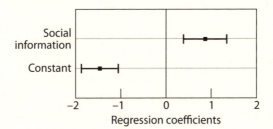

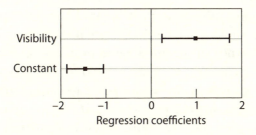

FIGURE 5.4 Round level analysis (logits)
Note: For the top model, we included all control rounds (154) and all rounds run under social information only (266). For the bottom model, we included all control rounds (154) and all rounds run under visibility only (42). We excluded all rounds run under both social information and visibility treatments (42).

only) were considerably more likely than the other scenarios to be funded, although social information also had a strong effect for the scenario relating to street lights, while visibility had a strong effect on the street party scenario. These results show that the scenarios used were affecting subjects' behaviour. However, the scenario effects (and the variations in the control condition shown in the graph) are to a large extent explained by the different levels of importance that subjects ascribed to the scenarios, for which we controlled in all regression analyses.

THE EFFICIENCY OF SOCIAL INFORMATION

As discussed in Chapter 2, social media exert social influence on individuals deciding whether to participate in collective action, notably social information and visibility. In this chapter, we have aimed to simulate a social media environment with a laboratory experiment to investigate the relative impact of these two forms of social influence.

We confirm the importance of visibility of people's actions as a powerful determinant of their propensity to participate in collective action, something that has been demonstrated in offline contexts in previous research.[27] We also show that the impact of social information about the actions of others is not revealed at the individual level; social information can have both positive and negative effects at different stages in a mobilization, which can cancel each other out. Our subjects appear to have behaved strategically by using social information to participate if their contribution would make a difference to the good being provided, and not to participate if the contribution to collective action would be wasted, either because the good was clearly not going to be provided, or because the good was going to be provided regardless of their contribution.

In contrast, we find that both social information and visibility have similar impacts at the aggregate or round level, which can correspond to the community or collective. The provision of social information can help communities provide collective goods just as much as making potential contributors visible, in spite of the greater positive effect of visibility at the individual level. Such a finding shows social information to be the more efficient form of social influence in terms of the collective, encouraging individuals to target their contributions where they feel they will make the most difference. Basically, although the proportions of rounds funded under both treatments are approximately the same, those run under the social information treatment were funded with fewer overall contributions than those run under visibility. Assuming that any contribution to a cause has some kind of opportunity cost, in terms of time, money, or effort, that could have been devoted elsewhere (as suggested by the findings of the natural experiment in Chapter 3), then social information emerges as the optimal form of social influence for maximising the chances of providing the public good.

Our findings are to some extent born out by the Ice Bucket Challenge, which used visibility to good effect in shaming people to partake. Visibility pushed people to opt to undertake an unpleasant and even painful act, operating through the twin influences of shame and desire for prestige, or at least attention. But visibility was also conspicuous in its absence as soon as the video finished, melting away as people contemplated donating away from the gaze of their social networks; in the United Kingdom, while one in six people took part in the challenge, only 10 percent of those went on to donate, and although this figure was higher in the United States, the majority there also did not donate. In the aggregate, as in our experiment, visibility exhibited inefficiency, with allegations that the ALS association spent most of the donations on advertising, promotion, and exorbitant salaries for top officials, while the rest went to 'the pockets of Big Pharma' already investing heavily in ALS research, with huge profits in sight.[28]

These findings could have relevance for the design of platforms geared at civic engagement, or for decisions over which social media platforms to use for which endeavour. Making participants visible as they participate (as is the case on some charitable donation sites and petition platforms) may be useful for increasing participation. But it may not be the most efficient way to do so in some contexts, such as when sufficient levels of contributions have been collected already or mobilization has already shown itself to be non-viable. Here social information can be a more valuable tool to encourage participants to behave strategically and direct their resources where they will have the utmost effect.

Likewise, the effect of visibility will be very context-dependent and needs to be adjusted accordingly. In the context we simulated in this experiment, participants (or at least most of them) clearly wanted to be perceived as having contributed. Other work has shown that the visibility of contributors' names makes people more likely to make charitable donations, as discussed above. The Ice Bucket Challenge relied on the strongest form of visibility discussed in Chapter 2, that is where participants' actions are visible but also the participants themselves are identified in person and linked to the action. In other contexts, as in the early stages of the Egyptian and Tunisian revolutions of 2011, for example, it might be crucially important for participants to remain anonymous while their actions remain visible. In this case, their actions constitute an anonymous form of social information that, as it scales up, may exert influence on other people considering whether to participate.

Up until now in the empirical part of this book, we have assumed that all individuals will react similarly to these different forms of social influence. However, with both social information and visibility, we might also expect various forms to exert different influences on different types of people, even within the same context. For example, while some individuals may appreciate the visibility enabled by social media, proudly displaying their 'I voted today' button on their Facebook page, for example, others may shy away from having their contributions made public (these people might have donated to the ALS association, but would not have participated in the Ice Bucket Challenge). We might also expect some people to be particularly susceptible to high (or low) levels of social information, with others more willing to act unilaterally, irrespective of what other people are doing. We investigate these possible sources of individual-level difference in reactions to social influence in the next chapter.

CHAPTER 6

PERSONALITY MATTERS

The second half of 2014 saw a wave of protests and civil disorder in the United States, in response to the treatment of African Americans by white police offers. As we discussed in Chapter 2, unrest began in August after the fatal shooting of Michael Brown and continued into November after a jury declined to indict the police officer who had shot him. The protests, which mobilized strong feelings among Ferguson's largely black population, were coordinated on social media via hashtags such as #HandsUpDontShoot (Brown's alleged last words) and #Ferguson, which trended on Twitter and Facebook around the world, and was sustained by other incidents of a similar nature that reoccurred during the year, including the death of another unarmed black man in police custody, Eric Garner, as we showed with data from Twitter and Facebook in Chapter 2. In December, when a grand jury decided not to indict the white police officer who put a chokehold on Eric Garner, public protest erupted again, including the Millions March in Oakland in December and trending of the hashtag #ICantBreathe. At the end of the year, the *Huffington Post* remembered 'The Year in Police Killings' under the byline 'Has the country reached a tipping point?'[1] The difference between this and previous years was not the number of police killings (research has since shown that between 2010 and 2012 young blacks were twenty-one times more likely to be killed than white males in that age range at the hands of police).[2] The difference that brought the issue to the *Huffington Post* was the level of public protest and demonstration. Although some of these protests involved gratuitous violence and opportunistic looting—that is, private participation geared at private goods—they also represented the beginning of a new, largely peaceful rights-based movement composed of people who, under the traditional view of demographics as a predictor of political behaviour, would not be inclined to participate.

How might we understand participation in this new movement? As argued throughout this book, social media are drawing new people into political activities by offering them, at least in the first instance, a low-cost form of participation, such as sharing a post or otherwise drawing attention to hashtags like #ICantBreathe, which acts as a local, national, or even global focal point for expressions of feeling and opinion. When deciding whether to participate in this way, people are exposed to two key forms of social influence discussed in Chapters 4 and 5: social information and visibility. Up until this point we have assumed that people approach the decision to participate in a mobilization uniformly, perceiving costs, benefits, and rewards in the same way. Indeed, applications of the rational actor approach have been based on such assumptions. Under such a view, people react in a homogeneous way to the social influences exerted by social media. But do people react in the same way to these influences? Would we not expect different types of people to react differently to information about other participants or to being visible or anonymous? We suggest that, to assess fully the relative impact of visibility and social information, research needs to appraise differences between individuals who may react differently to these influences when moderated by context.

The traditional social science method to understand differences in people's political behaviour and their response to social influence is through their socioeconomic status (often abbreviated as SES) and demographic profile, typically broken down into categories of gender, income, education, ethnic group, and age. But the surge of political protest and demonstration among African Americans of low socioeconomic status poses a challenge to this mainstream approach. They represent the classic latent group who are unlikely to be able to participate or coordinate due to lack of resources and geographical dispersion in Olson's terms.[3] We argue here that these categories are less relevant for understanding differences in political behaviour in an online context, such as differential susceptibility to social information and visibility. Demographic analysis can do little to explain the protests against racist policing in the United States in 2014 or many of the other movements based on social media involving other demographic groups traditionally viewed as limited in political participation, such as the young.

We turn instead to personality, a measure of individual difference that implies that people perceive and respond to the same stimuli in fundamentally different ways. We follow work that has given weight to personality in recent years, in particular the 'Big Five' traits. The Big Five is a scheme developed by psychologists that simplifies the large number of possible personality traits into five broad categories. It can be used more generically in social science research, such as that carried out by political scientists, who suggest these variables should play a part in research designs in political behaviour, while psychologists have found them to shape social media use. In addition, we employ social value orientation, the individual difference variable favoured by economists.

To assess claims relating to different forms of social influence on different personality types, we use data from the public goods experiment introduced in the previous chapter. But first we review existing research on individual-level difference in collective action, examining demographics and then personality. Second, we analyse our experimental data at the individual level using a number of typologies of personality, and draw implications for our understanding of how individuals differ in their susceptibility to these two types of social influence.

THE ATTENUATION OF DEMOGRAPHICS

A long line of political sociologists have ascribed importance to socioeconomic variables as a source of inequality in political behaviour,[4] with differences in age, gender, race, income, and education all being viewed as structuring most political activities and attitudes, from voter turnout through to political engagement, environmental concerns, and complaining.[5] In liberal democracies, it is usually the older, richer, and more educated male, white individuals who are more likely to participate in politics,[6] although the wide literature on the topic reveals a more nuanced picture according to context and the type of participation under observation, and whole subfields of research have grown up around the issue of underrepresentation according to socioeconomic and demographic groupings such as gender and race.

Of course, all forms of online political participation are subject to inequality in Internet access, and using the Internet requires skills and capacity that are not equally distributed in the population.[7] Mossberger et al. define digital citizens as those who use the Internet every day, with regular means of access (usually at home), some technical skill, and the educational competencies to find and use web-based information and communicate with others on the Internet.[8] Their argument is based on the assumption that the explosion of political information and opportunities to participate on the Internet means that 'digital citizenship is an enabling factor for political citizenship, whether practiced online or offline'.[9] The research of Mossberger and others reveals a number of inequalities in both access and use of the Internet, with wide variation in the ability to participate online, structured by age, education, income, race, and ethnicity.[10] It is inevitable therefore that scholars looking at online political behaviour have also focused on demographic effects, investigating the possible impact of Internet use on inequalities in political participation across different socioeconomic and demographic categories. As discussed briefly in Chapter 2, research from the early 2000s tended to conclude that traditional inequalities in political behaviour across groups were either normalized (that is, it did not reduce inequality) or even reinforced by the Internet, leading to various arguments of the 'politics-as-usual' variety—that the kinds of politics that existed before the expansion of the Internet, where inequality was prevalent, would prevail in the online age.

Later research, however, has started to provide evidence for the 'new mobilization' thesis, which argues that the Internet may facilitate the mobilization of new individuals and groups of individuals who have traditionally not participated before.[11] These studies provide evidence that groups that have previously been regarded as participating at lower levels (such as young people) are now participating more, and also may explain the apparent increases in various forms of unconventional participation, such as protests, demonstrations, and product boycotts.

Given the focus of this book on social media and Internet users, however, demographic distinctions are not going to be so helpful, given that most of the socioeconomic and demographic distinctions that have traditionally been viewed as shaping political participation also shape Internet use, particularly income and education. Some of the demographic differences in political participation are not as strong within Internet users as between Internet users and non-Internet users: those who have access to the Internet already have a higher SES. However, there is evidence that traditional political participatory acts, such as contributing money to candidates, contacting officials, and communicating with political groups, are still stratified socioeconomically when done online,[12] but there is less evidence that the new micro-acts of participation possible on social media are structured in this way. There is a more complex relationship for age: traditionally older people have participated more in political activities, but younger people are more likely to use the Internet and social media. However, once people are using social media, there is no strong evidence or theory to suggest that their age will shape how susceptible they might be to social influence, the focus of this chapter. Many of the movements based on social media discussed in the book, such as the US protests, the 15-M movement in Spain, and the protests in Turkey and Brazil, have attracted large numbers of young people to political causes.

As we made clear in Chapter 1, this book is not about people who do not use the Internet. Even though the marginalization of groups that are digitally excluded is a problem for democracy, it is not the focus of this book. As Internet penetration continues to grow and reach equal diffusion as other forms of technology (for example, the mobile telephone), future students of the Internet might return to the thorny issue of demography and socioeconomic status. Here we map out the changes for politics more generally as we observe the innovators and opinion formers. In many ways, the impact of the Internet resembles that of technologies in past centuries, whereby large changes in social organization and politics were driven by a minority of the population, such as those who read printed books, generating profound changes in social and political behaviour that diffused to the rest in society once the shift to a new political order (or disorder) had taken place.

Demographic differences may be less important in Internet-enabled participation than they were in the pre-online era. As we outlined in the early chapters of this book, the key feature of social media is that they allow micro-donations of both time and money, extending the range of participatory acts available to citizens, partly because gaining access and passing information to others are easy. These acts have far lower participation and transaction costs than traditional participation (see Chapter 2), so people's decisions whether or not to undertake them are less likely to be structured by their socioeconomic resources. Income, for example, may determine whether someone is likely to make substantial charitable donations or pay a party membership fee, but will play far less of a role in determining whether that individual will participate on free social networking services such as Facebook or Twitter. Levels of education may shape how willing and able an individual is to undertake the offline information costs of finding out which party to vote for, but may have less impact on the person's ability to do so online in spite of the deluge of material that everyone receives, from flyers on front doors to broadcast media commentary. Likewise, individuals (such as single parents) who cannot contemplate attending political meetings are more likely to find themselves able to disseminate a political video or share a petition on a social media site. It is possible to argue that the demographic variables that have been associated with different levels of political participation will have less importance shaping an individual's decision to make one of these micro-donations of time or money. With less of a focus on socioeconomic status and demographics as sources of influence on participation, it is possible that other influences on collective action, in particular the moderating influences on the impact of social information and personality, may have greater prominence.

PERSONALITY ASCENDANT

We turn therefore to personality as an individual-level variable that mediates the relationship between social influence and propensity to participate in collective action. Personality denotes a particular combination of an individual's emotional, attitudinal, and behavioural response patterns that are stable over time and mediates how individuals respond to their context, meaning that different types of people will perceive and act on the same stimuli in fundamentally different ways. There has been a revival of interest in political science on the impact of personality on political behaviour and beliefs.[13] In this chapter and the next, we follow recent work that has given more weight to personality as a predictor of political behaviour and beliefs, in particular the Big Five traits,[14] suggesting they should be part of a more general research framework. Of particular pertinence to this book, researchers beyond political science have found such variables to shape the use of social media. For example, the Big Five traits correlate with the amount of time spent on Facebook,[15] the use of social media for social or informational purposes, and preferences for social media platforms such as Facebook or Twitter, with their different levels of anonymity and provision of social information.[16] We use an important insight from the research of Gerber et al. that the impact of personality is dependent on context, suggesting that there will be differential susceptibility to social influence.[17] However, it is less clear which personality types respond in which ways to social influence, and we argue that political scientists may wish to use other measures alongside the Big Five, such as social value orientation, as we do in both this chapter and the one that follows.

THE BIG FIVE

In the recent revival of interest in personality as a predictor of political behaviour, political scientists have utilized the Big Five personality traits, which have been foundational in psychological studies,[18] and for which a measurement instrument has been developed for situations requiring a short survey as opposed to the very long batteries of questions that psychologists often use.[19] Psychologists have reached a working consensus that these personality traits can be comprehensively conceptualized and reliably measured,[20] and are stable over time.[21] When used in political science, they have been shown to be significant predictors of political attitudes and propensity to participate, such as likelihood of turnout.[22]

The Big Five personality factors comprise openness, conscientiousness, extraversion, agreeableness, and neuroticism. Openness refers to an inventive and curious rather than cautious nature; conscientiousness is about being self-disciplined and efficient rather than easygoing or careless; extraversion is about being outgoing and energetic rather than shy or reserved, describing people with positive emotions who wish to seek stimulation in the company of others; agreeableness describes those who are friendly and compassionate rather than cold or unkind; and neuroticism (or emotional stability) describes even-temperedness and contrasts with a neurotic temperament and anxiety. Denny and Doyle found that personality was at least as associated with voter turnout as interest in politics, finding that those who are hardworking, even-tempered, and aggressive are more likely to vote than those with lazy, moody, and timid personalities.[23]

PRO-SELF AND PRO-SOCIAL

For the particular context examined here, we identify another typology of individual difference that we might use to predict the
susceptibility of individuals to social influence. Social value orientation may be important also in predicting collective behaviour,
a concept that has been used in a large economics literature that
examines the relationship between social value orientation and cooperation, which derives from interdependence theory.[24] Although
strictly speaking a measure of personal values rather than personality per se, social value orientation has been identified as a stable
individual difference variable in which three types of orientation
may be identified: cooperators (or pro-social individuals), who are
concerned with enhancing the outcomes and equality of outcomes
for both the self and others; competitors, who try to maximize the
difference between outcomes for the self and others; and individualists, who endeavour to maximize their own outcome with no
regard for the outcomes of others. The latter two are most usually
combined,[25] as we do here with the term 'pro-self'. This difference
in dispositions has been shown to affect people's actions: pro-
socials are systematically more willing to undertake the costs of
participation than pro-selves,[26] and express greater concern for the
welfare of others and the group as a whole.[27] Social value orientation is used extensively in economic research on cooperation and
competition, which has shown much within-individual consistency
in behaviour over various interactions and situations.[28] While it is
used far less in political science, pro-social behaviour has been associated with political participation and turnout.[29]

Social value orientation is used in the work on conditional cooperation discussed briefly in Chapter 4, including in laboratory
experiments involving public goods and cooperation games,[30] and,
more recently, field experiments in which subjects are provided
with varying levels of information about the participation of others.[31] Some of this work has shown that people differ strongly in

their contribution preferences,[32] and various authors have identified categorizations that develop the simple distinction between individualistic (pro-self) and pro-social individuals,[33] to identify some participants as 'strong free-riders', some as 'reciprocators', and some as 'conditional co-operators'.[34]

WHO CONTRIBUTES?

From the findings of political science research into the relationship between the Big Five traits and political behaviour, extraversion emerges as the strongest predictor of participation in collective action, particularly for group-oriented tasks and social forms of political activity. Mondak and Halperin found that extravert personalities were consistently associated with a higher propensity to participate in politics,[35] a finding verified by Gerber et al.;[36] although only with forms of political activity that involve interacting with others, rather than donating to campaigns, for example. For the other four traits, results are mixed. Openness to experience has been positively associated with some participatory acts,[37] and this finding has been replicated in most,[38] but not all studies.[39] Agreeableness has been associated with lower levels of participation in general, but several inconsistent effects have also been reported, indicating the importance of context for this variable.[40] Mondak and Halperin, Mondak et al., and Gerber et al. found that agreeableness was negatively associated with participation in electoral politics, such as voting, and positively associated with others (such as attending meetings and signing petitions);[41] Volk et al. showed that agreeableness was indicative of a greater preference for cooperation,[42] while Vecchione and Caprara found no results for agreeableness.[43] Conscientiousness, with subdimensions of industriousness, order, and responsibility, has been associated with performance in the workplace,[44] but has largely been shown to have no effect on civic engagement; Mondak and Halperin and Gerber et al. found no consistent pattern for conscientiousness,[45] while Mondak et al. found that its association with participation switched from positive for community engagement to negative for conflictive forms of engagement such as protest activity.[46] Finally, mixed results have been found for the association of neuroticism/ emotional stability and political participation. Parkes and Razavi and Vecchione and Caprara reported null results; Mondak and Halperin and Gerber et al. found a positive relationship between neuroticism and emotional stability and some forms of participation, but Mondak et al. found negative associations.[47]

From research based on the Big Five personality traits,[48] then, extraversion and agreeableness have emerged with the strongest findings, although results across studies are inconsistent. Comparing the predictive values of the Big Five traits and social value orientation, Volk et al. found agreeableness to be a more consistent predictor of cooperativeness than pro-social social value orientation.[49]

To compare our own findings with this earlier work, we used data from the experiment described in the last chapter. The experimental design included short personality questionnaires to assess the Big Five personality traits and social value orientation of the subjects, as well as their 'Rotter score' of locus of control (discussed in the next chapter). All questionnaires are shown in the Appendix. Social value orientation was assessed via a short series of questions referencing a game in which subjects are asked to imagine that they have been randomly paired with another person, and then have to make choices resulting in points for both the subject and the 'other' (see the Appendix), based on a frequently used instrument, the Triple-Dominance Measure of Social Values.[50] The measure classifies people as cooperators, individualists, or competitors if they make six out of nine choices.

We examine the relationship between the personality scores of individual subjects and the amount they contributed to the public good game by carrying out double-censored Tobit regressions (with standard errors clustered around individual subjects) on a collapsed form of the experimental data, in which each observation refers to one person-round. We ran regressions with all the personality measures included, which is justified on theoretical grounds and because they are not collinear, as shown in Table 6.1.

TABLE 6.1 Correlation matrix for personality measures (Big 5 & SVO)

	Extravert	Agreeable	Conscientious	Emotionally stable	Open	Pro-self	Pro-social
Extravert	1.00						
Agreeable	.19	1.00					
Conscientious	−.06	.02	1.00				
Emotionally stable	.29	.20	.29	1.00			
Open	.31	.00	.02	−.01	1.00		
Pro-self	−.18	.10	.06	.01	.04	1.00	
Pro-social	.11	−.11	−.05	−.02	−.10	−.89	1.00

The results of all our regressions (three of which are shown in Figures 6.1, 6.2, and 6.3) reveal, as expected based on the previous chapter, that the amount contributed by the subjects to each good increased with the importance they ascribed to the issue at hand and decreased with the size of the group in which they participated, as we would expect,[51] and we used these as control variables in all our analyses. Including variables for the scenarios increased the fit of models for the regressions (increasing the pseudo-R^2 by .005 for social information [Figure 6.1] and .013 for visibility [not shown]), but did not change the results, with the coefficients changing by less than 0.1 and never gaining or losing statistical significance.

Figure 6.1 also shows that the visibility treatment clearly has a significant effect ($p < .01$) on propensity to contribute at the individual level, as discussed in the last chapter. Of the Big Five personality variables, agreeableness has a highly significant negative effect ($p < .001$), while conscientiousness has a weaker negative effect ($p < .05$). Neuroticism/emotional stability has a significant positive effect on contributions ($p < .01$), as does openness to new experience (although the significance of this variable disappears if

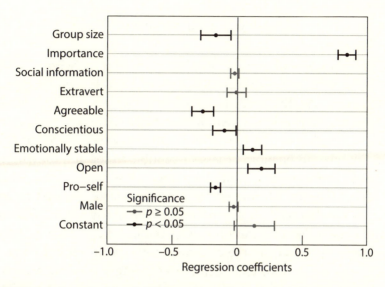

FIGURE 6.1 Contribution of different personality types to collective action
Note: For each variable, the point shows the size of the coefficient (measured on the x-axis) and the width of the line shows a 95 percent confidence interval for the coefficient. Only variables with confidence intervals that do not cross zero are significant at the 95 percent confidence level. We have controlled for social information, although (as we discussed in Chapter 5) it is not significant at the individual level.

we control for visibility). Extraversion has no statistically significant impact. Social value orientation also has a significant effect on propensity to contribute, with pro-social individuals contributing more, as we would expect, and pro-self individuals contributing significantly less. (While the two can't be shown in the same model since they correlate very strongly and would cause collinearity, we show pro-self in Figure 6.1, and the result for pro-social is similar but has the expected opposite sign.) Obviously we would expect this result for social value orientation because (in contrast to the other variables) we measured it by asking subjects to play a game that is not dissimilar to the game played in the experiment itself, so they are likely to react in similar ways. These results lay the ground for our interest in how social value orientation interacts with social information and visibility, and we describe this below.

WHO IS SUSCEPTIBLE?

We now turn to our key relationship of interest, between the different forms of social influence and personality. We would expect different personality types to be more or less susceptible to visibility, because previous research has shown that some people are more shameable than others. We would also expect different personality types to be more or less susceptible to social information; the large literature on conditional cooperation suggests that some people use social information to act strategically (indeed to cooperate conditionally) while others act consistently according to their social value orientation, for example by contributing their fair share (six tokens in the experiment we conducted) or more if they are pro-social, or consistently free-riding if they are pro-self. With respect to the far smaller body of work on the susceptibility of the Big Five personality types to social information and visibility, individuals low in extraversion and high in agreeableness would seem to be the most responsive to social information feedback regarding collective resource.[52]

These results are shown in Figure 6.2, where we introduce interaction terms with the visibility treatment. Here it seems that agreeable people contribute more under visibility, although they contribute less than the other personality types in the control and social information treatment. There is also a significant effect for extraversion: extraverts contribute less under visibility ($p < .05$). The visibility treatment also has a positive effect for pro-self individuals ($p < .001$); that is, pro-selves contribute more under the treatment, in contrast to our expectation that they would be unaffected by either treatment. We replaced the pro-self variable with pro-social (again, due to collinearity) and found that pro-social subjects are significantly and negatively affected by the visibility treatment (not shown). This result suggests that at least some members of the pro-self group were shameable, not wishing to be viewed as uncooperative. Both groups become less extreme under the visibility treatment.

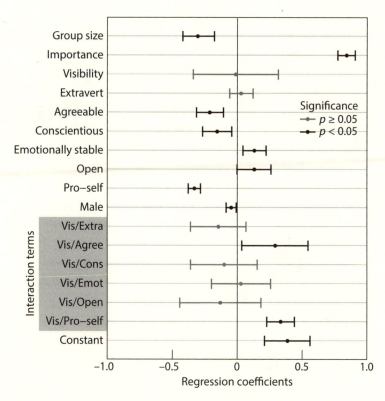

FIGURE 6.2 The relationship between personality and susceptibility to visibility

Next we carried out the same analysis for the social information treatment, shown in Figure 6.3. When interaction terms are used for the social information treatment, there is no interaction effect of the treatment for any of the Big Five traits. As demonstrated for visibility, those with a pro-social social value orientation contribute significantly less when they receive social information. When the pro-self variable is used instead of pro-social, there is a strongly significant effect; that is, pro-selves are more likely to be affected positively by social information and will contribute more under this treatment.

So it seems that our subject pool responded to both treatments in different ways according to their personality type. Of the Big

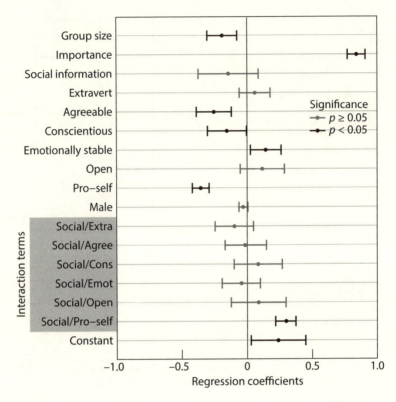

FIGURE 6.3 The relationship between personality and susceptibility to social information

Five personality types, we obtained the most significant results in interaction terms for agreeable and extravert. Agreeable people seem to contribute less in general (commensurate with some of the previous work outlined earlier in this chapter), but are affected positively by the visibility treatment; they contribute more when visible, in contrast to extraverts, who contribute less under visibility (the other Big Five types do not appear as interaction terms for this treatment). We do not find the same result for the social information treatment, to which they do not seem differentially susceptible.

Rather than the Big Five personality traits, it is social value orientation that predicts why individuals respond differently to both treatments across the subject pool. Pro-social people are significantly less likely to contribute under both visibility and social information than under control conditions, while pro-selves (who contribute less under control conditions) contribute significantly more under both treatments. It seems that pro-self people are shameable when visible and strategic when social information is available. In contrast, both visibility and social information have a negative effect on the propensity of pro-socials to contribute. These findings add new insight; they are not a product of the measurement used for social value orientation, because they reveal that pro-socials and pro-selves behave in opposite ways when exposed to different forms of social influence. These opposite effects on different personality types may explain why there was no overall effect for the social information treatment at the individual level, but that it was as significant as visibility at the round level. These results join previous work on conditional cooperation that has explored how people differ in their pro-social preferences,[53] but add insight to this literature by showing how these different individuals respond differentially to social influence.

THE SHAME OF PRO-SELVES

To investigate the precise nature of heterogeneity according to conditional cooperation, we looked at subject behaviour by social value orientation in Figure 6.4, which shows the difference between the mean contribution amount under control conditions and under both treatments, for pro-social and pro-self subjects. Without exception, all pro-selves in our experiment contributed more under the visibility treatment than under the control condition, suggesting that all were shameable under this strong form of social influence. Under the social information treatment, they also mostly contributed more, here suggesting that they used the

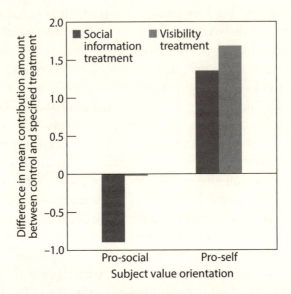

FIGURE 6.4 Behaviour of subjects with pro-social and pro-self social value orientations under visibility and social information treatments compared with the control condition

opportunities for strategic play, whereas under the control condition they did not contribute. This pattern suggests that these are individuals who do not automatically cooperate, but do so when they are provided with the information that their contribution will make a difference. The behaviour of pro-socials was more heterogeneous. Some pro-social individuals were more cooperative when visible in comparison with the control, but the majority were actually less cooperative, suggesting that this strong form of social influence actually discouraged them from contributing. It could be that these subjects were using the (generally high) levels of contribution shown on the projector screen and using it as a limited form of aggregated social information (they do not know which people were in their particular subgroup) to estimate that a large contribution would not be necessary to meet the target. It could be that they were negatively affected by the visibility treatment itself, where the feeling that there was an attempt to shame them to contribute actually discouraged them, similar to the crowding out of blood donation by incentivization that Titmuss used in an argument for voluntary as opposed to compensated blood donation or the negative effect of sanctions on altruistic cooperation demonstrated experimentally by Fehr and Rockenbach.[54]

A distinctive element of our experimental design is that we measured the personality of subjects using a tried and tested survey instrument, but also measured cooperative and free-riding behaviour under the treatments used. This aspect of the design allowed us to isolate the effect of the treatment and to identify different susceptibilities to the treatment of the different social value orientations. As noted in the reporting of the results above, the finding that pro-social individuals contribute more and pro-selves contribute less is not surprising. But the findings that show differential susceptibility to the treatments according to social value orientation shed new light on the issue of conditional cooperation. In all the models presented here, the inclusion of social value orientation variables significantly ($p < .001$) increases the fit of the models according to likelihood ratio tests. These tests can assess whether statistical models are different from each other. Most previous work has suggested that some pro-selves will always free ride and that the cooperation of most pro-socials is conditional on the behaviour of others.[55] In contrast, our research suggests that all pro-selves are likely to cooperate if a strong enough form of social influence (that is, visibility) is applied. In contrast, some pro-social personality types were resistant to this form of social influence (and indeed, were actively discouraged from contributing by this treatment). Most of our pro-socials were at their most cooperative when receiving no information about what other people were doing, while taking the opportunity to behave strategically when presented with social information about the behaviour of others. More research would be needed to corroborate this finding, but the insight that social influence can be used to persuade even the most persistent free riders to cooperate collectively, yet can have a negative effect on pro-social types, could be important for the design of information environments where cooperative behaviour is sought, contributing to the body of work that considers when—and when not—anonymity can be beneficial for maximizing contributions to collective goods.[56]

UNDERSTANDING DIFFERENCE

To understand the heterogeneous impact of social influence, in this chapter we have explored its interaction with personality, in particular the Big Five personality traits that have interested political scientists so much in the past decade. This chapter shows that other individual difference variables—in particular social value orientation, a measure favoured by economists—may also be useful in explaining levels of contribution to collective efforts under varying information environments. The finding that pro-social people contribute more confirms previous work, but the finding that pro-socials and pro-selves respond so differently to the two types of social influence explored here adds new insight.

Visibility makes pro-self people contribute more, pro-social people less. The mechanism appears to be shaming: pro-selves give more under conditions of visibility in a way that is consistent with this causal mechanism, while pro-socials seem more resistant to this form of social pressure. The effects are the same for social information: pro-selves give more than under control conditions, while pro-socials give less. This treatment identifies the conditional cooperators among the pro-selves; those who will cooperate when provided with the information that allows them to do so strategically.

With respect to the Big Five traits, our findings for agreeableness join those of Gerber et al., Mondak and Halperin, and Mondak et al. in finding it to be negatively associated with participation in the collective action we considered,[57] although they go against those of Volk et al. and other work that found that for certain types of non-conflictual political activity, agreeable people contribute more.[58] The negative association we found for conscientiousness and participation in collective action joins the mixed results of previous research, while the positive association we found for emotional stability is commensurate with the conclusions of Gerber et al., although not those of Mondak et al.[59] Our findings regarding the visibility treatment, which caused extravert people to contribute less and agreeable people to contribute more, add new insight to previous research, which has not focused on the differential effect of social influence on different personality types.

We thus provide a more integrated and precise account of the way in which social influence operates, in particular the importance of social pressure that comes from visibility. We identify social value orientation as an important source of heterogeneity in susceptibility to the experimental treatments for both visibility and social information. It is through the interaction of social influence and social value orientation that it is possible to predict how individuals will behave and whether collective actions will be viable. By looking within social value orientation, we can identify both hard-core pro-socials who contribute more when social information is not available and strategic or conditional cooperators who give only when it is available. These results also suggest that pro-selves are more shameable, that is, susceptible to the social influence of visibility, than hypothesized or revealed in previous research.

Such findings could help to understand certain types of success and failure in attempts to encourage civic engagement, and even inform platform design. When trying to encourage a community that is likely to be largely populated by pro-selves to make charitable donations (a group of city bankers, perhaps?), then visibility will be the tool to select. When trying to attract a community of cooperative pro-social people to contribute to a collective good, visibility may be counterproductive and actually discourage contributions.

This chapter has taken a step towards understanding individual difference in political participation in the age of social media. Working on the assumption that demographic differences matter less in an environment of almost costless participation, we have identified personality as a variable that could be an important predictor of who contributes and indicate who is most swayed by the influences that social media exert. In the next chapter, we extend our analysis of individual-level difference by looking at the effect of personality on people's propensity to take part early in a mobilization. Clearly the people who took to the streets of Ferguson, New York, Oakland, and other US cities in 2014 were undertaking higher-cost acts of participation, but those who were quick to make tiny contributions in retweeting, liking, or sharing posts on Twitter, Facebook, and other social media to create the momentum that led to the street protests played an important role in the formation of a nascent political movement, which is worthy of analysis.

CHAPTER 7
HOW IT ALL KICKS OFF

In May 2011 protests and demonstrations erupted across austerity-stricken Spain, starting in Madrid's Puerta del Sol and spreading to consume public squares in over fifty Spanish cities. Protestors demanded radical political changes and a response to the social and economic problems facing Spain, particularly its record-breaking unemployment rate of 27 percent (over half of young people in many regions). Inspired by the revolutions and uprisings of the Arab Spring, the movement was coordinated in the early days almost exclusively via social media, particularly Twitter and Facebook, with only negligible effects of news media until one-fifth of users had already joined the online exchange of protest information.[1] Around one-fifth of Spanish people have participated at some point. Called alternatively 15-M (Movimiento 15-M, after the date the first demonstration took place) and Los Indignados ('the discontented', to express the widespread feelings of outrage at conditions in Spain), the movement was born out of a myriad of groups, local organizations, and loose associations with highly nebulous and disparate aims, not the most auspicious circumstances for coordination or the growth of a social movement. Yet 15-M survived and became a force for change, even contributing to the Occupy movement and now considered to be 'part of modern Spain'.[2] As we will discuss in the final chapter, 15-M is one of the few movements of 2011—when demonstrations started kicking off everywhere, as Mason put it—that appears to be developing into a sustainable political force with the formation of the political party Podemos (meaning 'We Can') in 2014.[3]

How are mobilizations like 15-M launched? Chapter 4 showed that evidence of a critical mass of participants plays an important role in encouraging people to join in, and Chapter 5 showed how people respond strategically to social information; not participating when it seems as if a good will not be provided or when it is clear that it will be provided without their contribution. But how can a critical mass form if everyone waits for this point? Implicit in the critical mass argument is that some people are willing to join when there are few signals of viability, in order to lay the foundations for critical mass to form by encouraging others to join. If this assumption holds, then the social information effects—which are crucial in indicating both the viability of a mobilization and the most efficient way of influencing it—observed in the last two chapters will act differently on different people. But can we test this assertion? And if we can prove it to be so, what could explain this difference? What sorts of people are willing to start?

To tackle these questions, in this chapter we turn to threshold models of collective action,[4] building on the work of the economist Thomas Schelling and the sociologist Mark Granovetter from the 1970s. Both these scholars claim that people vary in their threshold for joining a mobilization (that is the proportion of other people that will propel them to mobilize); some people take the lead by participating when few others have done so, while others require high levels of participation before they will take part. They argue that the distribution of thresholds in a population will be crucial in determining whether a mobilization gains critical mass. If there are enough people with low thresholds to start a mobilization, then evidence of their participation will give a signal of viability to those with slightly higher thresholds, and so on in a series of chain reactions until there is enough of a sense of viability to suggest to those with thresholds somewhere in the middle that it is worth joining. At this point, critical mass will be attained and the majority of potential participants will join. If this series of chain reactions does not occur, then a mobilization will fail. In this way, the threshold model is closely related to the tipping points we identified in Chapter 4, when we looked at the arguments of Marwell and Oliver.[5]

In this chapter, we investigate the moments when different people join a mobilization (rather than what they contribute), looking for evidence of different thresholds and identifying the types of people associated with them. We use data from our laboratory-based experiment to test Schelling's assertion that a population will vary in thresholds for joining a mobilization;[6] some joining when the number of participants is very low, some when almost everyone is participating, and most joining somewhere in the middle.[7] Using measures of personality as we did in the last chapter, we develop the idea that personality may present the clue to understanding an individual's threshold. If so, then the pattern of starters and followers who progressively join a mobilization may present a way to understand how movements like 15-M can take off and build momentum. Previous research has shown that rather than this kind of collective action relying on a small subset of special individuals with disproportionate influence (such as the mass media), influence derives from a critical mass of 'common users' who in aggregate make chain reactions converge.[8] González-Bailón et al. usefully analysed chain reactions in the Twitter network relating to 15-M, finding that the protest managed to mobilize so many people in such a short time span because of reinforcing interactions between four categories of participants in the network: influentials (with high visibility), hidden influentials (with low visibility, but a central role), broadcasters, and grassroots users.[9] But these categories of protesters are based on roles in the network and in the diffusion of information, rather than any intrinsic characteristics and cannot, therefore, provide insight into differential thresholds.

THRESHOLDS FOR JOINING

The clue to identifying differential willingness to join at the start of a mobilization might come from the threshold model of collective behaviour. Schelling in the book *Micromotives and Macrobehaviour*

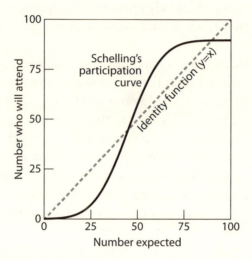

FIGURE 7.1 Schelling's participation curve

develops a model of mobilization, although not for a political context, pointing to examples of where a person's behaviour will vary
depending on information about how many other people are participating,[10] such as how many people attend an optional seminar,
how many applaud and clap loudly, and how many people leave
a failing school.[11] He argues that the number representing critical
mass varies by context, which can mean a proportion of potential participants (important when considering adopting a certain
fashion, for example) or an actual number (which might matter to
attendees at a seminar). He assumes that people have different individual thresholds for joining a mobilization and argues that where
such thresholds are normally distributed in a population, there will
be an S-shaped joining curve for any mobilization, illustrated in
its simplest form in Figure 7.1, where the number of people participating in an event is represented on the vertical axis, while the
number of people expected to participate is shown on the horizontal axis. There is a relationship between the numbers that people
think are going to turn out and how many eventually do so, based
on the effect that information about expected numbers has on any
one individual's decision to participate. The eye can follow the line

along the axes, so at low levels of expectation, this creates the self-fulfilling prophesy that even lower numbers turn up. As the numbers expected increase, so do the numbers who actually do show up, but at increasing proportion, so the numbers expected and actual numbers equalise. As the numbers get higher, so the numbers coming exceed those expected, which creates the critical mass for mobilization, in Marwell and Oliver's terms.[12] Schelling produces a variety of predictions from this basic form, showing how sometimes the mobilization curve will cross the diagonal line because the number of people expected to participate meets most people's threshold and the mobilization succeeds, whereas at other times the curve does not rise above the line and the mobilization fails.[13]

We do not test all aspects of Schelling's model here. Indeed as we observed in Chapter 2 for the mobilizations relating to US demonstrations against racist policing and noted in Chapter 3 with respect to petition signing, many mobilizations related to political issues show surprisingly little adherence to Schelling's S-shaped curve. Rather, we focus on his claim regarding thresholds for joining a mobilization. Likewise, Granovetter identified the concept of a threshold as key to the viability of collective behaviour, arguing that the distribution of thresholds within a population was a vital determinant of outcomes.[14] The threshold model suggests that individual behavioural disposition does not change before, during, or after collective decisions are made; these are contingent dispositions that act on the situation, even if actual behaviour may change. But there is no attempt to identify the origins of these dispositions; neither Schelling nor Granovetter 'consider how individuals happen to have the preferences that they do'.[15] In contrast, the aim of this chapter is to investigate empirically the distribution of thresholds in a population, focusing on the characteristics of the group of starters who are willing to join a collective action early.

In mobilizations initiated via social media, Schelling's 'number expected to attend' will be informed by the social information that most platforms provide, that is, an indication of the number of participants involved in a petition, a mass email campaign, a Facebook group, or a charitable donation page. Although Schelling makes the questionable assumption that people are able to estimate the 'number expected' figure in an offline setting, it may be that for the first time we can now test his claims.

WHO JOINS WHEN?

As discussed in the previous chapter, personality is a fundamental part of the human condition, and different types of people perceive and respond to the same stimuli in fundamentally different ways. As in the last chapter, we follow recent work that has used personality as a predictor of political behaviour and beliefs, in particular the Big Five traits,[16] using these variables as part of our research design to investigate whether people with particular personalities show a different propensity to join an action early.

When looking for clues as to which personality type is most likely to start, we look for traits that have been associated with leadership and leaders, given the connotations that these concepts have of showing initiative and leading others at the front. Our assumption is that propensity to join early (or start) could be related to some (although not all) of the personality traits associated with leadership. Previous research provides no clear picture of how personality traits relate to leadership,[17] and the results of these investigations 'have been inconsistent and often disappointing'.[18] For this reason, we select two alternative typologies of individual-level difference that have been associated with willingness to lead, rather than selecting a single one.

First, as in the previous chapter, we utilize the Big Five personality traits. In that chapter, we followed previous political science research in identifying extraversion and agreeableness as the most significant predictors of contributory behaviour, so we hypothesize here that they will be the most useful in understanding a person's willingness or reluctance to go early in mobilizations where there are few signals of viability.

Psychological research looks at two broad categories of leadership: leadership emergence and leadership effectiveness,[19] the latter being less relevant to the current study. Although much of that work focuses on leaders in the sense of other people's views of the potential leader, rather than the 'starter' criteria that we are interested in here, and some researchers have dismissed trait theory as obsolete in this context,[20] two extensive and detailed reviews of leadership research found evidence to suggest that the Big Five typology 'is a fruitful basis for examining the dispositional predictors of leadership'.[21] Of the Big Five characteristics, extraversion in particular has been positively associated to self and peer ratings of leadership.[22] In their meta-analysis of leadership and personality research, Judge et al. found that 'extraversion emerged as the most consistent correlate of leadership', particularly with respect to leader emergence,[23] although there were some findings for conscientiousness and openness to experience. For these reasons, we test all the Big Five personality traits while hypothesizing that extraversion will be the most important and the most likely to lead to a positive association with willingness to start.

We introduce here locus of control as another personality trait. In the field of organizational and applied psychology, internal locus of control (the extent to which people believe that they have control over their own fate) has been identified as an important personality trait with respect to all kinds of social roles, including leadership. Developed by Rotter into a measurable scale (later shortened by Carpenter and employed in Carpenter and Seki),[24] locus of control identifies 'internals', who are those people who believe that they are masters of their fate and who perceive a strong link between their actions and consequences, and 'externals', who do not believe themselves to have direct control of their fate and who perceive themselves in a passive role with regard to the external environment. In work settings, internal locus of control has been positively associated with favourable work outcomes and greater job motivation,[25] high job satisfaction and performance,[26] and more effective leadership.[27] In business studies and management research, people with internal locus of control have been identified as more likely to be leaders and to have superior leadership performance,[28] although Judge et al. found locus of control to be a weaker predictor of successful leaders than other personality traits reviewed.[29] In economics, Boone et al. found that 'internals' in social dilemma situations are more likely than 'externals' to try to influence the behaviour of others to achieve their goals, while externals behave less strategically.[30] With particular relevance for this study, locus of control has been associated with the tendency for people to exert active control over the environment,[31] to participate in social action,[32] and to engage in political activism.[33]

We may hypothesize therefore that extraversion and internal locus of control will be associated with low thresholds for joining a mobilization at an early stage. We may further hypothesize that the likelihood of a mobilization growing in its very early stages will increase as the number of individuals with low joining thresholds in the population increases.

LOOKING FOR STARTERS AND FOLLOWERS

We use data derived from the public goods laboratory experiment undertaken by the authors,[34] introduced in Chapter 5. To recap, the subjects were asked to contribute tokens to a collective good under control, visibility, and social information treatments (the instructions to the participants and post-experiment questionnaires are shown in the Appendix). In Chapter 6 we looked at the *amount* that individual subjects contributed under the different treatments, whereas here we examine the relationship between personality and the *order* in which subjects participated in each round. We use just those rounds where participants were aware of how many others in their group had contributed (the social information treatment) and whether they were leading or following at the precise moment that they decided to participate, thereby using the number of other participants as a surrogate for 'number expected' in Schelling's model. We look at the rank (first, second, third, and so on) at which individuals contribute, seeking consistent patterns in the rank at which they join rounds, to identify thresholds and then examining the relationship between personality and threshold, controlling for the importance that people ascribe to the issue under consideration. We also examine the relationship between the propensity of a round to get funded and the distribution of personality characteristics across the people in the group playing the round.

First, we looked at the propensity of individual subjects to contribute tokens in the early stages, when there was little or no evidence that others were participating, to see if we could identify subjects who consistently started or followed, providing evidence of stable personal thresholds. We examined the minimum, median, and mean rank at which subjects participated in a round as their threshold for participation (Figure 7.2). First, with respect to minimum rank, if an individual subject has a minimum rank of 1, it indicates that he or she is willing to start a mobilization with no other participants. Alternatively, if the participant's minimum rank across the twenty-eight rounds is 5, then a higher threshold is suggested. Figure 7.2a shows the distribution of minimum rank across our 185 subjects, showing that just over half of them were willing to start at some point. This result was quite surprising, suggesting a far from normal distribution of people's willingness to start a mobilization. To identify threshold, however, we need to determine consistent starters, rather than just people who are willing to start at some point. Therefore, second, we looked at median rank (Figure 7.2b). Here the figures are more evenly distributed, with a few subjects starting often (and therefore having a median rank of 1 or 2), a few almost always joining only at the end of the mobilization, and most being somewhere in between. The most common median rank is 3, suggesting people who are most likely to contribute when over 25 percent (two out of eight, the most common group size) have already done so. Third, Figure 7.2c shows the results for mean rank, again illustrating a distribution that appears normal and that fails all tests for non-normality.

Finally, we construct a variable to count the number of times a subject starts a round (propensity to start) normalized by the number of rounds the subject played. This variable exhibits an extremely skewed distribution (Figure 7.2d), with just under half of the participants never starting a round, and for whom the 'propensity to start'

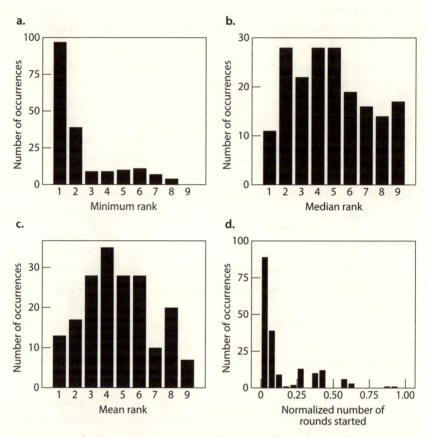

FIGURE 7.2 Distribution of subjects' (a) minimum, (b) median, and (c) mean ranks and distribution of (d) the number of times subjects started a round

variable is therefore zero. Of those subjects who do start a round at some point (i.e., who have at least one round with rank one and therefore a minimum rank of 1), the distribution is still left-skewed, with most individuals starting only one or two rounds.[35]

Each subject played between seven and fourteen rounds in the conditions investigated here. We calculated the standard deviation of each subject's ranks across these rounds as a measure of their consistency. Plotting this standard deviation score against the median rank of each participant (Figure 7.3) shows that nearly all subjects with a low or high average rank consistently contributed

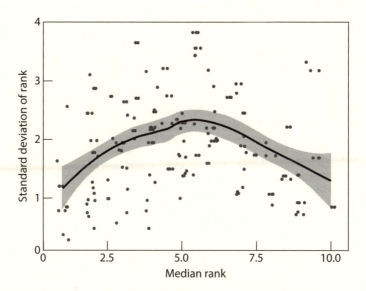

FIGURE 7.3 Median rank and standard deviation of rank per subject
Note: The best fit line is a locally weighted scatterplot smoothing (LOWESS) line with a 95 percent confidence interval shaded around the line.

early or late. In contrast, while some subjects with a median rank towards the middle also had a low standard deviation score, other subjects were much less consistent and had higher standard deviation scores. Standard deviations for subjects with a mean rank between 4 and 6 ranged from 0.488 to 3.827, with a mean deviation of 2.276 across subjects. These distributions show that the subjects have heterogeneous propensities to start or join a collective action and suggest that a few people have consistently low thresholds for joining, and some have consistently high thresholds. There is greater variability in subjects going near the middle, but early movers and late movers act more consistently.[36]

WHO STARTS, WHO FOLLOWS?

The analysis above has identified four possible ways to identify the threshold for individual subjects: minimum rank, median rank, mean rank, and propensity to start. All four measures exhibit variance

TABLE 7.1 Correlation matrix for personality measures (Big 5 & locus of control)

	Extravert	Agreeable	Conscientious	Emotionally stable	Openness	Internal locus
Extravert	1.00					
Agreeable	.19	1.00				
Conscientious	−.06	.02	1.00			
Emotionally stable	.29	.20	.29	1.00		
Open	.31	.00	.02	−.01	1.00	
Internal locus	.34	.05	.20	.34	.35	1.00

across individual subjects, supporting our aim to find some proxy for personal thresholds, by which we mean consistent behaviour in terms of participants joining a petition early, late, or somewhere in the middle. Before we could examine the relationship between these threshold measures and personality, we first examined the personality variables in our dataset for collinearity (Table 7.1). These results show that in general the variables are not highly correlated; even the correlations of .34 and .35 between Rotter score (the variable used to measure internal locus of control) and three of the Big Five variables (extravert, open, and emotionally stable) are not high enough to be problematic. Nonetheless, we ran separate regressions for the Big Five and Rotter score when testing our hypotheses, shown in separate panels of Table 7.2.

We ran Tobit regressions to test the association between the threshold measures and the various personality traits discussed above, in order to examine our hypotheses that people scoring highly on extraversion and internal locus of control would be more likely to start or go early. These results are shown in Table 7.2.[37] We tested for possible associations between demographic variables (income, age and ethnicity) and propensity to start, but none were found to be significant. We also found that social value orientation (as discussed in Chapter 6) was unrelated to people's propensity to start, in spite of the strong relationship between this

TABLE 7.2 Tobit regressions showing relationships between threshold measures and personality traits

A. Rotter score

	Rank			
	Mean	Median	Minimum	Propensity to start
Mean importance	–3.168*	–3.793*	–5.211*	0.115
	(1.34)	(1.65)	(2.54)	(0.21)
Rotter score	–2.226*	–3.065**	–5.674**	0.421**
	(0.92)	(1.14)	(1.81)	(0.15)
Constant	8.853***	9.673***	8.036***	–0.333
	(1.15)	(1.41)	(2.18)	(0.19)
N	177	177	177	177

B. 'Big Five' personality traits

	Rank			
	Mean	Median	Minimum	Propensity to start
Mean importance	–3.649**	– 4.164*	–5.454*	0.155
	(1.29)	(1.62)	(2.45)	(0.20)
Extravert	–1.788**	–2.073**	–3.428**	0.276**
	(0.61)	(0.78)	(1.20)	(0.10)
Agreeable	3.063***	2.936**	5.715***	–0.606***
	(0.71)	(0.90)	(1.44)	(0.12)
Conscientious	–0.154	–0.421	0.665	–0.033
	(0.79)	(1.00)	(1.60)	(0.12)
Emotionally stable	–0.166	–0.221	–0.635	0.186
	(0.63)	(0.80)	(1.25)	(0.10)
Open	0.394	0.240	0.238	0.214
	(0.88)	(1.12)	(1.72)	(0.14)
Constant	6.477***	7.253***	2.224	–0.086
	(1.27)	(1.61)	(2.43)	(0.20)
N	180	180	180	180

*$p < .05$. **$p < .01$. ***$p < .001$.

Note: Standard errors are in parentheses

variable and contribution behaviour identified by economists and ourselves in the previous chapter.[38] In all regressions we controlled for the relative importance of the scenario at hand (as asked in the post-experiment questionnaire) for our subjects, as clearly the importance ascribed to an issue will be an important factor in the motivation of an individual to participate, something we have established in earlier work and in Chapter 4.[39] The post-experiment questionnaire included questions on whether the subjects agreed with the issue and how important they considered it to be. Both were significant, but as they were correlated we controlled for importance as it had the most predictive strength.

First, we found locus of control, the personality variable most often associated with leadership in the psychology and management literature, to be significantly associated with going early in mobilizations. The locus of control variable was a predictor of median rank, mean rank, minimum rank, and propensity to start across all issue subjects. So our hypothesis that internal locus of control would be associated with willingness to start is confirmed, although, as found in some earlier work,[40] locus of control was found to have a weaker effect than some of the other personality traits we investigated.

We found significant results for two of the Big Five personality traits. Across our measures of threshold, extraversion was consistently associated with joining early, and agreeableness was consistently associated with joining late. Table 7.2b shows agreeable people as being strongly associated with higher median ranks and higher mean ranks, and with a lower propensity to start. Extraversion is also an important personality variable. Extraverts have a significantly lower median rank ($p < .01$) and mean rank ($p < .01$) and are significantly more likely to have a high number of starts ($p < .01$). None of the other Big Five personality traits have a significant effect on these threshold variables. These results confirm our prediction that extraversion would be a predictor of low threshold to start or join early, with the additional finding for agreeableness, which has a consistently higher coefficient than those for extraversion.

WHAT MAKES FOR SUCCESS?

If successful mobilizations rely on a number of people with low thresholds in order to start them and if these people are those with extravert personalities (or a high internal locus of control), then it should be that rounds without people with one or other of these personality types will consistently fail. To test this hypothesis we collapsed the data at the round level, looking at the maximum, minimum, and mean scores for external/internal locus of control and extraversion/intraversion of the people participating in each round and the relationship between these variables and whether a round was funded or not.

We ran regressions for all personality variables separately while controlling for the mean importance attributed by all participants on the team to the scenario at hand and the amount of the first contribution. Basically, the higher the importance ascribed to the issue across the group of participants, the more likely it is to be supported. The amount of the first contribution in a round is also significant, reaffirming results of previous experimental research in economics investigating conditional cooperation in charitable giving, which showed that the larger the first contribution, the larger the total contributions are likely to be.[41] We control for these two variables in the regressions that follow.

Among all the personality variables tested, only extraversion was significant in explaining the likelihood of a round being funded. Two measures of the extraversion of the group, the mean and minimum, were significant, as shown in Figure 7.4. If we picture Schelling's mobilization curve (Figure 7.1), it seems that extraversion correlates with willingness to join the movement (Schelling's x-axis). Those high in extraversion are so motivated that they are willing to start, while those with more moderate levels of extraversion have a medium threshold to then join. Those with low levels of extraversion have a very low willingness to join, and too high a proportion of these individuals within a population hampers the possible success of a movement. A high minimum value

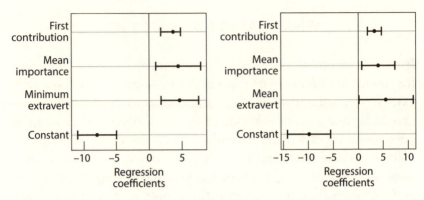

FIGURE 7.4 Logistic regressions to show the effect of personality on the round being funded
Note: N = 217.

for extraversion in any given round suggests that there are lower numbers of people with low extraversion (high thresholds), which is associated with a higher likelihood of a round being funded. Mean extraversion was also significant, showing again that generally high numbers of extraverts in the group were associated with a higher chance of a round being funded. We did not, however, find similar results for internal locus of control. Similarly, the minimum, maximum, and mean levels of agreeableness (and all the other personality variables) were not associated with the likelihood of a round's being funded.

STARTERS AND FOLLOWERS

We have identified heterogeneity in our experimental subjects in their willingness to join a collective action at an early stage, when there is little or no evidence that other people will join or that the common goal is likely to be attained. Some people were willing to start a mobilization more than once, some joined mobilizations only during the later stages, and most varied their behaviour across a middle range. We have also identified that for a proportion of subjects in our experiment, the rank (or willingness) at which they join is consistent, and we found most evidence of this consistency at the early and late stages of a mobilization. That is, we identified some people with consistently low thresholds, and some with consistently high thresholds for joining.

We have identified the personality characteristics associated with low or high thresholds, although not for all the personality variables that we investigated in our analysis. Internal locus of control is positively associated with a willingness to start, supporting the findings of research on leadership in psychology and management studies.[42]

Likewise, we find that extraversion is consistently associated with willingness to start. This joins the growing body of evidence from political science that points to a relationship between extraversion and political participation.[43] We might have expected that in online contexts where participants do not interact socially, such as the one we simulated here, extraversion would be less predictive (as Mondak et al. and Gerber et al. found for various 'nonsocial' types of participation, and we found in the previous chapter),[44] so the fact that it remained significant throughout our analysis in this chapter renders this finding more interesting and suggests that this personality trait acts endogenously to predispose individuals to start or initiate action even when there is no indication that others will do so. The positive association we found between the concentration of extraversion in a subject group, and the likelihood of a round getting funded, suggesting that a mobilization with higher numbers of people with high extraversion has a higher chance of success, reinforces this finding.

We have made the additional finding that agreeableness is positively associated with a tendency to go late, suggesting that agreeable people wait until it is clear that the mobilization will be funded before joining themselves. This joins the mixed results of previous research for this personality trait; agreeable people seem drawn to some types of participation and not to other, more conflictual activities. Starting an action where there are few other participants could fall into this category, confirming the importance of context and 'personality-relevant characteristics of each participatory act', as we found in the last chapter.[45] None of the other Big Five personality variables investigated is significantly associated with an individual's joining threshold, a result that adds to the mixed results for these traits in most previous political science research.[46]

These findings also support previous research on leadership showing that the Big Five typology is a fruitful basis for examining predictors of leadership and that extraversion is the most consistent correlate of leadership.[47] This previous research focused on leadership in organizations, whereas our findings for extraversion in the different context of collective action in a non-organizational setting are stronger and less equivocal. It may be that the strength of our results derives from extraversion being best suited to the starting element of leadership, and less so to the other activities required for leading in offline contexts, which require other dimensions of personality.

MOBILIZATION WITHOUT LEADERS, REVOLUTIONS WITHOUT ORGANIZATIONS

Analysis of large-scale transactional data from electronic petitions presented in Chapter 3 showed that the early days of a mobilization are crucial; success is reliant on a significant number of people being willing to act at this early point, when there is no social information to indicate viability. On social media, where people can be rapidly notified of new mobilizations through large-scale social networks, and social information is readily available, mobilizations can quickly reach critical mass; likewise, a movement may fail almost immediately as news of the mobilization slips down the news feed on social media platforms, and the starting moment is lost. By identifying heterogeneous thresholds for our subjects, consistent at least at the early and late stages of mobilizations, we have provided some evidence for this mechanism in action.

In this environment, leadership is the aggregate of many low-cost actions undertaken by those willing to start, rather than the high-cost actions and rare attributes usually associated with leadership. Of course, the group of starters will usually include at least one leader more in the traditional mould who has taken a higher cost action, for example, the person who sets up a petition and circulates it to close associates in her immediate social networks. But the number of starters needed to get the mobilization off the ground will be beyond that which could be obtained with strong ties to the initiator alone, but will be attained with weak ties, such as the friend of a friend on a social networking site, or the retweet of the retweet of a tweet. To obtain the five hundred signatures used as a measure of success for the first UK petition platform analysed in Chapter 3, an individual initiating a petition would probably have to go beyond his immediate social network; in 2011, the median number of friends on Facebook was 100,[48] and the median number of followers on Twitter was 85.[49] In the United States, where petitions must have 150 signatures before they can even be public on the petitions platform, a petition initiator could struggle to gain visibility for her petition using her own immediate social network alone. As requests to sign arrive through weaker and weaker ties, the raw information of how many signatures have been obtained will be a relatively important piece of social information, rather than the network attachment to the initiator. Many petitions on similar issues fail while one might succeed; it is not the existence of the leader who brings the success, but the existence of a sufficient number of starters with low thresholds, and the readily available and disseminated social information about other participants that draws in the followers with higher thresholds. By providing this social information, social media platforms circumvent the need for other activities traditionally performed by leaders.

If extraversion is a good predictor of low threshold, then the likelihood of a mobilization obtaining some measure of success will depend in part on the distribution of extraversion in the pool of people who care about the issue at hand and who are aware of the mobilization. A possible corollary of this finding is that mobilizations initiated by people with high levels of extraversion are more likely to succeed. Given that we might hypothesize that extravert people tend to select extravert friends;[50] given evidence to suggest that extravert people have more friends on social media;[51] and given that an individual is most likely to kick off a mobilization via her own online social networks, then an extravert's initiative might be immediately disseminated to a pool of people with greater than normal levels of extraversion and, if our findings are correct, low thresholds for joining.

The earlier work by Schelling and Granovetter discussed in the first section assumed that different individuals have different thresholds for joining a mobilization and based their models on this assumption. They did not investigate why individuals have the thresholds that they do, or what types of people have which types of threshold. In contrast, we have looked at the characteristics of people with low thresholds and identified a relationship between extraversion (and, to a less clear extent, internal locus of control) and low thresholds. From the evidence reported here, we cannot attempt to make any claims as to what the distribution of thresholds might be in any given context, as our findings are based on experimental data that did not purport to be a representative sample of any population. However, the findings suggest that future research aimed at understanding the distribution of thresholds might include secondary analysis of research into the distribution of extraversion or locus of control in different populations.

These findings also have a wider significance. The argument presented here combined with the evidence of previous chapters suggests that contemporary political mobilizations can become viable without leading individuals or organizations to undertake coordination costs, and proceed to critical mass and even achieving the policy or political change at which they are aimed. Our conclusions provide one plausible explanation for how the Spanish 15-M movement could mobilize without any national organization or clear leadership. It could be argued that this is the case with some of the uprisings of the Arab Spring, where dictators and their administrative apparatus were toppled by huge political mobilizations of people, but without institutions, political parties, or embryonic leaders in the wings to undertake the process of re-building the state.

The existence of movements like 15-M makes it more likely that discontent or other strong political emotions crystallise into concrete expression. The large resources of followers are potential voters, or can be mobilized to protest again, bringing further turbulence to political life. But Internet-based mobilization of this kind is no guarantee of sustained political change, as evidenced by some of the disappointments of the nascent political movements that emerged from 2011. In Egypt, for example, in spite of the huge waves of popular protest that toppled the Mubarak regime, the Muslim Brotherhood, as the only organized force on the political scene but with limited commitment to democracy, gained power in the first elections, leading to Mohamed Morsi becoming the first democratically elected head of Egypt in 2012. Even after a further year, when renewal of popular protests and demonstrations led to the removal of Morsi, it was the Egyptian military—again a pre-existing organization rather than a new organizational force—that returned to power with the election of President Abdel Fattah el-Sisi, previously the minister of defence.

In the final chapter, we pull together the arguments and evidence in this book, to see how new forms of collective action impact on the practice of politics more generally. We combine the experimental and big data evidence we have gathered about collective attention, critical mass, tipping points, thresholds, and personality effects to characterize the relationship between social media and collective action. We highlight how greater turbulence is the consequence of the processes we have traced. We identify a model of democracy that encapsulates this turbulence, and provides the basis to understand politics in the age of social media.

CHAPTER 8

FROM POLITICAL TURBULENCE TO CHAOTIC PLURALISM

We started this book with a question: how does the changing use of social media affect politics? This line of enquiry was suggested by the dramatic rise in the use of social media from the mid-2000s, built on the previous decade of expansion of Internet-enabled activities and fuelled by the widespread adoption of mobile telephones connected to the Internet. Such technologies have changed the way most people work, shop, and travel and how they manage their financial affairs, educate and entertain themselves, keep in touch with friends and family, and get involved in politics and interact with government. Of course, the medium itself could be entirely neutral, with electronic communications simply replacing activities that were once done on paper, by telephone, or in face-to-face contact. Even with this rapid adoption of new technologies, the same institutions and behaviours might carry on as they did before, just with the added convenience afforded by electronic forms of communication. But this has not happened. Instead, the Internet and social media are now inextricably intertwined with the political behaviour of ordinary citizens. So what can we say about the changing nature of politics?

The kind of politics we have observed and analysed is characterized by rapidly shifting flows of attention and activity. Social media extend the range of political activities that citizens can undertake, lowering the costs to an extent whereby people are offered the opportunity to make micro-donations of time and effort to political causes throughout their daily activities. In every decision over whether to undertake these tiny acts of participation, people are exposed to social influences: the knowledge of what other people are doing, or the knowledge that what they do will be visible to other people, so their own actions are interdependent with those of large numbers of other people, causing chain reactions that can scale up to large mobilizations—but usually do not. This is a turbulent politics, which is unstable, unpredictable, and often unsustainable.

In 2013 two countries started to experience the waves of protest and demonstration that typify this kind of political mobilization. In Turkey, demonstrations against plans to build a shopping mall on the Gezi Park in Istanbul grew into a sustained protest against the increasing authoritarianism of Prime Minister Recep Tayyip Erdogan. Two weeks of protests climaxed in a drastic response by riot police in which five people died; demonstrators sustained a silent vigil, with the 'standing man' Erdem Gunduz standing silently for eight hours in Taksim Square, a protest copied many times over across the country. In Brazil, as we noted at the start of Chapter 1, rallies that started in Sao Paulo in mid-June, triggered by a rise in bus and underground fares, swept across the country to around a hundred cities. Although the government reversed its original policy on transport pricing, the protests continued, based on a more generalized objection to a whole range of issues such as rising prices, continuing inequalities in society, and irrational spending on bringing the 2014 World Cup and 2016 Olympics to Brazil. Social media were implicated in the spread of both these movements. In Turkey, the Facebook page 'Diren Gezi Parki', set up to coordinate events, had 622,000 'likes' by mid-June, with 707,000 'talking about this', while an app to allow private messaging on a virtual network gained 120,000 users in a week. Even from Gezi Park itself, over 15,000 users sent at least one tweet during the first five days of the protest.[1] In Brazil, demonstrators carried banners proclaiming 'We are the Social Network!' Members of both movements described themselves as leaderless and resisted any institutional involvement, from political parties for example. Both started with relatively minor issues, but quickly grew in support, reflecting a more generalized dissatisfaction and greater distrust of the government and political leaders. Both appeared to melt away from global news in the year that followed, but could reemerge at any time. Both cases illustrate strongly all the trends and patterns we have identified in this book.

In this, the final chapter of the book, we outline our account of contemporary collective action, using the experimental and large-scale data analysis presented in the previous chapters to shed light on the dynamics of political turbulence. In so doing, we hope to provide the reader with a way of understanding mobilization in the twenty-first century. We investigate pluralism as a democratic model, identified in Chapter 1 as the best bet for the theoretical framework to encapsulate the changing form of politics. From the turbulent political world we have explored here, we seem to be able to discern a new kind of pluralism, highly decentred and chaotic in its operation, that might revive strands of thought from the earliest pluralist thinkers of the previous century, such as Dahl and Lindblom, while being based on a transformed notion of many of its principles, particularly the conception of interest groups as the basic building block of society and the state. We believe that the turbulence of contemporary politics is best captured by the term 'chaotic pluralism'. We explore the policy implications of this democratic model for the future, looking at possible state responses to the challenge of turbulent politics and the design options for groups seeking to maximize civic engagement and political participation. Finally, we assess the contribution this book makes to the research base and to the methods currently used in social science.

WHAT WE HAVE FOUND OUT

What have we found out? We have identified the capacity of social media to enable contribution of micro-donations of time and money that can scale up to mass mobilizations. These tiny acts of political participation may seem insignificant on their own, and they have been dismissed by sceptical commentators as mere 'slacktivism'—the idle and aimless tapping of keys and pressing of buttons with only vague political aims. But they represent a growing form of political participation, which in some countries and contexts is overtaking voting as the political act that people are most likely to undertake. They alter the costs and benefits of political action, reducing the transaction costs when compared to the costs of getting involved. When set against the possible benefits of political action, such a reduction of costs can tip an individual decision over into participation rather than apathy. When carried out by millions, as in the revolutions of the Arab Spring or the mass demonstrations in response to the 2008 financial crash, these tiny acts of participation are bringing about social and political change.

Social media platforms—by providing what can be termed zero-touch coordination for these micro-donations of time, effort, and money—are replacing organizations and institutions in some areas of political life. Indeed, organizations increasingly resemble social media platforms in the way they present themselves to the public, with facilities for commenting and encouraging the sharing of content on social media. These new forms of political participation are individually based, unmediated by organizations or institutions in at least the early stages, although the rules that private companies impose are a hidden form of mediation of course. We see this as an individualization of collective action in that individuals can quickly and easily make some small contribution to a political campaign or mobilization without interacting with the personnel of organizations and their representatives, such as politicians and interest group leaders. In this political landscape, citizens may express multiple allegiances to issues and support a heterogeneous range of causes without formal membership of any group.

By far the majority of these mobilizations will fail to attain any kind of measure of success, disappearing with little trace within hours of their initiation. But those few that succeed do so extremely rapidly, attaining critical mass and tipping over into large-scale participation. As we showed in Chapter 3, they seem to defy the expectations of formal political science theory, by showing no gradual buildup in a classic S-shaped curve, with an increase, maximum, and decrease of acceleration in the curve of changes over time. Rather, they shoot up and peak in the earliest stages, rendering them less predictable than any smooth buildup of support.

This dynamic generates a pattern of mobilization that has been shown in other areas of political science research, in particular the punctuated equilibrium model of Baumgartner and Jones. They show a leptokurtic or extreme distribution of changes to the policy agenda and other arenas, which implies that otherwise similar mobilizations can differ hugely in their level of success, an almost random allocation based on their falling just over or inside the tipping line. We see this pattern for mobilizations initiated on social media, suggesting that they contribute to punctuations in the policy agenda. That is, where political mobilizations using social media fail, they do not interrupt the period of stasis, and on the few occasions where they take off, they initiate or contribute to punctuations. This is a new ecology of mobilization, which promotes an even more intense process of competition, ensuring survival only of the fittest, with a large number of failures and a small number of unpredictable, extreme events. If this pattern is sustained across other areas of political life playing out on social media—and we have every reason to suppose it would be—then this kind of collective action will continue to act as an important influence on policy change. It will inject turbulence into every area of politics, acting as an unruly, unpredictable influence on political life.

In this book we have revealed the dynamics of these new kinds of mobilizations. We have tested the effects of two key forms of social influence that an individual experiences when deciding to participate using social media by simulating a social media environment in an experimental setting. First, we have analysed the effects of social information, real-time information about the participation of others. When levels of social information are high, they provide potential participants of a collective action with crucial signals of its likely viability that can encourage them to also participate. Second, we have looked at the effect of making individuals' actions visible to others when they make their participatory decision. Both these forms of social influence can encourage individuals to participate. At the individual level, visibility has the greater effect. But when we look at the collective, social information proves to be the more efficient. Under social information, rational individuals are able to behave more strategically. They can target their resources where they are needed most, where they will not be wasted on goods that will never be provided or will be provided anyway regardless of their contribution.

These forms of social influence do not act in a uniform way but differently affect different types of people. In mainstream social science research, the traditional way to distinguish between people in terms of their likelihood of participating politically has been to look at demographics, which have, for example, been a consistently good predictor of voter turnout. Where costs of participation are very small, demographics will be less useful as a determinant of whether people participate or not. With these factors less salient, other factors, which were always present, can come to the fore. We have been inspired by recent political science research that uses personality as a useful predictor of political behaviour. We have identified the personality types that are resistant to these forms of influence and those that are particularly susceptible. We have shown that those with emotionally stable personalities consistently give more, while agreeable and conscientious people consistently contribute less—it appears that some disagreeableness is a precondition of political action. Behaviours determined by some personality types are relatively resistant to social information. But when it comes to visibility, we find large differences at the individual level. Agreeable people contribute more under visibility, while extravert people contribute less. In particular, those individuals who have a pro-self, or individualist, social value orientation contribute significantly more when they are visible, whereas pro-social or cooperative types contribute less. Individualists it seems are more shameable than we might have thought, whereas cooperative people can be put off participation by the same shaming mechanism. Such a finding can inform the design of online initiatives seeking to encourage civic engagement, matching design to constituency, for example, by using visibility when dealing with individualist groups, and social information for more cooperatively oriented communities.

We find that collective action is dependent upon the distribution of individual thresholds for action, elaborating and extending Schelling and Granovetter's earlier work on threshold models. That is, we have taken some steps towards identifying the distinct thresholds people have for joining mobilizations. For critical mass to form, some people with low thresholds obviously have to join at the earliest stages, when there are no signals of viability, and their participation will send a signal to those with slightly higher thresholds. The personality type most associated with this willingness to join early (or to start) is extraversion, although a high internal locus of control can also play a part. A mobilization needs a minimum number of extraverts in the population to get off the ground. In contrast, agreeable people tend to have high thresholds and will join only in the later stages. Most people are likely to join somewhere in the middle. This distribution of thresholds will be crucial in determining whether a mobilization can assemble a chain reaction of starters, ensuring a succession of followers with gradually increasing thresholds that allows a campaign to become viable.

Such a pattern means that mobilizations can launch without leaders, needing only sufficient people with low thresholds who are willing to start when there are few signals of viability. That poses a real challenge for their sustainability. Many of the most prominent protest movements of the past decade have faded away. In many of the countries of the Arab Spring, even where the rebellions of 2011 were seemingly successful in forming critical mass and achieving revolutionary change (as in Egypt), they provided no leaders in the wings, and none of the organizational trappings of pre-Internet revolutions. The post-revolution period was dominated by the one long-standing organization that was present on the political scene of the region, the Muslim Brotherhood, even though their participation in the revolutions had been limited and their commitment to democracy questionable. In some countries, mobilizations have now started to engage with the mainstream, as in Spain where some elements of the Indignados protest movement formed the political party Podemos (We Can), now a viable electoral entity, with 8 percent of the vote in the 2014 European elections. Podemos gained 600,000 supporters on Facebook between May and July 2014 and by the end of October had 200,000 members, who could sign up on their website for free, challenging and posing a credible alternative to all the established political parties in Spain in an increasingly turbulent 2015 following the election of the left-wing Syriza party in Greece in January. Podemos candidates were extremely successful in mayoral elections in May 2015, particularly in Barcelona and Madrid: 'the agendas of Spain's two largest cities will be driven by the priorities of anti-establishment parties with roots in Spain's indignado movement'.[2] But even now their sustainability must be in question if comparisons are made with other antiestablishment parties in Europe, as in the case of the Five Star Movement led by Beppe Grillo in Italy, which gained 25 percent of the electoral support in national elections in 2013 but remained incapable of forming a parliamentary bloc in the Chamber of Deputies, the lower house of the Italian Parliament.

FROM POLITICAL TURBULENCE TO A CHAOTIC SYSTEM?

Our core claim is that social media, as an indelible part of the way people interact in the twenty-first century, are creating a new kind of politics, characterized by turbulence, meaning 'full of commotion' (in Latin) or a 'state of conflict or confusion'. In fluid dynamics, turbulence is a flow regime characterized by chaotic property changes, including 'rapid variation of pressure and velocity in space and time', which seems to provide an adequate metaphor for what we have described. But there is a sense in which the idea of political turbulence could go beyond being merely a metaphor. Turbulence, or turbulent flow, is one kind of a chaotic system, a dynamic system with unpredictable behaviour despite the fact that its governing rules are known and deterministic. The reason for this is the high sensitivity of such systems to the initial conditions and slight perturbations while they evolve in time, and since measurements of the initial conditions of a system by the observer have errors (albeit very tiny), predicting the long-term behaviour of the system is impossible.

The classic example of a chaotic system is weather. In essence long-term weather forecasting is impossible, not because of unknown mechanisms but because of the sensitivity of the governing rules and dynamical equations to the initial conditions and parameters, such as wind speed and humidity, which cannot be measured with perfect accuracy. Even if precise measurement were possible, any future tiny perturbation, invisible to detection tools, could alter and totally transform the predicted scenarios. The famous example is known as the butterfly effect, a theory coined by Philip Merilees as 'Does the flap of a butterfly's wings in Brazil set off a tornado in Texas?' The answer is possibly yes, although it is not too likely. This example indicates that a tiny perturbation in one system parameter, as small as a flap of a butterfly's wings, could usher in a huge difference in the long-term trajectory of a nonlinear chaotic system like the global weather system. The important point here is that although the system looks random, it is not. As mentioned above, a chaotic system is deterministic in terms of mechanisms, but lack of exact knowledge of the initial conditions and tiny undetectable noises make the future behaviour of the system unpredictable to the observer. Chaotic systems are different to stochastic systems and quantum systems, in both of which the uncertainty comes as an intrinsic feature of the system, whereas the unpredictability of chaotic systems originates from the lack of precise measurements of the initial conditions magnified by nonlinear sensitive mechanisms.

The essential features of a chaotic system are non-linearity and a high degree of interconnectivity, which creates positive and negative feedback, causing changes to take place exponentially faster. Chaos theory has been successfully applied to explain a wide range of phenomena in physics, biology, and economics, including turbulent flow but also population fluctuations and financial crises. Simple chaotic models of social phenomena to explain many of the near-random and difficult-to-explain empirical patterns observed in the social world have proved elusive.[3] Although one of the key conditions for chaos often applies, the complexity, high noise, and lack of long-running datasets have worked against their application in the social sciences. However, recent commentary points to a development that offers renewed hope, in that 'new models inspired by complex systems build social systems from the bottom up; behaviour is simulated for individual agents, then taken to the aggregate level either through analytic methods or through explicit computer simulations', providing a model that is less mechanical and that uses simpler, better-defined assumptions about small-scale behaviour, which may well become important in the future, even outside the 'low-noise world of experimental physics'.[4]

The transition of our daily lives into a super-connected world embedded in and provided by online social media, with the very low (tending to zero) cost of participation in collective movements, could have brought political systems into a chaotic state, where small perturbations or micro-contributions could eventually lead to large social phenomena. The same micro-contributions would have been dampened and neglected in a pre-Internet society with high barriers to free communication and high transaction costs. At the same time social media and digital life records could also be of help in order to measure the real current state of a system more precisely to avoid being surprised by its long-term behaviour, unpredictable due to our lack of knowledge of its current state, to develop the kind of models that LeBaron proposes.[5] In his book *The Signal and the Noise*, the political forecaster Nate Silver argued that just as meteorologists have become better at predicting the weather with a combination of long-running, large-scale data sources, and calibration through analysis of previous forecasts and actual meteorological patterns, we ought to be able to predict economic and social phenomena such as financial crises and elections, as he himself did with great success in the 2012 US elections.[6] As these kinds of data sources become available through social media, such methods might be applied to other forms of collective action.

DEMOCRACY AND TURBULENT POLITICS

We need to understand not only the current form of political turbulence, but also its implications for democracy, representation, and governance. What model of democracy and representation helps us to understand what has happened to politics as a result of the greater use of social media—the empirical reality of turbulent politics and the emergence of a chaotic system? In Chapter 1, we expressed great caution about the idea of the Internet as a new public sphere, which has been particularly associated with Habermas's idea of a network for communicating information and points of view, where citizens can express their opinions, deliberate, and formulate some kind of common view or will. The main ideas from his approach are based around the notion that the Internet provides a kind of public sphere for public discussion and deliberation, in the same way that the coffeehouses of Vienna provided the forum for Habermas's original conception of the public sphere.[7]

We believe that the political world on social media that we have analysed here is too heterogeneous, too individualized, too chaotic, and too ill-suited to deliberation to represent the revival of the public sphere beloved of communication theorists.[8] This is not to say that we accept Sunstein's gloomy prediction of a fragmented public discourse of echo chambers in which individual citizens experience the political world as an extension of their own narrow pre-existing interests and concerns.[9] Sunstein believes that the ability to control the content they see and follow would mean that people would chose to follow only organizations, information, and friends that reflected their own viewpoint, thereby reinforcing it. Rather than individuals being subjected to a diversity of views— one of the key elements of a democratic polity—they would not be challenged, simply existing in a small bubble of the 'Daily Me'.[10] But neither Sunstein nor anyone else has demonstrated any evidence for this self-exclusion applying more online than offline, while others have argued persuasively that the Internet is too vast, too dynamic, too interconnected for such a state of affairs to exist in practice, particularly in comparison with conventional media channels.[11] As we discussed in Chapter 2, social media allow individuals to conduct their lives in a 'time-based world stream', pumping out and receiving information and social influence, in which they are exposed to many contradictory and overlapping currents of information, views, influences, causes, campaigns, and concerns that widen rather than narrow their political experience. Rather, our claim is that what has emerged is a new form of pluralism: what we call chaotic pluralism. In the following sections, we discuss why this is the case, and its potential for conceptualizing turbulent politics.

WHAT IS PLURALISM?

To make the argument for a more pluralistic politics, we need to set out the context and offer a definition. For that we need first to return to the intellectual debate of the 1950s and 1960s when pluralism became a dominant account of the operation of democratic political systems promoted by some of the key figures in post-1945 political science, such as Robert Dahl, David Truman, Charles Lindblom, and Nelson Polsby.[12] The key idea of pluralism is that society is made up of many competing and varied elements, which form into groups and associations. This diversity penetrates and structures the operation of political institutions and the making of public policy, which limits the exercise of power by a small group or ruling organization and ensures that power is spread throughout the political system. The pluralism of the political system reflects the diversity of societies as a whole with their different elements and groups. In politics these interests tend to balance out in the struggle for influence. If one group is strong, then another will counter-mobilize so as to undermine the monopolistic exercise of power. Forms of pluralism can exist even in authoritarian states, as in what was called the state pluralism of the former Soviet Union,[13] characterized by factionalism and the delegation of power to different elements within the bureaucracy. Pluralism, however, is best promoted by differentiated institutions and democratic mechanisms of liberal democracy, what Dahl calls polyarchy, whereby elections ensure that leaders will seek to balance out interests and aim for a winning coalition.[14] There are multiple access points for interest groups to influence public policy, enabled by fragmentation of institutions, such as that caused by the separation of powers and federalism. In liberal democracies, policy emerges as a result of balance and the mediation of interests. No one interest is dominant.

Almost as soon as the ink was dry on these classic works, critics targeted pluralism as an unrealistic description of the operation of politics, most notably in its account of power.[15] Even what appear to be pluralist interactions may disguise power relations that operate even when interest groups are negotiating with each other in the political process. The pervasive impact of economic and social inequality determines the allocation of resources and the nature of authoritative decisions that emerge from political systems. In fact, Dahl and Lindblom spent most of their careers worrying about the impact of economic inequality on political representation, and concluded that pluralism was itself one-sided as business tended to win or to be advantaged, even if societies could still benefit from the underlying diversity of interest groups and points of view.[16] As E. E. Schattschneider put it much earlier, 'the flaw in the pluralist heaven is that the heavenly chorus sings with a strong upper-class accent'.[17] In response to these concerns, pluralism morphed into neo-pluralism, with more recognition of how representation worked imperfectly, favouring business and the wealthy.[18]

In spite of generations of political scientists poring scorn on pluralism, it has proved surprisingly resilient as a political concept, with writers often returning to it after decades spent in the opposite camp.[19] In part, most thinkers and empirical researchers realize that pluralism is not just a description of the operation of political systems, but also an aspiration that could be promoted by reforms that give the right incentives and offer an appropriate institutional framework. Such an interest reflects a perception that the age of dominance of a few ideologies grounded in basic ethical principles is at an end: the world is simply too diverse to create much more than an operating consensus on the rules of political interactions, and such agreement on the rules might be all that can be achieved. Societies can agree on certain matters such as free elections and free media, but not much else. The question then becomes, in all this diversity and differentiation, what kind of political system is most appropriate for it? This search encourages political scientists to focus on incipient trends as an indication of a return to a more fluent form of politics, such as the pluralism of interest intermediation in the European Union.[20]

Pluralism has been rediscovered as the property of thinkers from the late nineteenth century and early twentieth who promoted older values of association and pre-state forms of mobilization. These pluralist traditions had been shut out in the age of ideological conflicts based on left and right, which had created powerful political parties seeking a monopoly of political action and control of the state. Such was the project of the English pluralists, William Morris, G.D.H. Cole, and Harold Laski, who argued that a more community-based mobilization could overcome some of the limitations of state intervention. In his later work, Paul Hirst picked up on these concerns and argued that the world emerging in the 1980s was becoming more diverse again, in a way that gives these older pluralist arguments more traction. He wrote, 'Associationalism makes accountable representative democracy possible again by limiting the scope of state administration, without diminishing social provision. It enables market based societies to deliver social goals desired by citizens, by embedding the market system in a social network of coordinative and regulatory institutions'.[21] The model of pluralism we see emerging is not based on such gradualism, but what these associational arguments show is that social and political change is organic, resting on developments that are outside the state. Like us, Hirst believed that associationalism would counter the logic of collective action, though in his case by rediscovering the social basis to political action rather than the transaction cost argument we pursue here.

More recently, the political theorist William Connolly has offered an alternative revisionist perspective on earlier pluralist work, developing a kind of postmodern pluralism reflecting the proliferations of 'minorities of many types', 'a world of interlocked minorities' of immigrants, alternative lifestyle movements, religious groups, feminist movements, and ethnic minorities, in which the national majority is a 'symbolic centre consisting of fewer people than the sum of the minorities'.[22] His view of minority groups appreciating the fallibility of their own beliefs and thereby coexisting in a system of partisan mutual adjustment is reminiscent of the early pluralists and also Hirst's associationalism, but has further parallels with the political world we have described where 'new political demands often unsettle existing configurations of identity'[23] in unstable systems 'marked by an element of internal unpredictability'.[24] It is not necessary to adopt a postmodern perspective to be able to use these insights and to recognise them in the political world unfolding today where the drivers for change are embedded in society, outside the state. Although some have argued that Connolly's pluralism represents a break with the pluralism of postwar American political thought,[25] others have argued that in contrast, 'Connolly's work is best understood as the resumption and enhancement of a distinct canon of pluralism in American political thought'.[26]

WHY TURBULENT POLITICS IS PLURALIST

Even in the relatively short time since Paul Hirst or William Connolly wrote, the political world has continued to become more diverse and fragmented. The use of social media is magnifying this diversity and empowering different elements within it, helping to foster different kinds of movement that have their origins outside existing forms of representation and institutional structures.

The Internet and social media may embody some pluralist ideas in their ability to rebalance power relationships, blur organizational boundaries, enable bottom-up dynamism, and reclaim politics by society. The theories and models we have presented—through their emphasis on peer-to-peer social information, the influence provided by social media platforms, and the stressing of individual-level difference—represent a theory of society rather than the state, as indeed did pluralism. What is different about chaotic pluralism is the absence of groups as we know them: for every interest there will be some kind of mobilization—maybe even a whole constellation of mobilizations—but not necessarily an organized group, at least not one organized in conventional ways.

Given the clear potential of the Internet to facilitate the formation of networked groups, matching people with similar beliefs and preferences, lowering coordination and organization costs, and allowing new forms of mass mobilization based on weak-tie associations, it is inevitable that it has been associated with a revival of pluralist thought. As early (in Internet time) as 1998, Bruce Bimber was writing of accelerated pluralism through the Internet,[27] in which the Internet would contribute to 'the on-going fragmentation of the present system of interest-based group politics and a shift toward a more fluid, issue-based group politics with less institutional coherence'.[28] In his 2003 work, *Information and American Democracy*, Bimber developed the idea of post-bureaucratic pluralism, where 'the structure of collective action is less tightly coupled than in the past to a marketplace of formal political organizations',[29] but one that would be constrained by the market dynamics of the traditional mass media, and the structure of the state apparatus itself: 'the need for collective action organizations to orient themselves to the structures and processes of largely unchanging institutions of the state creates limits on the advantages of postbureaucratic forms'.[30]

What is more surprising is that there has been little attention paid to a revival of Internet-fuelled pluralism as a model of democracy since then, far less than there has been for republicanism, even as social media have emerged with the potential to challenge traditional political institutions and overcome some of the earlier constraints on postbureaucratic pluralism. Bimber's most recent book,[31] with its plea for bringing organizations back into collective action, mentions neither pluralism nor Dahl, in spite of his early and prescient predictions noted above. A 2014 collection of articles on *Online Collective Action*, many using some of the methodological approaches that we have explored here, makes no mention of pluralism or pluralists.[32] It seems as though pluralism in the age of social media has diverged too far from the original pluralist dream, perhaps because it was seen as too disorganized, disordered, and chaotic to be viewed as a coherent model of politics at all. The early notions of pluralism, such as those of Dahl and Lindblom, were ordered and organized; pluralists had a vision of a system of interest groups applying continual pressure on the state, but each fulfilling a distinctive need and engaging in a process of mutual accommodation. Bimber's theory of 'accelerated pluralism' was based on the idea that 'the processes of group-oriented politics will show less coherence and less correspondence with established private and public institutional structures', but that this process (1) would still be based on the idea of issue group formation and action and (2) would not alter the overall interest of individuals in public affairs or their 'ability to assimilate and act on political information'.[33] He analysed the history of assimilation of other technologies (such as television into society), to argue that there was no link between increased political information and political participation. Dismissing populist and communitarian arguments about the influence of the Internet on political life, he argued that the basic logic of pluralism would remain unchanged: 'No less now than when David Truman wrote about American pluralism, Americans will associate themselves in groups, and structure their political participation and engagement through those associations'.[34] This still sounds like old-school pluralism.

In contrast, we emphasize the breakdown of existing structures and organizations, such as interest groups. We focus on the speed of interaction and rapid growth (but also decay) of mobilizations.

This changed environment puts government on the back foot, disrupting traditional institutional strategies for engaging with society. The disordered and unpredictable nature of this chaotic pluralism, which makes some contemporary societies harder to govern, is one of the key weapons of those people who have mobilized with social media. Just as an earlier generation of political activists thought non-violent tactics would disarm those in power, such as the flower in the rifle butt as a symbol of non-violent protest in the 1960s, so tweeting and liking have become the instruments of the new turbulent politics.

CHAOTIC PLURALISM

We use the term 'chaotic pluralism' to reflect a key divergence between the changes we have observed, and either pre-Internet pluralism or Bimber's accelerated or postbureaucratic pluralism. Classic notions of pluralism were group-based and surprisingly ordered (particularly the English version, where neat and tidy guilds and unions provided a structured environment within which political activism could take place). Even Paul Hirst's revision for the post-1989 era, associationalism, is characterized by a commitment to gradual reform. Corporatism, which is an account of the tripartite institutions that help govern relations between state actors and representatives of producer groups, saw politics as an orderly process of mutual accommodation among state, unions, and business. This practice is very much in retreat, accounting for the formal relationships only in some European states. This aspect of pluralism in no way represents the vision we have presented here, where mobilizations spring from the ground, facilitated by technological platforms rather than organizations, and where organizational boundaries are blurred and sometimes disappear altogether. We have in mind a variant of pluralism that reflects the degree of disorganization and speed of change in political mobilization that has taken place, more aligned to Connolly's postmodern pluralism or the radical pluralism of William James, based on the idea that 'the overlapping forces propelling the world are themselves messy. Pluralism is the philosophy of a messy universe'.[35]

A pluralist pattern is emerging, but rather than being based on stable, ordered forms of association, it is characterized by mobilizations that spring from the bottom up, highly reactive to events. We call this model chaotic pluralism to build on the idea of political turbulence as a chaotic system discussed above. Such a model conceptualizes politics as a natural system and uses scientific models of chaos theory in natural systems to understand its operation, employing the kind of big data or social data science methods we have used in this book. In this model, the tiny acts of political participation that take place via social media are the units of analysis, the equivalent of particles and atoms in a natural system, manifesting themselves in political turbulence. The laws that guide them, however, derive from social influences exerted by social media and the heterogeneity of people who undertake these tiny acts. A model of chaotic pluralism will require also a social science understanding of human behaviour, including personality, social influence, and all the other things that shape political preferences and willingness to act upon them. Such understanding cannot come from big data alone, as such sources tend to be stripped of any information about the people involved and without benchmarks or control groups for comparison. To understand this piece of the pluralist puzzle, we need the second key method we used in this book: experiments, which hold out the possibility of causal inference. Experiments can allow us to understand how different people behave differently when they use social media, how series of chain reactions can form, and why some mobilizations succeed while most do not. We hope that the experiments used here have begun to show how this method can reveal the mechanisms at work in contemporary, chaotic pluralism.

There are pointers to this melding of natural science and social science perspectives in the recent revival of pluralist thought in political theory, outlined above. Connolly argues that the latest developments in evolutionary biology, neuroscience, and complexity theory show how 'the emergence of new formations is irreducible to patterns of efficient causality, purposive time, simple probability, or long cycles of recurrence', and therefore work against conventional methods of understanding politics;[36] that 'we find models of evolution where open systems possess powers of self-organization, and seemingly minor variations can initiate distinct new trajectories so that change cannot be fully predicted'; and that 'we need to come to terms with the idea that chaotic and unpredictable behaviours represent essential features of the evolution of political systems, and develop models of multi-linear, complex and emergent causality, and correspondingly intricate modes of inference'.[37] However, in his postmodern pluralism, operating at the intersection of neuroscience and cultural theory, Connolly does not discuss, as we have here, the mechanisms by which these developments play out in political systems, the relationship between pluralism and societal use of technology, or the empirical approaches that might be used to research them. In this book, by showing how social media play a role in political change and by highlighting some methodological approaches and modelling techniques from the natural sciences, we offer a more concrete framework for researching this turbulent and unpredictable political world.

WHAT FOR THE FUTURE? THE LIMITATIONS OF POLITICAL TURBULENCE AND CHAOTIC PLURALISM

To conceptualize political turbulence within a democratic model of chaotic pluralism poses a number of challenges. We need to be alert to the problems of classic pluralism, in particular the tendency for interest intermediation to be an unequal contest, benefiting those who have more resources and marginalizing others. These are not necessarily overcome just because the form is different to whatever happened or was conceived of before. The problems may reappear in the chaotic successor to pluralism. But we think these problems are less severe and may return our account of the world closer to those claimed by the early pluralists, and from which they retreated partly in recognition of the distortions provided by big business and the state with its corporatist and powerful institutions. Here we look to the future of the three main problems of pluralism: inequality, the power of the state, and the collective action problems of large groups.

First, inequality remains, even under chaotic pluralism. The classic accounts of political participation stress the importance of wealth, education, and parental socialization,[38] which reduce the access of the poor and those without cognitive resources to the political process. Such measures of socioeconomic status predict every kind of political act from voting, through membership of parties and interest groups, to complaining.[39] They are less influential in the dynamics of the mobilizations we have studied here because we have concentrated on those who use the Internet and social media, that is, people who are already likely to be in more economically privileged groups. Such an emphasis is, we feel, justified here by our aim to identify trends and patterns in contemporary collective action in the context of still-rising Internet penetration, where we can expect usage to reach that of the mobile phone (that is, near universal in developed nations and rapidly growing in developing countries) at some unspecified point in the medium-term future. But of course, in spite of growing wealth in Africa and Asia, inequalities remain in the social media age and will still shape collective action behaviour. And the Internet itself introduces new forms of inequality, such as those based on speed and cost of Internet access, and different levels of Internet expertise and skills. Indeed, as discussed in the book, many Internet-based activities exhibit power-law-like distributions, where attention is focused disproportionately on a small number of points, which could also increase inequality, as happens in natural systems at critical point.[40] But, we argue, the Internet will remain a force for redistribution of power because of the ease with which it assists mobilization, given that it can ensure that groups with the most resources do not always win, partly because the Internet can harness the power of large numbers of people making micro-donations. Because the costs of participation and transaction are lower, the online world increases the access of the poor to political action and reduces the relative advantage of the rich. By how much we cannot know at present, but we are sure that the equilibrium of power will be different to the one that existed during the twentieth century.

The second big drawback of pluralism is that it tends to downplay the influence of the state. Yet the state remains a powerful actor in terms of structuring the progress of group negotiation, especially when producer groups are also powerful, such as in the corporatist framework, for example, whereby the powers of the state and business and worker groups reinforce each other. The onslaught of mobilization under chaotic pluralism has the potential to weaken the influence of the state in ways that might have been attractive to the early pluralists. Governments have been slow and inefficient in taking advantage of the Internet. Large-scale bureaucracy was well suited to earlier information technologies, and in the early days of computer technology from the 1960s, governments led the way in developing huge information systems to undertake administrative operations.[41] However, as information technology became increasingly networked and interactive, bureaucratic culture in large states in particular mounted considerable barriers to innovation,[42] exacerbated by troubled contract relationships with global computer service providers.[43] With the Internet, the first information technology that is used by significant proportions of populations, governments have found it particularly difficult to innovate, lagging behind both private and voluntary sectors in terms of interacting or engaging with citizens, and being unable to respond to the swiftness of coordination enabled by social media. In the 2011 London riots, groups of looters armed with mobile phones running BlackBerry Messenger were able to outwit the technologically superior police forces, being able to coordinate their movements in real time. Similarly in the Arab Spring, citizens outmanoeuvred the less technologically savvy security services. States can fight back in ways that expose this limitation of the state's role in pluralist thought. They will employ various tactics in an attempt to catch up, often by piling massive resources into Internet surveillance or, in authoritarian states, blocking or censoring online access. Now that technological innovation has become domesticated in everyday life, protestors (and criminals) are likely to remain one or more steps ahead. But in formulating a response, the state faces the challenge of how to do so in a way that is commensurate with the principles of democratic legitimacy.

The third limitation is the difficulty of sustaining mobilizations that lack institutions or organization, a key theme of this book. Social media have proved time and time again to be useful in overcoming some elements of the collective action problem, through the kinds of mechanisms that we have analysed here. But some of the classic features of collective action problems will continue in the age of social media because there will remain an asymmetry between those contributing to groups, such as those who provide more content over those who consume it, with collective action failures happening as leaders get bored or fed up with providing collective goods for nothing, and followers become disillusioned by the lack of policy responses to campaigns, protests, demonstrations, and even revolutions. And of course the Internet and social media have ushered in a whole cast of corporate actors to the political stage: Google, Facebook, Twitter, and so on. The potential of handing over power to civil society may be limited by Internet giants like Google, new stakeholders in public policy, who have started to take on some of the traditional activities of the state, such as counterterrorism, but with no democratic accountability. Will the chorus of the pluralist heaven now sing with a Californian accent? Our argument is that even with these tendencies the cost-benefit equation has changed, meaning that it is harder for any larger group to dominate for long. The speed of change affects corporations too, which can find it hard to stay ahead of the game. Witness Google's attempts to break into this market with Google+, for example, or the continual process of mergers and acquisitions among social media companies as the popularity of social networking sites peaks and falls. Companies that were dominant may become so large they cannot innovate, often because they cannot keep up with the fast-changing predilections, fads, and interests of the very groups that use their products.

Finally, in addition to these three main limitations, the greater levels of instability that chaotic pluralism brings to political systems, by amplifying perturbations that otherwise would have been stamped out, have both advantages and disadvantages. The advantage is that an unstable agenda can benefit those who challenge older established agendas by offering new opportunities and ensuring that old routines and defences do not work; but the disadvantage might be that some depend on a degree of stability to follow and to shape the agenda, and if events are moving too fast those with good access and their finger on the pulse will benefit purely for those reasons. It may be that in spite of bringing new actors into the political process chaotic pluralism might exclude those without the time and resources to invest in following the twists and turns of the social media agenda. Again this is for future empirical investigation.

Certainly, political turbulence poses major challenges to both governments and citizens. For politicians, there is a tension in learning to deal with the current state of play in the new democratic climate in ways that are consistent with the objectives of democratic pluralism. For citizens making micro-donations to large-scale mobilizations that circumvent the need for organized groups, there is the challenge that in the end, institutions may be required to achieve sustained policy or regime change. And the mechanisms of chaotic pluralism do not lend themselves to institution building. The process of mutual accommodation, with the values of compromise and learning that underpinned the early models of pluralism, is extremely difficult to develop in a turbulent and disordered environment. If there are no leaders, how do groups bargain and compromise? The change engendered by the types of mobilizations we have discussed will be vulnerable to takeover.

HOW CAN STATES RESPOND TO POLITICAL TURBULENCE?

As the world observed the events in Turkey and Brazil in the summer of 2013, commentators in other countries noted that the same kind of dissatisfaction and unrest was also present at home: 'A crisis of legitimacy could strike Britain too' bemoaned the editorial of the *Observer*, indicating that 'modern politics is not fluent in the vocabulary of shifting power and empowering citizens'.[44] Clearly, the first step is to understand these new forms of collective action, even without the institutional road map of earlier forms of pressure and protest.

The second step is to take what plays out on social media seriously, rather than viewing it as peripheral to the political system. Political leaders have shown a tendency to play with the language of social media, or to use it as a glossy veneer for their offline activities. In Egypt in the summer of 2013, amid mass protests and demonstrations in Cairo and other cities across the country, President Morsi tweeted to say that he was 'with the protestors', but his speech later to the state television channels showed him to be in a very different place.[45] Likewise, after he had been ousted by the military, army leaders posted on Facebook on 5 July that they were not going to persecute the Muslim Brotherhood or other religious groups; but they then immediately started shutting down Islamist TV channels and rounding up and imprisoning Muslim Brotherhood leaders, while the president remained in prison. By these acts, both major protagonists showed that they did not take social media seriously as the venue in which the political future of the country was being decided. Rather, they saw social media as a way to feign that they were acting in the public interest and doing the right thing, not in the same league as conventional media. In contrast, the protestors in Egypt, Tunisia, Turkey, Brazil, and Hong Kong really are utilizing social media as the primary means of communication and coordination, and indeed for the general population there is early evidence to suggest that Facebook (for example) is overtaking conventional media as a trusted news source,[46] particularly in countries where there are reasons to distrust mainstream media. Ironically, it seems that former President Mubarak of Egypt really understood the significance of social media, as he blocked the Internet a few days into the revolution, as did the Turkish prime minster in the events of 2013, when he described social media as 'the worst menace to society'.[47]

States face a challenge in engaging with social media, in that they are bound to encounter scepticism as to their motive. In authoritarian states, engagement can be viewed as the development of an instrument to repel and quash demonstration and protest, and indeed this is often the case. Recent research has demonstrated this approach to be the key pillar in the highly sophisticated censorship regime developed by the Chinese government, whereby criticisms of the state, its leaders, and it policies are permitted on social media, which indeed are even used by the authorities to inform themselves about instances of corruption or incompetence within the state apparatus, but posts about 'real-world events with collective action potential' are censored.[48] In democratic states, any government collection of data pertaining to citizens can reveal major weaknesses and lack of trust in government-citizen relationships. Take the furore in 2013 surrounding the whistleblower Edward Snowden's revelations that the security agencies of the US and UK governments were collecting a significant proportion of all Internet traffic entering their respective countries. The response highlighted the public's distrust of government with respect to their data, a general view that nothing good would be done with them. Such views are exacerbated by a tendency of political leaders to use big data for private rather than public goods; the UK Prime Minister David Cameron operates an alert system that uses social media to predict which policy plans are accumulating so much opposition that they will be politically damaging to implement, rather than indicating illegitimacy or underlying societal problems. Only by developing an ongoing programme of working with this kind of data can states hope to institutionalize this kind of activity.

One way that states might develop such a programme would be to use some of the data sources and approaches that we have used in this book. Data generated from social media can allow policy makers to monitor and understand undercurrents of public opinion and dissatisfaction. They can be used to identify weaknesses in government services, such as failing schools or hospitals with deep-rooted problems with cleanliness or management style. They can be used to work out when policies are illegitimate, or impossible to implement. They can also be used to conduct reviews of government agencies, and to inform programmes of self-improvement. For example, in 2014 the UK Department of Work and Pensions commissioned a feasibility study on the use of social media data for social research and analysis at the department, focussing on recent changes to the UK benefits system, carried out by some of the authors of this book.[49] Likewise, the kind of randomized controlled trials (RCTs) that we have used here could be implemented to understand which policy and service designs work, and which do not. They can be used to illuminate the kinds of information environments that encourage citizens to engage with public policy and those that do not. In this way, experiments could be used to capitalize on citizens' evident willingness to make micro-donations of time and money to improve public goods. There is new enthusiasm among policy makers to conduct experiments, particularly in the United Kingdom, where the Behavioural Insights Team first operated from the Cabinet Office during the coalition government of 2010 to 2015. The team carried out a number of RCTs to nudge citizens towards socially efficient behaviour, such as timely payment of taxes and fines. These experiments were partly inspired by Thaler and Sunstein, who in their 2008 book *Nudge* presented a range of ways in which the choice architecture of policy initiatives could be designed to nudge citizens to undertake a certain kind of behaviour, in a rather paternalistic way. There might be other, more empowering ways that allow citizens to undertake a more proactive role in policy design, using feedback, reviews, and recommender systems for example, and experiments would be the way to design such systems.

If governments were to conduct such a programme of using data and insight generated by social media to understand the impact of non-linearities and chaos in social systems, the payoffs could be huge. As LeBaron observes, 'The control of nonlinear systems can actually be easier than the control of linear ones, because it might take only a small push to engender a big change in the system. In other words, small low-cost policy changes could have a large impact on overall social welfare'.[50] The key to such payoffs could be using the same methodological toolkit for understanding turbulent politics as we have used in this book: the analysis and modelling of large-scale data, and greater use of experiments.

Data generated by social media could be deployed by governments to understand trends and patterns in citizens' needs, preferences, concerns, behaviour, and complaints, as a barometer of their own legitimacy (or illegitimacy), and to identify the warning signals of critical transitions. Chaotic pluralism could allow them to work with rather than against the grain of citizens' willingness to act in pursuit of collective goods.

We hope that states do not react too rapidly or strongly to political turbulence, nor do we think they have the capacity to do so, outmanoeuvred as they often are. Citizens have much to gain in the world of chaotic pluralism through their new capacity to set the political agenda from outside the political system. In this sense, social media have unleashed a more citizen-based politics, which for all its turbulence can open up new kinds of transparency, freedom of expression, and representation, at least to a certain extent. Turbulence may dash the hopes of some progressive challengers to the system, who find the disordered and unruly nature of politics too complex and confusing to join in. But it does seem to bring swathes of people into politics who have not been involved before. It would probably be an impossible task to systematically compare levels of political engagement before and after the advent of social media, particularly given our inclusion of new, previously unavailable tiny acts at the lower end of the ladder of political participation, and it is not one that we have undertaken here. But we do believe that the waves of online mobilization that we have described and analysed offer political possibilities to people who would, prior to 2005, have eschewed politics altogether.

RESEARCHING THE FUTURE

To understand the turbulent world of chaotic pluralism requires new approaches, which could have profound implications for social science research. We have only embarked upon them here. Our aim for this book was not to be comprehensive, but to start to understand the causal mechanisms behind online mobilizations, generic to whatever applications are being used, which could be corroborated or refuted in the next wave of research. As promised in Chapter 1, we analysed large-scale, fine-grained data related to petition signing: a dataset of real-time transactional data of a kind that was rarely available to social scientists in the pre-Internet era. Researchers in the growing field of computational social science or social data science have seized the opportunities afforded by these kind of data. But mainstream social science has been rather slower to capitalize on the new possibilities, particularly outside the United States. We believe that this kind of social data science analysis should and will grow common as researchers realize its potential. To make this happen, social scientists will need to work more closely with researchers in the mathematical, physical, and life sciences in future years. This will present a challenge to conventional social science departments, where faculty may lack the technical and multidisciplinary expertise required to generate, analyse, and model big data. The authors of this book comprise two political scientists, one physicist and a computer scientist, but such a research team would be difficult to form in a traditional social science department.

The payoffs of collaboration between the social sciences and mathematical, physical, and life sciences may be great, in terms of understanding social systems as chaotic systems. Other research from the scientific world has shown that in various non-linear, highly interconnected complex systems (most of them with chaotic characteristics) there can be tipping points at which a sudden shift to a different dynamical regime may occur.[51] Although traditionally the prediction of such critical points has been very difficult, research is starting to suggest that there may be generic indicators of the approach of a tipping point or critical transition, with obvious relevance for political turbulence. These early warning signals could come as particular temporal and spatial patterns such as slowing down, symmetry breaking, scaling of fluctuations, or the emergence of non-regular geometrical patterns such as fractals and scale-free distributions. Data science approaches to understand the world of collective action would need to develop far further than hitherto, but it might be that an understanding of patterns of communication or interaction on data generated from social media could provide such early warning signals in social systems in general, and in political turbulence in particular.

Of course, we should acknowledge some challenges to developing these approaches. We have used two key methodologies in this book: social data science (or computational social science) approaches and experiments or RCTs. Both these methods face technical, ethical, and logistical barriers that have restricted the range of sources that we could use within the scope of one book. Our large and comprehensive data on petition signing in two countries, including Twitter data relating to petitions, involved a three-year programme of hourly data collection, which was technically complex and time-consuming to both generate and analyse. The Google analytics data we presented in Chapter 3 resulted from a long-term relationship with the Government Digital Service; such data-sharing arrangements take time to establish, and we were able to do so in only one government department. Historical Twitter data, as presented in Chapter 2, are most easily obtained through the use of commercial data providers, as we did here, which are usually costly and subject to technical and legal considerations. Although we were able to obtain a limited amount of Facebook data, it is not possible to access data on private posts that users have shared only with their social networks, and we had to extrapolate from data on public posts. Other social media platforms that delete posts after they are shared, such as Snapchat, pose far greater challenges to data capture, and we did not attempt to generate data from any of these platforms. Field experiments on online political behaviour, as we presented in Chapter 4, offer far greater external validity than laboratory experiments but usually rely on collaborations with social media platforms to implement the intervention and measure outcomes. We developed such a collaboration with the social enterprise mySociety, but we did not do so with any of the major social media platforms, as James Fowler did with Facebook in his 2012 voter turnout experiment.[52] In fact, Kramer et al.'s experiment with Facebook on emotional contagion on social networks, which received a great deal of negative publicity for Facebook amid accusations that the experimental team had manipulated Facebook users' emotions, has soured the company's enthusiasm for such experiments, probably for many years to come.[53] We could have appraised the importance of Google's suite of applications and the way in which they use social information, in search algorithms, for example, were it not that these strategies are closely held secrets and those data are unavailable for research. There are numerous research projects underway that do expand the range of data science approaches and experimental methodologies beyond those used here, and the authors of this book are engaged in several of them.

We stress the urgency of pursing this research agenda at this particular time. At the World Economic Forum in 2015, the CEO of Google, Eric Schmidt, argued that 'the Internet will soon be so pervasive in every facet of our lives that it will effectively "disappear" into the background'. Before this happens, and the Internet and social media dissolve into the ether, we need to understand the generic influences on digital behaviour, like social information and visibility, while we can still disentangle their effects. Furthermore, from a data perspective, we are at a turning point. As Schmidt observed, 'there will be so many sensors, so many devices, that you won't even sense it, it will be all around you',[54] but sensors and devices operate across multiple cross-cutting networks, presenting a data universe that is opaque, fragmented, and often proprietary, owned and jealously guarded by the corporations that market these devices. It may be difficult to derive data from some social media platforms—such as Facebook, as discussed above—but it is not beyond the ingenuity of Internet researchers to work out ways of doing so.[55] It will be a very different task to obtain data from drones, from wearable technology, from heavily commercialized gaming environments using immersive technologies, from mobile medical devices, from driverless cars, or from all the devices that make up the Internet of Things. Before the Internet becomes too ubiquitous, researchers and policy makers need to seize the current moment to understand the profound political changes already underway.

We believe that the empirical and methodological paths we have started to take in this book reflect important developments for social science research. They must be accompanied by theoretical development, based on social scientific understanding and modes of enquiry and asking wide-ranging questions about social behaviour and societal development. Social scientists will need the collaboration of researchers from the mathematical, physical, and life sciences. There is no doubt of the value of observations and empirical laws of Johannes Kepler in the astronomy of the solar system and understanding of planetary motion, but it took nearly one century before Isaac Newton discovered his universal gravitation theory based on them. Only then did we become able to make accurate predictions about the behaviour of planets in a general framework and beyond the specific case of the solar system. Theoretical development of chaotic pluralism must be inspired by and validated against empirical observations and experiments. But to reveal the 'universal laws' governing political turbulence, we need to go beyond observations limited to a specific platform or phenomenon, and generate theories that address more fundamental aspects of collective human behaviour. We hope with this book to have taken a step in that direction.

APPENDIX

EXPERIMENT INSTRUCTIONS AND QUESTIONNAIRE

This appendix provides the background to the experiment reported in Chapters 5, 6, and 7. First, we give the instructions provided to subjects before starting the experiment; second, we outline the scenarios shown to subjects during the experiment; and third, we list the post-experiment questionnaire completed by all subjects after the experiment and before payment.

A1. INSTRUCTIONS TO SUBJECTS

Thanks very much for taking part in this experiment. This is an experiment looking at how people decide to support activities that benefit the whole community or neighbourhood. The experimenter will explain the procedure of this session to you, but all the information is reproduced below for your reference.

What You Will Do in This Experiment

This experiment will last about 1 hour and 15 minutes in total. After reading this sheet and hearing the introduction from the organizers, you will begin with a test round to become familiar with the interface before the experiment itself will start. Once the whole experiment is finished, you will be asked to complete a post-questionnaire, in which your answers are kept anonymous. In this experiment you will participate to 28 separate rounds in which you interact with other participants. In each round, you will be shown a scenario in which some local activity is being organized that will benefit the whole community or neighbourhood. You are given 10 tokens at the beginning of each round, and your task is to decide how much you want to contribute to the proposed issue. Whatever you do not contribute, you keep for yourself. Also, if enough people support the activity (total contributions reach a specific number of tokens), then everyone including you will get some extra money.

Interaction with Other Participants

At the start of each round, all participants are assigned to one of two small groups. These groups are reshuffled at each round and are thus almost never exactly the same from one round to the next. The other members of your group will never know your identity nor will you know their identity. Indeed, all decisions you make in this experiment are anonymous. Each round lasts 50 seconds. If you or another participant in your group contributes during the 5 last seconds of elapsed time, then 5 more seconds are added to the timer. You can only contribute once to each round, and cannot revise your decision once it has been submitted. Some scenarios that you will be presented are shown several times. Please treat each as if it were the first time you saw it. Please do not look at other monitors and do not communicate with any of the other participants for the duration of the experiment. If you need any assistance, please raise your hand and a member of the project team will come to help you.

Payment

You've already earned £6 for showing up on time to the experiment. Your additional earnings are calculated based on the tokens you choose to keep for yourself and the additional bonus of £6.50

if the activity was supported. The following table summarises your payoff in each possible case.

Your contribution in tokens	Money you receive if total tokens in round were lower than group aim	Money you receive if total tokens in round were higher or equal than group aim
0	£8.50	£15.00
1	£8.25	£14.75
2	£8.00	£14.50
3	£7.75	£14.25
4	£7.50	£14.00
5	£7.25	£13.75
6	£7.00	£13.50
7	£6.75	£13.25
8	£6.50	£13.00
9	£6.25	£12.75
10	£6.00	£12.50

We will select **one single round** at random for which you will be paid. Since you cannot predict which is the paid round, you are advised to treat each round as it were the paid one (regardless of what happens in the other rounds). Your payment will be paid out to you in cash immediately after the experiment.

Details of the project for which this experiment is undertaken:
Principal investigators   xxxxx
Address for enquiries   xxxxx

A2. SCENARIO WORDINGS

The following scenarios were shown to subjects in the course of the experiment.

Cycle path: An environmental group is trying to persuade the council to create a cycle and pedestrian walkway into town from the area where you live. The group members are seeking funds to help them achieve their goals, will you support them?

Disaster recovery appeal: Your local charity shop has set up a campaign to raise money towards the reconstruction of homes for victims of the recent earthquake in Haiti.

Hospital closure: Your hospital trust is planning to close the Accident and Emergency department of your nearest hospital, so everyone in your area will have to travel much further if they require emergency assistance. A local group is campaigning to reverse the decision and is seeking funds to help them achieve their goals.

Public Wi-Fi: A group of residents in your area is campaigning for a public wireless network which will give free Internet access to everyone in your area. The residents are seeking funds to help them achieve their goals.

Snow clearance: The area outside where you live has gotten blocked in the recent snowfall and a number of elderly people have slipped over. People in the street are talking about having a plan so that neighbours clear the snow as soon as it falls. It needs to have a plan and for neighbours to contribute shovels and store grit.

Street lights: You live in a long street with inadequate street lighting and one of your neighbours was recently mugged in a dark part of the street. A group of neighbours is now lobbying the council for more streetlights. The group of neighbours are seeking funds to help them achieve their goals

Street party: People in the street do not know each other very well. There is an idea to organize an annual summer party. People need to buy refreshments, decorate the street, cook food, and be around on the day.

A3. POST-EXPERIMENT QUESTIONNAIRE

All questions were optional and defaulted to a missing value. Questions for which the responses were not used in any of the analysis have been omitted.

In order to help us interpret the results of that experiment, we would like to ask you some further questions. Please rest assured that all data are kept anonymous.

Please indicate your gender:

· Male
· Female

Please indicate your age:
What is your nationality? (*drop-down list of country names*)
What is your ethnicity? (*drop-down list of ethnicities*)
What is the last type of educational institution that you have attended or are attending now? (*drop-down list of educational institutions*)
Do you have a health problem or disability which prevents you from doing everyday tasks at home, work, or school or which limits the kind (or amount) of work you can do?

· No
· Yes

Which of the following best describes your current situation?

· Working full-time (30 hours a week or more)
· Working part-time (8–29 hours a week)
· Retired
· Unemployed
· Permanently sick or disabled
· In community or military service
· Undergraduate student
· Postgraduate student
· In full-time education (not degree or higher)
· In part-time education (not degree or higher)
· Doing housework, looking after children or other persons
· None of the above
· Prefer not to answer

Which figures best represents the total income of your household before tax?

- Up to £12,500 per year
- £12,501 to £25,000 per year
- £25,001 to £37,500 per year
- £37,501 to £50,000 per year
- More than £50,000 per year

Please indicate to what extent you agree with the issues you were presented earlier, and how important you find them.
For each scenario, participants could choose one response from the following options:

- Agree strongly
- Agree moderately
- Agree a little
- Neither agree nor disagree
- Disagree a little
- Disagree moderately
- Disagree strongly

And one response from these options:

- Highly important
- Important
- Somewhat important
- Neutral
- Minor
- Not important at all

The following questions were used to determine subjects' Big Five personality scores and Rotter scores. (The information in parentheses following each statement indicates how the answer was used. This information was not included in the post-experiment questionnaire).

Please indicate to what extent you agree with the following statements:
Participants could choose from:

- Agree strongly
- Agree moderately

- · Agree a little
- · Neither agree nor disagree
- · Disagree a little
- · Disagree moderately
- · Disagree strongly

'I believe my success depends on ability rather than luck' (*Rotter score*)

'I dislike taking responsibility for making decisions' (*Rotter score*)

'I make decisions and move on' (*Rotter score*)

'I believe that unfortunate events occur because of bad luck' (*Rotter score*)

'I tend to analyse situations too much and therefore miss opportunities' (*Rotter score*)

'I see myself as extraverted, enthusiastic' (*extraversion*)

'I see myself as critical, quarrelsome' (*agreeableness, reverse coded*)

'I see myself as dependable, self-disciplined' (*conscientiousness*)

'I see myself as anxious, easily upset' (*emotional stability, reverse coded*)

'I see myself as open to new experiences, complex' (*openness*)

'I see myself as reserved, quiet' (*extraversion, reverse coded*)

'I see myself as sympathetic, warm' (*agreeableness*)

'I see myself as disorganized, careless' (*conscientiousness, reverse coded*)

'I see myself as calm, emotionally stable' (*emotional stability*)

'I see myself as conventional, uncreative' (*openness, reverse coded*)

The answers to the following questions were used to determine a subject's social value orientation. We scored these questions as in Lange et al. (1997). That is, an individual was classified into one category if he or she made six or more consistent choices. With this, we had 112 pro-social (cooperative) subjects, 59 pro-self (individualistic) subjects, and 15 inconsistent subjects (15 subjects who did not choose six or more consistent choices). No subjects chose six or more competitive options.

In this task we ask you to imagine that you have been randomly paired with another person, whom we will refer to simply as the 'Other'. This other person is someone you do not know and that you will not knowingly meet in the future. Both you and the 'Other' person will be making choices by circling either the letter A, B, or C. Your own choices will produce points for both yourself and the 'Other' person. Likewise, the other's choice will produce points for him/her and for you. Every point has value: the more points you receive, the better for you, and the more points the 'Other' receives, the better for him/her. Before you begin making choices, please keep in mind that there are no right or wrong answers—choose the option that you, for whatever reason, prefer most. Also, remember that the points have value: the more of them you accumulate the better for you. Likewise, from the 'other's' point of view, the more points s/he accumulates, the better for him/her.

For each of the options below, participants are asked:
Which option do you prefer?

- A
- B
- C

	A	B	C
You get	480	540	480
Other gets	80	280	480

	A	B	C
You get	560	500	500
Other gets	300	500	100

	A	B	C
You get	520	520	580
Other gets	520	120	320

	A	B	C
You get	500	560	490
Other gets	100	300	490

	A	B	C
You get	560	500	490
Other gets	300	500	90

	A	B	C
You get	500	500	570
Other gets	500	100	300

	A	B	C
You get	510	560	510
Other gets	510	300	110

	A	B	C
You get	550	500	500
Other gets	300	100	500

	A	B	C
You get	480	490	540
Other gets	100	490	300

If you would like to share any other comments, please write them in the text field below. We appreciate your feedback! (*free text question*).

NOTES

CHAPTER 1: COLLECTIVE ACTION GOES DIGITAL

1 See Ituassu 2013.
2 Gladwell 2010; Walt 2011.
3 Kaplan and Haenlein 2010.
4 Hendler et al 2008.
5 World Bank 2015.
6 According to the ITU World Telecommunication/ICT Indicators 2013 database, there were nearly 2.4 times as many 'active mobile-broadband subscriptions' as 'fixed (wired)-broadband subscriptions' worldwide in 2012.
7 *Arab Social Media Report*, May 2014.
8 *Business Insider*, 26 September 2014.
9 Sandler 1992.
10 Olson 1965.
11 Colomer 2011: 19.
12 Verba and Nie 1972; Parry et al. 1992.
13 See Parry et al. 1992.
14 Public Administration Select Committee 2000; Margetts 2006.
15 See Christensen 2011.
16 Morozov 2011.
17 Gladwell 2010.
18 Salganik et al. 2006; Salganik and Watts 2009.
19 Gerber et al. 2008.
20 Cotterill et al. 2013.
21 Ariely et al. 2009.
22 Pastor-Satorras and Vespignani 2007.
23 See, for example, Etling et al. 2009; Hale 2014b; Hindman 2008; González-Bailón et al. 2011; Segerberg and Bennett 2011; Aral and Walker 2011.
24 Verba et al. 1995.
25 Schlozman et al. 2005.
26 See, for example, Mondak 2010; Gerber, Green, et al. 2010; Gerber et al. 2011.
27 Schelling 1978, 2005; Granovetter 1978, 1983.
28 Gladwell 2000.
29 Ghonim 2012: 293.
30 Mason 2013: 148.
31 Clauset et al. 2009; Miotto and Altmann 2014; Mryglod et al. 2015.
32 Barabási 2002; Barabási et al. 2006.
33 Karsai et al. 2012.

34 Baumgartner and Jones 1993; Jones and Baumgartner 2005.
35 Mason 2013: 65.
36 Hawthorne 1991.
37 Abdelrahman 2013a.
38 See, for example, Etling et al. 2009; Hindman 2008; González-Bailón et al. 2011; Segerberg and Bennett 2011; Aral and Walker 2011; Goel et al. 2012; Hale 2014a.
39 Mayer-Schönberger and Cukier 2013.
40 Pentland 2014.
41 Lazer et al. 2009; Conte et al. 2012; Pentland 2014.
42 Morton and Williams 2010.
43 Centola 2010; Aral and Walker 2011; Bond et al. 2012.
44 Gerber and Green, 2002 2012; Morton and Williams 2010; Druckman et al. 2011; John 2013.
45 Dunning 2012.
46 Cook and Campbell 1979; Shadish et al. 2002.
47 Olson 1965; Hardin 1982.
48 Lupia and Sin 2003; Bimber et al. 2005, 2012; Bennett and Segerberg 2011, 2012, 2013.
49 We thank one of the anonymous reviewers of the manuscript for suggesting this summary of our intellectual project.
50 Bimber 2003; Bimber et al. 2005; Lupia and Sin 2003: 318.
51 Norris 2001; Bimber 2001.
52 Tolbert and McNeal 2003; Gibson et al. 2005; Anduiza et al. 2010; Anduiza, Gallego, and Cantijoch 2010; Borge and Cardenal 2011.
53 Benkler 2006.
54 Shirky 2008.
55 Chadwick 2006.
56 Chadwick 2013.
57 Bimber 2003: 104–7.
58 Bimber et al. 2012.
59 Bennett and Segerberg 2011, 2012, 2013.
60 Bimber et al. 2012.
61 Watts 2004.
62 Watts 2003; Watts and Strogatz 1998; Milgram 1967.
63 Lazer et al. 2009. For example, Aral 2012; Aral and Waller 2011; Centola 2010; Goel et al. 2012; Suri and Watts 2011 (for Twitter); Bakshy et al. 2011; Karsai et al. 2014.
64 See, for example, Christakis and Fowler 2009; Bond et al. 2012.
65 The 2013 Oxford Internet Survey showed that in the United Kingdom, 72 percent of the 22 percent of non-users of the Internet 'could definitely' or 'could probably' get someone to use the Internet on their behalf (Dutton and Blank 2013).
66 Sunstein 2007.
67 Smith et al. 2009; John et al. 2011.
68 Margetts 1999; Dunleavy et al. 2006, 2007; Margetts and Dunleavy 2013.

CHAPTER 2: TINY ACTS OF POLITICAL PARTICIPATION

1 E.g., Bimber 1999, 2003; Bimber et al. 2005; Lupia and Sin 2003.
2 Lupia and Sin 2003: 318.
3 Lohmann 1998.

4 See Bimber 2003: 87, 189.
5 Gibson and Ward 2009; Gibson et al. 2003.
6 John and Margetts 2003.
7 Bimber 2003: 188.
8 Margolis and Resnick 2000: 60–61.
9 Karpf 2012.
10 Karpf 2010.
11 Karpf 2010.
12 *Forbes* 2008.
13 Jordan and Taylor 2004: 6.
14 Jordan 2008; Jordan and Taylor 2004.
15 Barlow 1996.
16 Margolis and Resnick 2000; Norris 2003, 2006.
17 Margolis and Resnick 2000; Norris 2001; Bimber 2001, 2003.
18 Olson 1965.
19 Farrell and Drezner 2008; Pew Research Center 2005.
20 See Shirky 2003: chap. 1; Farrell and Drezner 2008; Hindman 2008.
21 Shirky 2008.
22 Koltsova and Koltcov 2013.
23 Alexa 2015.
24 See, for example, Benkler 2006; Loubser 2010.
25 Benkler 2006.
26 https://www.youtube.com/yt/press/en-GB/statistics.html.
27 http://en.wikipedia.org/wiki/List_of_the_most_subscribed_users_on_YouTube.
28 Madar 2012.
29 Dennis et al. 2013.
30 Alexa 2015.
31 'Twitter Third Quarter 2014 Selected Company Metrics and Financials', https://investor.twitterinc.com/results.cfm, accessed 3 February 2015.
32 Sajuria et al. 2014.
33 King et al. 2013, 2014.
34 http://wearesocial.net/blog/2014/01/social-digital-mobile-worldwide-2014/, accessed 25 February 2015.
35 Pew Research Center 2014.
36 http://wearesocial.net/blog/2014/01/social-digital-mobile-worldwide-2015/, accessed 22 May, 2015.
37 Madar 2012.
38 Eynon and Geniets 2012.
39 Shirky 2008.
40 Bennett and Segerberg 2012: 745.
41 Biezen et al. 2012; Whiteley 2011, 2012.
42 Dalton and Wattenberg 2002.
43 Dalton 2012.
44 Margetts 2006.
45 Putnam 2000.
46 Hall 1999; Andersen et al. 2006.
47 Grenier and Wright 2003.
48 *GlobalPost*, 22 March 2013.
49 This quotation was added to Wikipedia in May 2012 (http://en.wikipedia.org/w/index.php?title=Anonymous_%28group%29&oldid=493596695#Membership)

and endorsed by Anonymous on Facebook (for example, https://www.facebook
.com/phanonymous/posts/442388705809415) and AnonSweden (http://www
.anonsweden.se/?page_id=11) (all accessed 27 May 2015).

50 Smith 2013.
51 Smith 2013.
52 Pew Research Center 2012.
53 Borge and Cardenal 2011.
54 Anduiza et al. 2010; Anduiza, Gallego, and Cantijock 2010; Gibson et al. 2005.
55 Norris 2009.
56 Borge and Cardenal 2011.
57 Wilcox 2008.
58 'Runner-Up: Malala Yousafzai, the Fighter', *Time*, 19 December 2012, http://poy
    .time.com/2012/12/19/runner-up-malala-yousafzai-the-fighter/, accessed 28 Febru-
    ary 2015.
59 *Huffington Post*, 20 December 2013.
60 Gelertner 2013.
61 Naughton 2013.
62 Sunstein 2007.
63 boyd 2009.
64 Diani and McAdam 1993; González-Bailón et al. 2011; Knoke 1994.
65 As in Castells 2000.
66 Aral 2012: 212.
67 His original articulation of the argument in 1973 had over thirty thousand cita-
    tions on Google Scholar as of January 2015.
68 Granovetter 1973: 1377.
69 Granovetter 1973: 1378.
70 Bond et al. 2012.
71 Centola 2010.
72 Watts 2003.
73 Goel et al. 2012.
74 Goel et al. 2012.
75 Goel et al. 2014.
76 Suri and Watts 2011.
77 Fowler and Christakis 2010.
78 Frey and Meier 2004; Fischbacher et al. 2001.
79 Schultz 1999; Cotterill et al. 2013.
80 Gerber et al. 2008.
81 Marwell and Oliver 1993.
82 *New Yorker*, 5 July 1993.
83 Cotterill et al. 2013.
84 Gerber et al. 2008.
85 Mayer-Schönberger 2009.
86 Bimber 2003; Bimber et al. 2005.
87 Bimber et al. 2012.
88 Karpf 2012.
89 Bennett and Segerberg 2011, 2012, 2013.
90 Bennett and Segerberg 2012, 2013.
91 Following from Castells 2000, 2012.

CHAPTER 3: TURBULENCE

1 Salganik et al. 2006.
2 Baumgartner and Jones 1993.
3 Whyte et al. 2005.
4 Carpenter 2003; Carpenter and Moore 2014.
5 Smith et al. 2009.
6 Escher 2012; Chadwick 2013.
7 http://www.mysociety.org/projects/no10-petitions-website/.
8 http://www.whitehouse.gov/blog/2012/09/24/happy-birthday-we-people.
9 See Lindner and Riehm 2011; Jungherr and Jürgens 2010.
10 Wright 2012; Margetts et al. 2011; Hale et al. 2013.
11 Carpenter 2003; Carpenter and Moore 2014.
12 See below and Hale et al. 2013.
13 Hale et al. 2013.
14 Goel et al. 2012.
15 Centola 2013; Granovetter 1978; Schelling 1978; Rogers 1995.
16 Wu and Huberman 2007.
17 John and Margetts 2003; Baumgartner and Jones 1993; Jones and Baumgartner 2005.
18 Jones and Baumgartner 2005.
19 John and Margetts 2003.
20 See John and Margetts 2003; Breunig and Jones 2011.
21 Shapiro and Wilk 1965.
22 Chakravarti et al. 1967: 392–94.
23 Dunning 2012: 302.
24 Dunning 2012: 63.
25 Narayanan and Kalyanam 2011.
26 E.g., Buscher et al. 2009.
27 Borge and Cardenal 2011.
28 To check the stability of the forthcoming measurements, we repeated them for a shorter period, six months, starting from December 2012. The results were all broadly similar, with differences only in the decimal digits, and we therefore conclude that the results are stable at the reported precision.
29 Salganik et al. 2006; Salganik and Watts 2009.
30 Salganik et al. 2006: 855.
31 Jones and Baumgartner 2005.
32 Baumgartner and Jones 1993.
33 The authors have shared these findings with the UK Government Digital Service and the House of Commons Procedure Committee, and they were used during 2014–15 to inform the redesign of the petitions platform.

CHAPTER 4: HOW SOCIAL INFORMATION CHANGES THE WORLD

1 Pfeffer and Salancik 1978; Salancik and Pfeffer 1977.
2 Salganik et al. 2006.

3 Schelling 1978.

4 See Frey and Meier 2004: 1721.

5 *BBC News*, 16 February 2003.

6 Olson 1965.

7 Olson 1965: 62.

8 Bimber 2001, 2003; Bimber et al. 2005; Klotz 2004; Krueger 2002; Lev-On and Hardin 2007; Lupia and Sin 2003.

9 Lupia and Sin 2003.

10 Olson 1965: 63n8.

11 Lupia and Sin 2003: 324.

12 Frey and Meier 2004; Fischbacher et al. 2001; Fischbacher and Gächter 2010; Shang and Croson 2009.

13 Croson and Shang 2008; Shang and Croson 2006, 2009.

14 Brooks 2004; Shang and Croson 2009: 1426.

15 Marwell and Oliver 1993.

16 Oliver and Marwell 1988: 6.

17 Schelling 1978; Granovetter 1978.

18 Noelle-Neumann 1974.

19 Marsh 1985.

20 See Nadeau et al. 1993.

21 For a review, see Nadeau et al. 1993 and Cain 1978.

22 Nadeau et al. 1993.

23 Marsh 1985.

24 Glynn et al. 1997.

25 Frey and Meier 2004.

26 Olson 1965; Lupia and Sinn 2003.

27 Oliver et al. 1985; Schelling 1978.

28 Marsh 1985.

29 Frey and Meier 2004.

30 Goldstein et al. 2008.

31 Schultz 1999.

32 Gerber et al. 2008.

33 E.g., Panagopoulos 2010, 2011, 2013.

34 Fischbacher et al. 2001; Keser and van Winden 2000.

35 Frey and Meier 2004; Andreoni and Scholz 1998; Shang and Croson 2009.

36 Nadeau et al. 1993.

37 Glynn et al. 1997: 461.

38 We use a probit regression with submitting a letter as the dependent variable with the treatment (seeing numbers) and an interaction term of seeing the signatures and their number (which is the number of others writing). Compared to those in the low group, those in the medium group send more letters, but the difference is not significant ($z = 1.9, p = .55$). The difference between those in the low group and those in the high group is also non-significant ($z = 1.7, p = .09$).

39 This is also reported in Margetts et al. 2011. We also carried out a pilot experiment in the laboratory to inform the design, which is described in this article.

40 Goel et al. 2009; Salganik et al. 2006; Salganik and Watts 2009.

41 Salganik et al. 2006.

42 Margetts and Stoker 2010; Nosek et al. 2002; Skitka and Sargis 2006.

43 See Margetts et al. 2011 for a full description of the analysis.

44 See Margetts et al. 2011 for details.

45 See, for example, Ariely et al. 2003.
46 Lupia and Sin 2003.
47 Frey and Meier 2004; Shang and Croson 2009.
48 Frey and Meier 2004.
49 Oliver and Marwell 1988: 1.

CHAPTER 5: VISIBILITY VERSUS SOCIAL INFORMATION

1 *Guardian*, 27 August 2014.
2 Crandell 2014.
3 Gerber et al. 2008.
4 Cardy 2005; Panagopoulos 2010.
5 Gerber et al. 2008.
6 Green and Gerber 2010: 331.
7 Panagopoulos 2010, 2013.
8 Gerber et al. 2008.
9 Ariely et al. 2009, 546.
10 Ariely et al. 2009.
11 Harburgh 1998.
12 Cotterill et al. 2013.
13 Mann 2010.
14 Panagopoulos 2010.
15 Panagopoulos 2010, 2013.
16 As in Gerber et al. 2008.
17 Panagopoulos 2010, 2011, 2013; Gerber, Green, and Larimer 2010.
18 Panagopoulos 2013.
19 Gerber, Green, et al. 2010.
20 Panagopoulos 2010, 2011, 2013.
21 Although see Goldstein et al. 2008.
22 Levitt and List 2007a, 2007b.
23 Ariely et al. 2009.
24 Bardsley 2000.
25 Cf. Croson and Marks 2000.
26 Cf. Isaac and Walker 1988.
27 Gerber et al. 2008; Panagopoulos 2010, 2011, 2013; Gerber, Green, and Larimer 2010.
28 Crandell 2014.

CHAPTER 6: PERSONALITY MATTERS

1 *Huffington Post*, 29 December 2014.
2 *Blackvoices*, 6 January 2015; Pro Publica 2014.
3 Olson 1965.
4 E.g., Verba et al. 1995.
5 John 2009.
6 Verba et al. 1995.
7 Mossberger 2009.
8 Mossberger 2009: 173; Mossberger et al. 2008.

9 Mossberger et al. 2008: 173.
10 Norris 2001; Mossberger et al. 2008; Warschauer 2003; Mossberger 2009: 184.
11 Tolbert and McNeal 2003; Gibson et al. 2005; Anduiza et al. 2010; Anduiza, Gallego, and Cantijoch 2010; Cantijoch 2009; Borge and Cardenal 2011.
12 Schlozman et al. 2005; Escher 2012.
13 See Mondak and Halperin 2008; Mondak 2010; Mondak et al. 2010, 2011; Gerber, Huber, et al. 2010; Gerber et al. 2011.
14 Mondak and Halperin 2008; Mondak 2010; Mondak et al. 2011; Gerber, Huber, et al. 2010; Gerber et al. 2011; Gallego and Oberski 2012.
15 Butt and Phillips 2008; Ryan and Xenos 2011.
16 Hughes et al. 2012.
17 Gerber, Huber, et al. 2010.
18 Wiggins 1996; John and Srivastava 1999: 121.
19 Gosling et al. 2003.
20 Gerber, Huber, et al. 2010.
21 Tickle et al. 2001.
22 Gerber, Huber, et al. 2010; Mondak and Halperin 2008: 360.
23 Denny and Doyle 2008, 309.
24 For a review, see Lange et al. 2007.
25 See De Cremer 2000; Lange et al. 1997.
26 E.g., Cameron et al. 1998; Van Vugt et al. 1995.
27 De Cremer 2000.
28 Lange et al. 1997.
29 Fowler and Kam 2007.
30 Fischbacher et al. 2001; Keser and van Winden 2000.
31 Frey and Meier 2004; Andreoni and Scholz 1998; Shang and Croson 2009.
32 Fischbacher and Gächter 2010.
33 See Suleiman and Rapoport 1992; Weiman 1994; Fischbacher et al. 2001; Fischbacher and Gächter 2010.
34 Kurzban and Houser 2001, 2005.
35 Mondak and Halperin 2008.
36 Gerber et al. 2011.
37 Mondak 2010.
38 Mondak et al. 2011; Vecchione and Caprara 2009.
39 Gerber et al. 2011.
40 Gerber et al. 2011.
41 Mondak and Halperin 2008; Mondak et al. 2010; Gerber et al. 2011.
42 Volk et al. 2011.
43 Vecchione and Caprara 2009.
44 Mondak et al. 2011: 215.
45 Mondak and Halperin 2008; Gerber et al. 2011.
46 Mondak et al. 2011.
47 Parkes and Razavi 2004; Vecchione and Caprara 2009; Mondak and Halperin 2008; Gerber et al. 2011; Mondak et al. 2010.
48 See in particular Koole et al. 2001.
49 Volk et al. 2011.
50 Lange et al. 1997; see also earlier research by Messick and McClintock 1968 and Kuhlman and Marshello 1975.
51 See Isaac and Walker 1988.
52 Koole et al. 2001.

53 Fischbacher and Gächter 2010.
54 Titmuss 1970; Fehr and Rockenbach 2003.
55 See Fischbacher and Gächter 2010.
56 Reinstein and Hugh-Jones 2010; Hugh-Jones and Reinstein 2009.
57 Gerber et al. 2011; Mondak and Halperin 2008; Mondak et al. 2011.
58 Volk et al. 2011; Gerber et al. 2011.
59 Gerber et al. 2011; although not Mondak et al. 2010.

CHAPTER 7: HOW IT ALL KICKS OFF

1 González-Bailón et al. 2013.
2 BBC, 15 May 2012.
3 Mason 2013.
4 This chapter adapts and builds upon work previously published as Margetts et al. 2014. We are thankful to *Political Studies* and our anonymous reviewers for their thoughtful comments.
5 Marwell and Oliver 1993.
6 These results were reported in Margetts et al. 2014.
7 Schelling 1978, 2005.
8 González-Bailón et al. 2013; Bakshy et al. 2011; Watts and Dodds 2007.
9 González-Bailón et al. 2011, 2013.
10 Schelling 2005.
11 Schelling 2005: 94.
12 Marwell and Oliver 1993.
13 Schelling 2005: 95–110.
14 Granovetter 1978, 1983.
15 Granovetter 1978: 1421.
16 Mondak and Halperin 2008; Mondak 2010; Mondak et al. 2011; Gerber, Huber, et al. 2010; Gerber et al. 2011; Gallego and Oberski 2012.
17 Andersen 2006.
18 Judge et al. 2002: 765.
19 Lord et al. 1986.
20 Conger and Kanungo 1998.
21 Lord et al. 1986; Judge et al. 2002: 773.
22 Gough 1990; Judge et al. 2002.
23 Judge et al. 2002: 773.
24 Rotter 1966; Carpenter and Seki 2006.
25 Ng et al. 2006.
26 Judge et al. 2002.
27 Spector 1982.
28 Anderson and Schneier 1978.
29 Judge et al. 2002.
30 Boone et al. 1999.
31 Ng et al. 2006.
32 Gore and Rotter 1963.
33 Carlson and Hyde 1980; Guyton 1988; Milbrath and Goel 1977.
34 Margetts et al. 2014.
35 Skewness ranges between 1.015 and 1.05 depending on the method used from the three specified in Joanes and Gill 2002.

36 Subjects with a mean rank greater than 6 have a mean standard deviation of 1.796. Subjects with a mean rank less than or equal to 4 have a standard deviation of 1.666.
37 We use double-sided Tobit because the dependent variable is censored. Participants cannot give fewer than zero tokens or more than ten in any round. Thus the sum of a participant's contributions has a floor and ceiling.
38 Gächter et al. 2010.
39 Margetts et al. 2011.
40 Judge et al. 2002.
41 See Shang and Croson 2009; Bøg et al. 2012.
42 Anderson and Schneier 1978; Spector 1982; Gore and Rotter 1963; Carlson and Hyde 1980; Guyton 1988; Milbrath and Goel 1977.
43 Mondak and Halperin 2008; Gerber et al. 2011.
44 As Mondak et al. 2010 and Gerber et al. 2011.
45 Gerber et al. 2011: 692.
46 Mondak 2010; Mondak and Halperin 2008; Vecchione and Caprara 2009; Gerber et al. 2011.
47 Lord et al. 1986; Gough 1990; Judge et al. 2002.
48 Backstrom 2011.
49 Bakshy et al. 2011.
50 Selfhout et al. 2010.
51 Amichai-Hamburger and Vinitzky 2010; Moore and McElroy 2012.

CHAPTER 8: FROM TURBULENT POLITICS TO CHAOTIC PLURALISM

1 González-Bailón and Barbera 2013.
2 Kassam 2015.
3 Kiel and Elliott 1997; LeBaron 2002.
4 LeBaron 2002.
5 LeBaron 2002.
6 Silver 2012.
7 Boeder 2005.
8 See Papacharissi 2009 for a review.
9 Sunstein 2007.
10 Negroponte 1995.
11 O'Hara 2002.
12 Dahl 1961; Truman 1951; Lindblom 1959; Polsby 1963. See Dunleavy and Dryzek 2009: chap. 2 for a review.
13 Hough 1982.
14 Dahl 1961.
15 Bachrach and Baratz 1963; Lukes 1974.
16 Lindblom 1977; Dahl 1989.
17 Schattschneider 1960.
18 Dunleavy and Dryzek 2009: 131–34.
19 E.g., Hirst 1994.
20 Coen and Richardson 2009.
21 Hirst 1994: 12.
22 Connolly 2008: 27.
23 Connolly 1995.

24 Connolly 2002.
25 Chambers and Carver 2008.
26 Wenman 2015: 55.
27 Bimber 1998.
28 See also Norris 2003.
29 Bimber 2003: 104.
30 Bimber 2003: 107.
31 Bimber et al. 2012.
32 Agarwal et al. 2014.
33 Bimber 1998: 136.
34 Truman 1951; Bimber 1998: 155.
35 Wenman 2015; Connolly 2005: 70.
36 Connolly 2009: 222–25.
37 Wenman 2015: 70.
38 E.g., Verba et al. 1995.
39 See John 2009.
40 Stanley 1987.
41 Margetts 1999.
42 Margetts and Dunleavy 2013.
43 Dunleavy et al. 2006.
44 *Observer*, 23 June 2013.
45 Weaver and McCarthy 2013.
46 See Ingram 2013; Mason 2013.
47 *Guardian*, 2 June 2013; González-Bailón and Barbera 2013.
48 King et al. 2013, 2014.
49 https://www.gov.uk/government/publications/use-of-social-media-for-research-and
   -analysis.
50 LeBaron 2002.
51 Scheffer et al. 2009.
52 Bond et al. 2012.
53 Kramer et al. 2014.
54 Eric Schmidt's speech at the World Economic Forum in January 2015 was widely
   reported, including the *Science Times* (Wu 2015) and *Forbes* (Worstall 2015).
55 One way personal data might be accessed in the future is through individuals
   selling access to their personal data, as is envisioned in the patent of Bernardo
   Huberman, a physicist and computer scientist, for a market in unbiased private
   individual data. See https://www.google.com/patents/US8589292.

REFERENCES

Abdelrahman, M. (2013a) 'The Egyptian Opposition: From Protestors to Revolutionaries', *Open Democracy*, 22 April.

—— (2013b) *From Protests to Uprisings: Egypt's Permanent Revolution*. London: Routledge.

Ackland, R., and Gibson, R. (2006) *Hyperlinks and Horizontal Political Communication on the WWW: The Untold Story of Parties Online*. Canberra: Australian National University.

Agarwal, N., Lim, M., and Wigand, R. T. (eds.) (2014) *Online Collective Action: Dynamics of the Crowd in Social Media*. New York: Springer.

Alexa (2015) 'The Top 500 Sites on the Web', http://www.alexa.com/topsites/global, accessed 22 May 2015.

Almond, G., and Verba, S. (1963) *The Civic Culture*. Princeton: Princeton University Press.

Amichai-Hamburger, Y., and Vinitzky, G. (2010) 'Social Network Use and Personality', *Computers in Human Behavior*, 26(6): 1289–95.

Andersen, J. A. (2006) 'Leadership, Personality and Effectiveness', *Journal of Socio-Economics*, 35(6): 1078–91.

Andersen, R., Curtis, J., and Grabb, E. (2006) 'Trends in Civic Association Activity in Four Democracies: The Special Case of Women in the United States', *American Sociological Review*, 71(3): 376–400.

Anderson, C. R., and Schneier, C. E. (1978) 'Locus of Control, Leader Behavior and Leader Performance among Management Students', *Academy of Management Journal*, 21(4): 690–98.

Andreoni, J. (2006a) 'Leadership Giving in Charitable Fund-Raising', *Journal of Public Economic Theory*, 8(1): 1–22.

—— (2006b) 'Philanthropy', in L. A. Gerar-Varet, S.-C. Kolm, and J. Mercier Ythier (eds.) *The Handbook of Giving, Reciprocity and Altruism*, Handbooks in Economics: 1201–69. Amsterdam: North-Holland.

Andreoni, J., and Scholz, J. K. (1998) 'An Econometric Analysis of Charitable Giving with Interdependent Preferences', *Economic Enquiry*, 36(3): 401–28.

Anduiza, E., Cantijoch, M., Gallego, A., and Salcedo, J. (2010) *Internet y participación política en España*. Colección Opiniones y Actitudes, 63. Madrid: CIS.

Anduiza, E., Gallego, A., and Cantijoch, M. (2010) 'Online Political Participation in Spain: The Impact of Traditional and Internet Resources', *Journal of Information, Technology and Politics*, 7(4): 356–68.

Anduiza, E., Gallego, A., and Jorba, L. (2009) 'The Political Knowledge Gap in the New Media Environment: Evidence from Spain', Paper presented at the Joint Sessions of the ECPR, Lisbon, April.

Anstead, N., and Chadwick, A. (2009) 'Parties, Election Campaigning and the Internet', in Chadwick and Howard (2009): 56–71.

Aral, S. (2012) 'Social Science: Poked to Vote', *Nature*, 489: 212–14.

Aral, S., and Walker, D. (2011) 'Creating Social Contagion through Viral Product Design: A Randomized Trial of Peer Influence in Networks', *Management Science*, 57: 1623–39.

Ariely, D., Bracha, A., and Meier, S. (2009) 'Doing Good or Doing Well? Image Motivation and Monetary Incentives in Behaving Pro-socially', *American Economic Review*, 99(1): 544–55.

Ariely, D., Loewenstein, G., and Prelec, D. (2003) '"Coherent Arbitrariness": Stable Demand Curves without Stable Preferences', *Quarterly Journal of Economics*, 118(1): 73–105.

Auer, M. R. (2011) 'The Policy Sciences of Social Media', *Policy Studies Journal*, 39(4): 709–36.

Bachrach, P., and Baratz, M. (1963) 'Decisions and Nondecisions: An Analytical Framework', *American Political Science Review*, 57: 632–42.

Backstrom, L. (2011) 'Anatomy of Facebook', *Facebook Data Team's Notes*, http://www.facebook.com/notes/facebook-data-team/anatomy-of-facebook/10150388519243859, accessed 22 May 2012.

Bakshy, E., Hofman, J. M., Mason, W. A., and Watts, D. J. (2011) 'Everyone's an Influencer: Quantifying Influence on Twitter', in *Proceedings of the Fourth ACM International Conference on Web Search and Data Mining*: 65–74. New York: ACM.

Barabási, A.-L. (2002) *Linked: The New Science of Networks*. New York: Perseus.

Barabási, A.-L., and Albert, R. (1999) 'Emergence of Scaling in Random Networks', *Science*, 286: 509–12.

Barabási, A.-L., Newman, M., and Watts, D. J. (2006) *The Structure and Dynamics of Networks*. Princeton: Princeton University Press.

Bardsley, N. (2000) 'Control without Deception: Individual Behaviour in Free-riding Experiments Revisited', *Experimental Economics*, 3(3): 215–40.

Bardsley, N., Cubitt, R., Loomes, G., Moffatt, P., Starmer, C., and Sugden, R. (2010) *Experimental Economics: Rethinking the Rules*. Princeton: Princeton University Press.

Barlow, J. P. (1996) 'Declaration of the Independence of Cyberspace', https://projects.eff.org/~barlow/Declaration-Final.html, accessed 22 May 2015.

Baumgartner, F., and Jones, B. (1993) *Agendas and Instability in American Politics*. Chicago: University of Chicago Press.

Baumgartner, F., and Leech, B. (1998) *Basic Interests: The Importance of Groups in Politics and in Political Science*. Princeton: Princeton University Press.

Benkler, Y. (2006) *The Wealth of Networks: How Social Production Transforms Markets and Freedom*. New Haven: Yale University Press.

Bennett, L., and Segerberg, A. (2011) 'Digital Media and the Personalization of Collective Action: Social Technology and the Organization of Protests against the Global Economic Crisis', *Information, Communication & Society*, 14: 770–99.

—— (2012) 'The Logic of Connective Action', *Information, Communication & Society*, 15(5): 739–68.

—— (2013) *The Logic of Connective Action: Digital Media and the Personalization of Contentious Politics*. Cambridge: Cambridge University Press.

Best, M., and Wade, K. (2005) *The Internet and Democracy: The Global Catalyst or Democratic Dud?* Cambridge, MA: Berkman Center for Internet and Society.

Biezen, I. van, Mair, P., and Poguntke, T. (2012) 'Going, Going . . . Gone? The Decline of Party Membership in Contemporary Europe', *European Journal of Political Research*, 51(1): 24–56.

Bimber, B. (1998) 'The Internet and Political Transformation: Populism, Community and Accelerated Pluralism', *Polity*, 31(1): 133–60.

—— (1999) 'The Internet and Citizen Communication with Government: Does the Medium Matter?', *Political Communication*, 16(4): 409–28.

—— (2001) 'Information and Political Engagement in America: The Search for Effects of Information Technology at the Individual Level', *Political Research Quarterly*, 54(1): 53–67.

—— (2003) *Information and American Democracy: Technology in the Evolution of Political Power*. New York: Cambridge University Press.

Bimber, B., Caontijock Cunill, M., Copeland, L., and Gibson, R. (2015) 'Digital Media and Political Participation: The Moderating Role of Political Interest across Acts and over Time', *Social Science Computer Review*, 33(1): 21–42.

Bimber, B., Flanagin, A., and Stohl, C. (2005) 'Reconceptualizing Collective Action in the Contemporary Media Environment', *Communication Theory*, 15(4): 365–88.

—— (2009) 'Technological Change and the Shifting Nature of Political Organization', in Chadwick and Howard (2009): 72–85.

—— (2012) *Collective Action in Organizations*. Cambridge: Cambridge University Press.

Boeder, P. (2005) 'Habermas Heritage: The Future of the Public Sphere in the Network Society', *First Monday*, 10(9). http://dx.doi.org/10.5210/fm.v10i9.1280.

Bøg, M., Harmgart, H., Huck, S., and Jeffers, A. M. (2012) 'Fundraising on the Internet', *Kyklos*, 65: 18–30.

Bond, R., Fariss, C., Jones, J., Kramer, A., Marlow, C., Settle, J., and Fowler, J. (2012) 'A 61-Million-Person Experiment in Social Influence and Political Mobilization', *Nature*, 489: 295–98.

Boone, C., De Brabander, B., and van Witteloostuijn, A. (1999) 'Locus of Control and Strategic Behaviour in a Prisoner's Dilemma Game', *Personality and Individual Differences*, 27: 695–706.

Borge, R., and Cardenal, A. (2011) 'Surfing the Net: A Pathway to Participation for the Politically Uninterested?', *Policy and Internet*, 3(1): 1–29.

Boulianne, S. (2009) 'Does Internet Use Affect Engagement? A Meta-analysis of Research', *Political Communication*, 26: 193–211.

boyd, D. (2006) 'Friends, Friendsters, and MySpace Top 8: Writing Community Into Being on Social Network Sites', *First Monday*, 11(12). http://journals.uic.edu/ojs/index.php/fm/article/view/1418.

—— (2009) 'Streams of Content, Limited Attention: The Flow of Information Through Social Media', Paper presented at the Web 2.0 Expo, New York, 17 November.

boyd, D., and Ellison, N. (2007) 'Social Network Sites: Definition, History, and Scholarship', *Journal of Computer-Mediated Communication*, 13(1): 210–30.

Breunig, C., and Jones, B. D. (2011) 'Stochastic Process Methods with an Application to Budgetary Data', *Political Analysis*, 19(1): 103–17.

Brooks, A. C. (2004) 'What Do "Don't Know" Responses Really Mean in Giving Surveys?', *Nonprofit and Voluntary Sector Quarterly*, 33(3): 423–34.

Buscher, G., Cutrell, E., and Ringel Morris, M. (2009) 'What Do You See When You're Surfing? Using Eye Tracking to Predict Salient Regions of Web Pages', in *Proceedings of the SIGCHI Conference on Human Factors in Computing Systems (CHI '09)*: 21–30. New York: ACM.

Butt, S., and Phillips, J. G. (2008) 'Personality and Self Reported Mobile Phone Use', *Computers in Human Behavior*, 24(2): 346–60.

Cain, B. (1978) 'Strategic Voting in Britain', *American Journal of Political Science*, 22: 639–55.

Calvert, R. (1992) 'Leadership and Its Basis in Problems of Social Coordination', *International Political Science Review*, 13: 7–24.

Cameron, L. D., Brown, P. M., and Chapman, J. G. (1998) 'Social Value Orientations and Decisions to Take Pro-environmental Action', *Journal of Applied Social Psychology*, 28: 675–97.

Cardy, E. A. (2005) 'An Experimental Field Study of the GOTV and Persuasion Effects of Partisan Direct Mail and Phone Calls', *Annals of the American Academy of Political and Social Science*, 601(1): 28–40.

Carlson, J. M., and Hyde, M. S. (1980) 'Personality and Political Recruitment: Actualization or Compensation?', *Journal of Psychology*, 106(1): 117–20.

Carpenter, D. (2003) 'The Petition as a Recruitment Device: Evidence from the Abolitionists' Congressional Campaign', http://people.hmdc.harvard.edu/~dcarpent/petition -recruit-20040112.pdf.

Carpenter, D., and Moore, C. D. (2014) 'When Canvassers Became Activists: Antislavery Petitioning and the Political Mobilization of American Women', *American Political Science Review*, 108(3): 479–98.

Carpenter, J. P., and Seki, E. (2006) 'Competitive Work Environments and Social Preferences: Field Experimental Evidence from a Japanese Fishing Community', *B.E. Journal of Economic Analysis and Policy*, 5(2): article 2.

Castells, M. (1996) *The Rise of the Network Society, The Information Age: Economy, Society and Culture Vol. I*. Oxford: Blackwell. 2nd ed. 2000.

——— (1997) *The Power of Identity: The Information Age: Economy, Society and Culture Vol. II*. Oxford: Blackwell. 2nd ed. 2004.

——— (1998) *The End of Millennium: The Information Age: Economy, Society and Culture Vol. III*. Oxford: Blackwell.

——— (2000) 'Materials for an Exploratory Theory of the Network Society', *British Journal of Sociology*, 51(1): 5–24.

——— (2009) *Communication Power*. Oxford: Oxford University Press.

——— (2012) *Networks of Outrage and Hope: Social Movements in the Internet Age*. London: Polity.

Centola, D. (2010) 'The Spread of Behaviour in an Online Social Network Experiment', *Science*, 329: 1194.

——— (2013) 'Homophily, Networks, and Critical Mass: Solving the Start-Up Problem in Large Group Collective Action', *Rationality and Society*, 25: 3–40.

Chadwick, A. (2003) 'Bringing E-Democracy Back In', *Social Science Computer Review*, 21(4): 443–55.

——— (2006) *Internet Politics: States, Citizens, and New Communication Technologies*. Oxford: Oxford University Press.

——— (2013) *The Hybrid Media System: Politics and Power*. Oxford: Oxford University Press.

Chadwick, A., and Howard, P. N. (eds.) (2009) *The Handbook of Internet Politics*. New York: Routledge.

Chakravarti, I. M., Laha, R. G., and Roy, J. (1967) *Handbook of Methods of Applied Statistics*. Vol. 1. New York: John Wiley.

Chambers, S. A., and Carver, T. (eds.) (2008) *William E. Connolly: Democracy, Pluralism and Political Theory*. New York: Routledge.

Christakis, N. A., and Fowler, J. H. (2009) *Connected: The Surprising Power of Our Social Networks and How They Shape Our Lives*. New York: Little, Brown.

Christensen, H. (2011) 'Political Activities on the Internet: Slacktivism or Political Participation by Other Means?', *First Monday*, 16(2). http://firstmonday.org/ojs/index.php/fm/article/view/3336, accessed 27 May 2015.

Cialdini, R., and Goldstein, J. (2004) 'Social Influence: Compliance and Conformity', *Annual Review of Psychology*, 55: 592–621.

Clauset, A., Shalizi, C. R., and Newman, M.E.J. (2009) 'Power-Law Distributions in Empirical Data', *SIAM Review*, 51(4): 661–703.

Coen, D., and Richardson, J. (eds.) (2009) *Lobbying in the European Union: Institutions, Actors and Issues*. New York: Oxford University Press.

Coleman, S. (2004) 'Connecting Parliament to the Public via the Internet: Two Case Studies of Online Consultations', *Information Communication and Society*, 7(1): 1–22.

—— (2005) 'The Lonely Citizen: Indirect Representation in an Age of Networks', *Political Communication*, 22(2): 197–214.

—— (2009) 'Making Parliamentary Democracy Visible: Speaking To, With, and For the Public in the Age of Interactive Technology', in Chadwick and Howard (2009): 86–98.

Colomer, J. (1995) *Game Theory and the Transition to Democracy: The Spanish Model*. Aldershot: Edward Elgar.

—— (2011) *The Science of Politics*. New York: Oxford University Press.

Conger, J. A., and Kanungo, R. N. (1998) *Charismatic Leadership in Organizations*. Thousand Oaks, CA: Sage.

Connolly, W. E. (1995) *The Ethos of Pluralization*. Minneapolis: University of Minnesota Press.

—— (2002) *Neuropolitics: Thinking, Culture, Speed*. Vol. 23. Minneapolis: University of Minnesota Press.

—— (2005) *Pluralism*. Durham, NC: Duke University Press.

—— (2008) *Capitalism and Christianity, American Style*. Durham, NC: Duke University Press.

—— (2009) 'A World of Becoming', in A. Finlayson (ed.) *Democracy and Pluralism: The Political Thought of William E. Connolly*: 222–35. London: Routledge.

Conte, R., Gilbert, N., Bonelli, G., Cioffi-Revilla, C., Deffuant, G., Kertesz, J., . . . Helbing, D. (2012) 'Manifesto of Computational Social Science', *European Physical Journal Special Topics*, 214(1): 325–46.

Cook, T. D., and Campbell, D. T. (1979) *Quasi-Experimentation: Design and Analysis Issues for Field Settings*. Boston: Houghton Mifflin.

Cotterill, S., John, P., and Richardson, L. (2013) 'The Impact of a Pledge Campaign and the Promise of Publicity: A Randomized Controlled Trial of Charitable Donations', *Social Science Quarterly*, 94(1): 2000–2016.

Crandell, C. (2014) 'Critics Throw Cold Water on the Ice Bucket Challenge', *World News Group*, 21 August, wng.org, accessed 15 January 2015.

Croson, R. T., and Marks, M. B. (2000) 'Step Returns in Threshold Public Goods: A Meta- and Experimental Analysis', *Experimental Economics*, 2(3): 239–59.

Croson, R. T., and Shang, J. (2008) 'The Impact of Downward Social Information on Contribution Decisions', *Experimental Economics*, 11(3): 221–33.

—— (2009) 'Field Experiments in Charitable Contribution: The Impact of Social Influence on the Voluntary Provision of Public Goods', *Economic Journal*, 119(540): 1422–39.

Dahl, R. (1961) *Who Governs?* New Haven: Yale University Press.

—— (1989) *Democracy and Its Critics*. New Haven: Yale University Press.

Dai, X., and Norton, P. (eds.) (2007) 'The Internet & Parliamentary Democracy in Europe', special issue of *Journal of Legislative Studies*, 13(3).

Dalton, R., and Klingemann, H. (eds.) (2007) *The Oxford Handbook of Political Behaviour*. Oxford: Oxford University Press.

Dalton, R., and Wattenberg, M. (eds.) (2002) *Parties without Partisans: Political Change in Advanced Industrial Democracies*. Oxford: Oxford University Press.

Dalton, X. (2012) *The Apartisan American: Dealignment and Changing Electoral Politics*. Washington DC: CQ Press.

Danziger, J., Dutton, W., Kling, R., and Kraemer, K. (1982) *Computers and Politics: High Technology in American Local Governance*. New York: Columbia University Press.

Davis, R. (1999) *The Web of Politics: The Internet's Impact on the American Political System*. New York: Oxford University Press.

De Cremer, D. (2000) 'Leadership Selection in Social Dilemmas—Not All Prefer It: The Moderating Effect of Social Value Orientation', *Group Dynamics: Theory, Research and Practice*, 4(4): 330–37.

Deibert, R. (2009) 'The Geopolitics of Internet Control: Censorship, Sovereignty, and Cyberspace', in Chadwick and Howard (2009): 323–36.

Deibert, R., Palfrey, J., Rohozinski, R., and Zittrain, J. (2008) *Access Denied: The Practice and Policy of Global Internet Filtering*. Cambridge, MA: MIT Press.

Delli Carpini, M. X. (2000) 'Gen.com: Youth, Civic Engagement, and the New Information Environment', *Political Communication*, 17(4): 341–49.

Dennis, E., Martin, J., and Wood, R. (2013) *Media Use in the Middle East: An Eight-Nation Survey*. Qatar: Northwestern University in Qatar.

Denny, K., and Doyle, O. (2008) 'Political Interest, Cognitive Ability and Personality: Determinants of Voter Turnout in Britain', *British Journal of Political Science*, 38(2): 291–310.

Diani, M., and McAdam, D. (2003) *Social Movements and Networks: Relational Approaches to Collective Action*. Oxford: Oxford University Press.

Downs, A. (1957) *An Economic Theory of Democracy*. New York: Harper & Row.

Drew, D., and Weaver, D. (2006) 'Voter Learning in the 2004 Presidential Election: Did the Media Matter?', *Journalism and Mass Communication Quarterly*, 83(1): 25–42.

Drezner, D. (2010) 'Weighing the Scales: The Internet's Effect on State-Society Relations', *Brown Journal of World Affairs*, 16(2): 31–44.

Druckman, J., Green, D., and Kuklinski, J. (eds.) (2011) *Cambridge Handbook of Experimental Political Science*. Cambridge: Cambridge University Press.

Dunleavy, P., and Dryzek, J. (2009) *Theories of the Democratic State*. Basingstoke: Palgrave Macmillan.

Dunleavy, P., Margetts, H., Bastow, S., Pearce, O., and Tinkler, J. (2007) *Government on the Internet: Progress in Delivering Information and Services Online*. Value for Money Study by the UK National Audit Office, HC 529. London: HMSO.

Dunleavy, P., Margetts, H., Bastow, S., and Tinkler, J. (2006) *Digital Era Governance: IT Corporations, the State, and E-government*. Oxford: Oxford University Press.

Dunning, T. (2012) *Natural Experiments in the Social Sciences: A Design-Based Approach*. Cambridge: Cambridge University Press.

Dutton, W. H. (2009) 'The Fifth Estate Emerging through the Network of Networks', *Prometheus*, 27(1): 1–15.

Dutton, W., and Blank, G. (2011) *Next Generation Users: The Internet in Britain*. Oxford: Oxford Internet Institute.

——— (2013) 'Oxford Internet Survey 2013 Report: The Internet in Britain. Cultures of the Internet', Oxford: Oxford Internet Institute.

Earl, J., and Kimport, K. (2011) *Digitally Enabled Social Change: Activism in the Internet Age*. Cambridge, MA: MIT Press.

Ellison, N. B., Steinfield, C., and Lampe, C. (2007) 'The Benefits of Facebook "friends": Exploring the Relationship between College Students' Use of Online Social Networks and Social Capital', *Journal of Computer-Mediated Communication*, 12(4): 1143–68.

Escher, T. (2011) 'TheyWorkForYou.com. Analysis of Users and Usage for UK Citizens Online Democracy'. London: UK Citizens Online Democracy.

———— (2012) 'Does Use of the Internet Further Democratic Participation?', doctoral diss., University of Oxford.

Escher, T., and Margetts, H. (2007) 'Understanding Governments and Citizens On-line: Learning from E-commerce', Paper presented at the Annual Conference of the American Political Science Association, Chicago, 31 August.

Escher, T., Margetts, H., Petricek, V., and Cox, I. (2006) 'Governing from the Centre? Comparing the Nodality of Digital Governments', Paper presented at the Annual Meeting of the American Political Science Association, Philadelphia, 31 August–4 September.

Etling, B., Kelly, J., Faris, R., and Palfrey, J. (2009) *Mapping the Arabic Blogosphere: Politics, Culture and Dissent*. Berkman Center Research Publication no. 2009-06. Cambridge, MA: Berkman Center.

Eynon, R., and Geniets, A. (2012) 'On the Periphery? Understanding Low and Discontinued Internet Use amongst Young People in Britain', Report for the Nominet Trust, http://www.oii.ox.ac.uk/research/publications/Lapsed_Internet_Users_Report_2012.pdf.

Farrell, H., and Drezner, D. (2008) 'The Power and Politics of Blogs', *Public Choice*, 134: 15–30.

Fehr, E., and Rockenbach, B. (2003) 'Detrimental Effects of Sanctions on Human Altruism', *Nature*, 422(6928): 137–40.

Fischbacher, U., and Gächter, S. (2010) 'Social Preferences, Beliefs, and the Dynamics of Free Riding in Public Goods Experiments', *American Economic Review*, 100(1): 541–56.

Fischbacher, U., Gächter, S., and Fehr, E. (2001) 'Are People Conditionally Cooperative? Evidence from a Public Goods Experiment', *Economics Letters*, 71: 397–404.

Forbes (2008) 'When Small Loans Make a Big Difference', 6 March, http://www.forbes.com/2008/06/03/kiva-microfinance-uganda-ent-fin-cx_0603whartonkiva.html, accessed 22 May 2015.

Fowler, J. H., and Christakis, N. A. (2010) 'Cooperative Behavior Cascades in Human Social Networks', *Proceedings of the National Academy of Sciences*, 107(12): 5334–38.

Fowler, J., and Kam, C. (2007) 'Beyond the Self: Social Identity, Altruism, and Political Participation', *Journal of Politics*, 69(3): 813–27.

Francisco, R. A. (2010) *Collective Action: Theory and Empirical Evidence*. New York: Springer.

Frey, B. S., and Meier, S. (2004) 'Social Comparisons and Pro-social Behavior: Testing Conditional Cooperation in a Field Experiment', *American Economic Review*, 94: 1717–22.

Gächter, S., Nosenzo, D., Renner, E., and Sefton, M. (2010) 'Who Makes a Good Leader? Cooperativeness, Optimism, and Leading-by-Example', *Economic Inquiry*, 50(4): 953–67.

Gallego, A., and Oberski, D. (2012) 'Personality and Political Participation: The Mediation Hypothesis', *Political Behavior*, 34: 425–51.

Gelertner, D. (2013) 'The End of the Web, Search and Computer as We Know It', *Wired*, 1 February, http://www.wired.com/2013/02/the-end-of-the-web-computers-and-search-as-we-know-it/, accessed 27 May 2015.

Gerber, A., and Green, D. (2002) 'Reclaiming the Experimental Tradition in Political Science', in I. Katznelson and H. Milner (eds.) *Political Science: State of the Discipline*: 805–32. New York: Norton.

—— (2012) *Field Experiments: Design, Analysis , and Interpretation*. New York: Norton.

Gerber, A., Green, D., and Larimer, C. (2008) 'Social Pressure and Voter Turnout: Evidence from a Large-Scale Field Experiment', *American Political Science Review*, 102(1): 33–48.

—— (2010) 'An Experiment Testing the Relative Effectiveness of Encouraging Voter Participation by Inducing Feelings of Pride or Shame', *Political Behavior*, 32(3): 409–22.

Gerber, A. S., Huber, G. A., Doherty, D., and Dowling, C. M. (2012) 'Assessing the Stability of Psychological and Political Survey Measures', *American Politics Research*, 41: 54–75.

Gerber, A., Huber, G., Doherty, D., Dowling, C. M., and Ha, S. E. (2010) 'Personality and Political Attitudes: Relationships across Issue Domains and Political Contexts', *American Political Science Review*, 94(1): 1717–22.

—— (2011) 'Personality Traits and Participation in Political Processes', *Journal of Politics*, 73(3): 692–706.

Ghonim, W. (2012) *Revolution 2.0: The Power of the People Is Greater Than the People in Power*. London: Fourth Estate.

Gibson, R. K., Lusoli, W., and Ward, S. (2005) 'Online Participation in the UK: Testing a "Contextualised" Model of Internet Effects', *British Journal of Politics and International Relations*, 7: 561–83.

Gibson, R., Nixon, P., and Ward, S. (eds.) (2003) *Net Gain? Political Parties and the Internet*. London: Routledge.

Gibson, R., and Ward, S. (2009) 'Parties in the Digital Age—A Review Article', *Representation*, 45: 87–100.

Gladwell, M. (2000) *The Tipping Point*. Boston: Little, Brown.

—— (2010) 'Why the Revolution Will Not Be Tweeted', *New Yorker*, 4 October.

Glynn, C., Hayes, A., and Shanahan, J. (1997) 'Perceived Support for One's Opinions and Willingness to Speak Out: A Meta-analysis of Survey Studies on the "Spiral of Silence"', *Public Opinion Quarterly*, 61(3): 452–63.

Goel, S., Anderson, A., Hofman, J., and Watts, D. (2014) 'The Structural Virality of Online Diffusion,' http://www.jakehofman.com/inprint/twiral.pdf, accessed 28 February 2015.

Goel, S., Muhamad, R., and Watts, D. (2009) 'Social Search in "Small World" Experiments', in *Proceedings of the 18th International Conference on World Wide Web*: 701–10. New York: ACM.

Goel, S., Watts, D., and Goldstein, D. (2012) 'The Structure of Online Diffusion Networks', in *Proceedings of the 13th ACM Conference on Electronic Commerce*: 623–38. New York: ACM.

Goldstein, J., and Wu, T. (2008) *Who Controls the Internet? The Illusions of a Borderless World*. New York: Oxford University Press.

Goldstein, N., Cialdini, R., and Griskevicius, V. (2008) 'A Room with a Viewpoint: Using Social Norms to Motivate Environmental Conservation in Hotels', *Journal of Consumer Research*, 35: 472–82.

González-Bailón, S., and Barbera, P. (2013) 'The Dynamics of Information Diffusion in the Turkish Protests', *Monkey Cage*, http://themonkeycage.org/2013/06/09/30822/.

González-Bailón, S., Borge-Holthoefer, J., Rivero, A., and Moreno, Y. (2011) 'The Dynamics of Protest Recruitment through an Online Network', *Scientific Reports*, 1(197): doi:10.1038/srep00197.

—— (2013) 'Broadcasters and Hidden Influentials in Online Protest Diffusion', *American Behavioral Scientist*, 57(7): 943–65.

—— (2014) 'The Spanish "Indignados" Movement: Time Dynamics, Geographical Distribution, and Recruitment Mechanisms', in Agarwal, Lim, and Wigand (2014): 155–72.

Gore, P. M., and Rotter, J. B. (1963) 'A Personality Correlate of Social Action', *Journal of Personality*, 31: 58–64.

Gosling, S., Rentfrow, P. J., and Swann, W. B. (2003) 'A Very Brief Measure of the Big-Five Personality Domains', *Journal of Research in Personality*, 37(6): 504–28.

Gough, H. G. (1990) 'Testing for Leadership with the California Psychological Inventory', in K. E. Clark and M. B. Clark (eds.) *Measures of Leadership*: 355–79. West Orange, NJ: Leadership Library of America.

Gould, R. (1993) 'Collective Action and Network Structure', *American Sociological Review*, 58: 182–96.

Granovetter, M. (1973) 'The Strength of Weak Ties', *American Journal of Sociology*, 78(6): 1360–80.

—— (1978) 'Threshold Models of Collective Behavior', *American Journal of Sociology*, 83(6): 1420–43.

—— (1983) 'Threshold Models of Diffusion and Collective Behavior', *Journal of Mathematical Sociology*, 9(3): 165–79.

Green, D., and Gerber, A. (2010) 'Introduction to Social Pressure and Voting: New Experimental Evidence', *Political Behavior*, 32(3): 331–36.

Grenier, P., and Wright, K. (2003) 'Social Capital in Britain: An Update and Critique of Hall's Analysis', International Working Paper Series 14, Centre for Civil Society, London School of Economics and Political Science.

Groshek, J. (2008) 'Freedom and "New" Media: Examining the Relationship between Communication Technologies and Democracy Cross-Nationally from 1946 to 2003', doctoral diss., Indiana University.

Guyton, E. M. (1988) 'Critical Thinking and Political Participation: Development and Assessment of a Causal Model', *Theory & Research in Social Education*, 16(1): 23–49.

Hale, S. A. (2014a) 'Global Connectivity and Multilinguals in the Twitter Network', in *Proceedings of the 32nd International Conference on Human Factors in Computing Systems*: 833–42. New York: ACM.

—— (2014b) 'Multilinguals and Wikipedia Editing', in *Proceedings of the 6th Annual ACM Web Science Conference*: 99–108. New York: ACM.

Hale, S. A., Margetts, H., and Yasseri, T. (2013) 'Petition Growth and Success Rates on the UK No. 10 Downing Street Website', in *Proceedings of the 5th Annual ACM Web Science Conference*: 132–38. New York: ACM.

Hall, P. (1999) 'Social Capital in Britain', *British Journal of Political Science*, 29: 417–61.

Harburgh, W. (1998) 'What Do Donations Buy? A Model of Philanthropy Based on Prestige and Warm Glow', *Journal of Public Economics*, 67: 269–84.

Hardin, R. (1982) *Collective Action*. Baltimore: Johns Hopkins University Press.

Hatuka, T. (2012) 'Transformative Terrains: Counter Hegemonic Tactics of Dissent in Israel', *Geopolitics*, 17(4): 926–51.

Hawthorne, G. (1991) *Plausible Worlds: Possibility and Understanding in History and the Social Sciences*. Cambridge: Cambridge University Press.

Hendler, J., Shadbolt, N., Hall, W., Berners-Lee, T., and Weitzner, D. (2008) 'Web Science: An Interdisciplinary Approach to Understanding the Web', *Communications of the ACM*, 51(7): 60–69.

Henriks, J., and Denton, R. (2010) *Communicator-in-Chief: How Barack Obama Used New Media Technology to Win the White House*. Plymouth: Lexington.

Hindman, M. (2008) *The Myth of Digital Democracy*. Princeton: Princeton University Press.

Hirst, P. (1994) *Associative Democracy: New Forms of Economic and Social Governance*. Cambridge: Polity.

Hough, J. (1982) 'Pluralism, Corporatism, the Soviet Union', in S. Gross Solomon (ed.) *Pluralism in the Soviet Union*: 167–83. New York: St. Martin's.

Howard, P. (2011) *The Digital Origins of Dictatorship and Democracy: Information Technology and Political Islam*. New York: Oxford University Press.

Howard, P. N., and Hussain, M. M. (2011) 'The Upheavals in Egypt and Tunisia: The Role of Digital Media', *Journal of Democracy*, 22(3): 35–48.

——— (2013) *Democracy's Fourth Wave? Digital Media and the Arab Spring*. New York: Oxford University Press.

Howe, J. (2006) 'The Rise of Crowdsourcing', *Wired*, 14 June, http://archive.wired.com/wired/archive/14.06/crowds.html, accessed 27 May 2015.

Huberman, B. A., Romergo, D. M., and Wu, F. (2009) 'Social Networks That Matter: Twitter under the Micro-scope', *First Monday*, 14(1): http://firstmonday.org/article/view/2317/2063.

Hughes, D. J., Rowe, M., Batey, M., and Lee, A. (2012) 'A Tale of Two Sites: Twitter vs. Facebook and the Personality Predictors of Social Media Usage', *Computers in Human Behavior*, 28(2): 561–69.

Hugh-Jones, D., and Reinstein, D. (2009) 'Secret Santa: Anonymity, Signaling, and Conditional Cooperation', Jena Economic Research Papers 2009,048, http://hdl.handle.net/10419/31757.

Ingram, M. (2013) 'For Some in Arab Nations, Facebook Is the Only News Source That Matters', *Gigaom*, 19 June, http://gigaom.com/2013/06/19/for-some-in-arab-nations-facebook-is-the-only-news-source-that-matters.

Isaac, R. M., and Walker, J. M. (1988) 'Group Size Effects in Public Goods Provision: The Voluntary Contributions Mechanism', *Quarterly Journal of Economics*, 103(1): 179–99.

Ituassu, A. (2013) 'Brazil, a Crisis of Representation', http://www.opendemocracy.net/arthur-ituassu/brazil-crisis-of-representation, accessed 30 July 2013.

Janssen, M., Holahan, R., Lee, A., and Ostrom, E. (2010) 'Lab Experiments for the Study of Social-Ecological Systems', *Science*, 328(5978): 613–17.

Joanes, D. N., and Gill, C. A. (2002) 'Comparing Measures of Sample Skewness and Kurtosis', *Journal of the Royal Statistical Society: Series D*, 47(1): 183–89.

John, O. P., and Srivastava, S. (1999) 'The Big 5 Trait Taxonomy: History, Measurement and Theoretical Perspectives', in L. A. Pervin and O. P. John (eds.) *Handbook of Personality: Theory and Research*: 102–38. New York: Guilford.

John, P. (2009) 'Can Citizen Governance Redress the Representative Bias of Political Participation?', *Public Administration Review*, 69(3): 494–503.

——— (2013) 'Field Experiments in Political Science Research', in *Oxford Bibliographies Online: Political Science*: http://www.oxfordbibliographies.com/view/document/obo-9780199756223/obo-9780199756223-0092.xml.

John, P., Bertelli, A., Jennings, W., and Bevan, S. (2013) *Policy Agendas in British Politics*. Basingstoke: Palgrave.

John, P., Cotterill, S., Richardson, L., Moseley, A., Smith, G., Stoker, G., and Wales, C. (2011) *Nudge, Nudge, Think, Think: Experimenting with Ways to Change Civic Behaviour*. London: Bloomsbury.

John, P., and Margetts, H. (2003) 'Policy Punctuations in the UK: Fluctuations and Equilibria in Central Government Expenditure since 1951', *Public Administration*, 81(3): 411–32.

Johnson, T., and Kaye, G. (2003) 'A Boost or Bust for Democracy? How the Web Influenced Political Attitudes and Behaviours in the 1996 and 2000 Presidential Elections', *Harvard International Journal of Press-Politics*, 8(3): 9–34.

Jones, B. D., and Baumgartner, F. R. (2004) 'Representation and Agenda Setting', *Policy Studies Journal*, 32(1): 1–24.

—— (2005) *The Politics of Attention: How Government Prioritizes Problems*. Chicago: University of Chicago Press.

Jordan, T. (2008) *Hacking: Digital Media and Technological Determinism*. Cambridge: Polity.

Jordan, T., and Taylor, P. (2004) *Hactivism and Cyber Wars: Rebels with a Cause*. London: Routledge.

Judge, T., Ilies, R., Bono, J., and Gerhardt, M. (2002) 'Personality and Leadership: A Qualitative and Quantitative Review', *Journal of Applied Psychology*, 87(4): 765–80.

Jungherr, A., and Jürgens, P. (2010) 'The Political Click: Political Participation through E-Petitions in Germany', *Policy & Internet*, 2(4): 131–65.

Kaplan, A. M., and Haenlein, M. (2010) 'Users of the World, Unite! The Challenges and Opportunities of Social Media,' *Business Horizons*, 53(1): 59–68.

Karpf, D. (2010) 'Online Political Mobilization from the Advocacy Group's Perspective: Looking beyond Clicktivism', *Policy and Internet*, 2(4): 7–41.

—— (2012) *The MoveOn Effect: The Unexpected Transformation of American Political Advocacy*. New York: Oxford University Press.

Karsai, M., Iñiguez, G., Kaski, K., and Kertész, J. (2014) 'Complex Contagion Process in Spreading of Online Innovation', *Journal of the Royal Society Interface*, 11(101), http://rsif.royalsocietypublishing.org/content/11/101/20140694.

Karsai, M., Kaski, K., Barabási, A. L., and Kertész, J. (2012) 'Universal Features of Correlated Bursty Behaviour', *Scientific Reports*, 2: doi:10.1038/srep00397.

Kassam, A. (2015) 'Spain's Indignados Could Rule Barcelona and Madrid after Local Election Success', *Guardian*, 25 May, http://www.theguardian.com/world/2015/may/25/spains-indignados-ada-colau-elections-mayor-barcelona, accessed 27 May 2015.

Keser, C., and van Winden, F. (2000) 'Conditional Cooperation in Voluntary Contribution to Public Goods', *Scandinavian Journal of Economics*, 102(1): 23–39.

Kiel, L., and Elliott, E. (1997) *Chaos Theory in the Social Sciences: Foundations and Applications*. Ann Arbor: University of Michigan Press.

King, G., Pan, J., and Roberts, M. E. (2013) 'How Censorship in China Allows Government Criticism but Silences Collective Expression', *American Political Science Review*, 107(2): 1–18, http://j.mp/LdVXqN.

—— (2014) 'Reverse-Engineering Censorship in China: Randomized Experimentation and Participant Observation', *Science*, 345(6199): 1–10, http://j.mp/1KbwkJJ.

Kinnick, K., Krugman, D., and Cameron, G. (1996) 'Compassion Fatigue: Communication and Burnout toward Social Problems', *Journalism and Mass Communication Quarterly*, 73: 687–707.

Klotz, R. (2004) *The Politics of Internet Communication*. Lanham, MD: Rowman & Littlefield.

Knoke, D. (1990) *Organizing for Collective Action: The Political Economies of Associations*. New York: de Gruyter.

—— (1994) *Political Networks: the Structural Perspective*. Cambridge: Cambridge University Press.

Koltsova, O., and Koltcov, S. (2013) 'Mapping the Public Agenda with Topic Modeling: The Case of the Russian LiveJournal', *Policy & Internet*, 5(2): 207–27.

Koole, S., Jager, W., van den Berg, A. E., Vlek, C., and Hofstee, W. (2001) 'On the Social Nature of Personality: Effects of Extraversion, Agreeableness, and Feedback about Collective Resource Use on Cooperation in a Resource Dilemma', *Personality and Social Psychology Bulletin*, 27(3): 289–301.

Kramer, A., Guillory, J. E., and Hancock, J. T. (2014) 'Experimental Evidence of Massive-Scale Emotional Contagion through Social Networks', *Proceedings of the National Academy of Sciences*, 111(24): 8788–90.

Krueger, B. (2002) 'Assessing the Potential of the Internet: Political Participation in the United States: A Resource Approach', *American Politics Research*, 30: 476–98.

Kuhlman, M. D., and Marshello, A. (1975) 'Individual Differences in Game Motivation as Moderators of Preprogrammed Strategic Effects in Prisoner's Dilemma', *Journal of Personality and Social Psychology*, 32: 922–31.

Kurzban, R. O., and Houser, D. (2001) 'Individual Differences in Cooperation in a Circular Public Goods Game', *European Journal of Personality*, 15: 37–52.

—— (2005) 'Experiments Investigating Cooperative Types in Humans: A Complement to Evolutionary Theory and Simulations', *Proceedings of the National Academy of Sciences of the United States of America*, 102: 1803–7.

Lange, P., Cremer, P., Dijk, E. V., and Vugt, M. V. (2007) 'Self-Interest and Beyond: Basic Principles of Social Interaction', in A. W. Kruglanski and E. T. Higgins (eds.) *Social Psychology: Handbook of Basic Principles*, 2nd ed.: 540–61. New York: Guilford.

Lange, P., Otten, W., Bruin, P., and Joireman, J. (1997) 'Development of Prosocial, Individualistic, and Competitive Orientations: Theory and Preliminary Evidence', *Journal of Personality and Social Psychology*, 73: 733–46.

Laudon, K. (1977) *Communications Technology and Democratic Participation*. New York: Praeger.

Lazer, D., Pentland, A., Adamic, L., Aral, S., Barabási, A.-L., Brewer, D., et al. (2009) 'Computational Social Science', *Science*, 323: 721–23.

LeBaron, B. (2002) 'Has Chaos Theory Found Any Useful Application in the Social Sciences?', http://people.brandeis.edu/~blebaron/ge/chaos.html, accessed 28 May 2015.

Levitt, S. D., and List, J. A. (2007a) 'Viewpoint: On the Generalizability of Lab Behaviour to the Field', *Canadian Journal of Economics*, 40: 347–70.

—— (2007b) 'What Do Laboratory Experiments Measuring Social Preferences Reveal about the Real World?', *Journal of Economic Perspectives*, 21: 153–74.

Lev-On, A., and Hardin, R. (2007) 'Internet-Based Collaborations and Their Political Significance', *Journal of Information Technology and Politics*, 4(2): 5–27.

Liben-Nowell, D., and Kleinberg, J. (2008) 'Tracing Information Flow on a Global Scale Using Internet Chain-Letter Data', *Proceedings of the National Academy of Sciences*, 105(12): 4633.

Lindblom, C. (1959) 'The Science of Muddling Through', *Public Administration Review*, 19: 79–88.

—— (1977) *Politics and Markets: The World's Political-Economic Systems*. New York: Basic Books.

Lindner, R., and Riehm, U. (2011) 'Broadening Participation through E-Petitions? An Empirical Study of Petitions to the German Parliament', *Policy & Internet*, 3(1): 1–23.

Lohmann, S. (1998) 'An Information Rationale for the Power of Special Interests', *American Political Science Review*, 92(4): 811.

Lord, R. G., De Vader, C. L., and Alliger, G. M. (1986) 'A Meta-analysis of the Relation between Personality Traits and Leadership Perceptions: An Application of Validity Generalization Procedures', *Journal of Applied Psychology*, 71: 402–10.

Loubser, M. (2010) 'Organisational Mechanisms in Peer Productions: The Case of Wikipedia', doctorate thesis, Oxford Internet Institute, University of Oxford.

Loughlin, J., Hendriks, F., and Listrom, A. (eds.) (2011) *The Oxford Handbook of Local and Regional Democracy in Europe*. Oxford: Oxford University Press.

Lukes, S. (1974) *Power: A Radical View*. London: Macmillan.

Lupia, A., and Philpot, T. S. (2005) 'Views from Inside the Net: How Websites Affect Young Adults' Political Interest', *Journal of Politics*, 67: 1122–42.

Lupia, A., and Sin, G. (2003) 'Which Public Goods Are Endangered? How Evolving Communication Technologies Affect the Logic of Collective Action', *Public Choice*, 117: 315–31.

Madar (2012) 'Arab ICT Use and Social Networks Adoption Report'. Dubai: Madar Research and Development.

Mann, C. B. (2010) 'Is There Backlash to Social Pressure? A Large-Scale Field Experiment on Voter Mobilization', *Political Behavior*, 32: 409–22.

Margetts, H. (1999) *Information Technology in Government: Britain and America*. London: Routledge.

——— (2006) 'The Cyber Party', in R. Katz and W. Crotty (eds.) *Handbook of Party Politics*: 528–35. London: Sage.

——— (2009) 'The Internet and Public Policy', *Policy and Internet*, 1(1): 1–21.

Margetts, H., and Dunleavy, P. (2013) 'The Second Wave of Digital-Era Governance: A Quasi-paradigm for Government on the Web', *Philosophical Transactions of the Royal Society A: Mathematical, Physical and Engineering Sciences*, 371(1987): http://classic .rsta.royalsocietypublishing.org/content/371/1987/20120382.full.

Margetts, H., John, P., Escher, T., and Reissfelder, S. (2009) 'Experiments for Web Science: Examining the Effect of the Internet on Collective Action', Paper presented at the Web-Sci2009 Conference, Athens, 18–20 March.

——— (2011) 'Social Information and Political Participation on the Internet: An Experiment', *European Political Science Review*, 3(3): 321–44.

Margetts, H. Z., John, P., Hale, S. A., and Reissfelder, S. (2014) 'Leadership without Leaders? Starters and Followers in Online Collective Action', *Political Studies*, 63(2): 278–99.

Margetts, H., Reissfelder, S., and Escher, T. (2010) 'Information Effects on Citizens' Propensity to Seek Redress in Public Services: An Experimental Analysis', Paper presented at the 60th Political Studies Association Annual Conference, Edinburgh, 29 March– 1 April.

Margetts, H., and Stoker, G. (2010) 'The Experimental Method: Prospects for Laboratory and Field Studies', in D. Marsh and G. Stoker (eds.) *Theory and Methods in Political Science*, 3rd ed.: 308–24. Basingstoke: Palgrave.

Margolis, M., and Moreno-Riaño, G. (2009) *The Prospect of Internet Democracy*. Burlington, VT: Ashgate.

Margolis, M., and Resnick, D. (2000) *Politics as Usual: The 'Cyberspace Revolution'*. Thousand Oaks, CA: Sage.

Marsh, C. (1985) 'Back on the Bandwagon: The Effects of Opinion Polls on Public Opinion', *British Journal of Political Science*, 15: 51–74.

Marwell, G., and Oliver, P. (1993) *The Critical Mass in Collective Action*. Cambridge: Cambridge University Press.

Marwell, G., Oliver, P., and Prahl, R. (1988) 'Social Networks and Collective Action: A Theory of the Critical Mass III', *American Journal of Sociology*, 94: 502–34.

Mason, P. (2013) *Why It's Still Kicking Off Everywhere: The New Global Revolutions*. 2nd ed. London: Verso. 1st ed. 2012.

Mayer-Schönberger, V. (2009) *Delete*. Princeton: Princeton University Press.

Mayer-Schönberger, V., and Cukier, K. (2013) *Big Data*. London: John Murray.

Messick, D. M., and McClintock, C. G. (1968) 'Motivational Basis of Choice in Experimental Games', *Journal of Experimental Social Psychology*, 4: 1–25.

Milbrath, L., and Goel, M. L. (1977) *Political Participation*. 2nd ed. Chicago: Rand McNally.

Milgram, S. (1967) 'The Small World Problem', *Psychology Today*, 2(1): 60–67.

Miller, D. (1995) 'Citizenship and Pluralism', *Political Studies*, 43: 432–50.

Miotto, J. M., and Altmann, E. G. (2014) 'Predictability of Extreme Events in Social Media', *PLOS ONE*, 9(11): e111506.

Mondak, J. (2010) *Personality and the Foundations of Political Behavior*. Cambridge: Cambridge University Press.

Mondak, J., Canache, D., Seligson, M., and Hibbing, M. (2011) 'The Participatory Personality: Evidence from Latin America', *British Journal of Political Science*, 41(1): 211–21.

Mondak, J., and Halperin, K. (2008) 'A Framework for the Study of Personality and Political Behavior', *British Journal of Political Science*, 38(2): 335–62.

Mondak, J., Hibbing, J., Canache, D., Seligson, M., and Anderson, M. R. (2010) 'Personality and Civic Engagement: An Integrative Framework for the Study of Trait Effects on Political Behavior', *American Political Science Review*, 104: 85–110.

Moore, K., and McElroy, J. (2012) 'The Influence of Personality on Facebook Usage, Wall Postings, and Regret', *Computers in Human Behaviour*, 28(1): 267–74.

Morozov, E. (2011) *The Net Delusion: The Dark Side of Internet Freedom*, Washington DC: Public Affairs.

Morton, R. B., and Williams, K. C. (2010) *Experimental Political Science and the Study of Causality: From Nature to the Lab*. Cambridge: Cambridge University Press.

Mosca, L., and Santucci, D. (2009) 'Petitioning Online. The Role of E-petitions in Web Campaigning', in S. Baringhorst, V. Kneip, and J. Niesyto (eds.) *Political Campaigning on the Web*: 121–46. Bielefeld: transcript Verlag.

Mossberger, K. (2009) 'Toward Digital Citizenship: Addressing Inequality in the Information Age', in Chadwick and Howard (2009): 173–85.

Mossberger, K., Tolbert, C. J., and McNeal, R. S. (2008) *Digital Citizenship: The Internet, Society, and Participation*. Cambridge, MA: MIT Press.

Mryglod, O., Fuchs, B., Szell, M., Holovatch, Y., and Thurner, S. (2015) 'Interevent Time Distributions of Human Multi-Level Activity in a Virtual World', *Physica A: Statistical Mechanics and Its Applications*, 419: 681–90.

Nadeau, R., Cloutier, E., and Guay, J.-H. (1993) 'New Evidence about the Existence of a Bandwagon Effect in the Opinion Formation Process', *International Political Science Review*, 14: 203–13.

Narayanan, S., and Kalyanam, K. (2011) 'Measuring Position Effects in Search Advertising: A Regression Discontinuity Approach', Working Paper.

Naughton, J. (2012) *What You Really Need to Know about the Internet: From Gutenberg to Zuckerberg*. London: Quercus.

——— (2013) 'Why a Stream of Consciousness Will Kill Off Websites', *Observer*, 10 February, http://www.theguardian.com/technology/2013/feb/10/stream -consciousness-computer-desktop, accessed 27 May 2015.

Negroponte, N. (1995) *Being Digital*. London: Hodder and Stoughton.

Ng, T. W. H., Sorensen, K. L., and Eby, L. T. (2006) 'Locus of Control at Work: A Meta-analysis', *Journal of Organization Behavior*, 27: 1057–87.

Noelle-Neumann, E. (1974) 'The Spiral of Silence: A Theory of Public Opinion', *Journal of Communication*, 24: 43–51.

—— (1993) *The Spiral of Silence: Public Opinion—Our Social Skin*. 2nd ed. Chicago: University of Chicago Press.

Norris, P. (2001) *Digital Divide: Civic Engagement, Information Poverty and the Internet Worldwide*. Cambridge: Cambridge University Press.

—— (2003) 'Preaching to the Converted? Pluralism, Participation and Party Websites', *Party Politics*, 9(1): 21–45.

—— (2006) 'Did the Media Matter? Agenda-Setting, Persuasion and Mobilization Effects in the 2005 British General Election', *British Politics*, 1(2): 195–221.

—— (2009) 'The Impact of the Internet on Political Activism: Evidence from Europe', in C. Romm-Livermore and K. Setzekorn (eds.) *Social Networking Communities and E-dating Services*: 123–41. Hershey, PA: I-Global.

Nosek, B., Banaji, M., and Greenwald, A. (2002) 'E-research: Ethics, Security, Design and Control in Psychological Research on the Internet', *Journal of Social Issues*, 58(1): 161–76.

O'Hara, K. (2002) 'The Internet: A Tool for Democratic Pluralism', *Science as Culture*, 11(2): 287–98.

Oliver, P. (1980) 'Rewards and Punishments as Selective Incentives for Collective Action: Theoretical Investigations', *American Journal of Sociology*, 85: 1356–75.

Oliver, P., and Marwell, G. (1988) 'The Paradox of Group Size in Collective Action: A Theory of the Critical Mass. II', *American Sociological Review*, 53: 1–8.

Oliver, P., Marwell, G., and Teixeira, R. (1985) 'A Theory of the Critical Mass. Interdependence, Group Heterogeneity, and the Production of Collective Action', *American Journal of Sociology*, 91(3): 522–56.

Olson, M. (1965) *The Logic of Collective Action*. Cambridge, MA: Harvard University Press.

O'Neil, M. (2009) *Cyber Chiefs: Autonomy and Authority in Online Tribes*. New York: Pluto Press.

Oostveen, A., and van den Besselaar, P. (2006) 'Non-technical Risks of Remote Electronic Voting', in A. Anttiroiko and M. Malkia (eds.) *The Encyclopedia of Digital Government*: 502–7. Hershey, PA: Idea Group.

Oxford Internet Survey (OXIS) (2007) *The Internet in Britain*. Oxford: Oxford Internet Institute.

Panagopoulos, C. (2010) 'Affect, Social Pressure and Prosocial Motivation: Field Experimental Evidence of the Mobilizing Effects of Pride, Shame and Publicizing Voting Behavior', *Political Behaviour*, 32: 369–88.

—— (2011) 'Thank You for Voting: Gratitude Expression and Voter Mobilization', *Journal of Politics*, 73(3): 707–17.

—— (2013) 'Positive Social Pressure and Prosocial Motivation: Evidence from a Large-Scale Field Experiment on Voter Mobilization', *Political Psychology*, 34(2): 1467.

Panagopoulos, C., Larimer, C., and Condon, M. (2014) 'Social Pressure, Descriptive Norms, and Voter Mobilization', *Political Behaviour*, 36: 451–69.

Papacharissi, Z. (2009) 'The Virtual Sphere 2.0: The Internet, the Public Sphere and Beyond', in Chadwick and Howard (2009): 230–45.

Parkes, K., and Razavi, T. (2004) 'Personality and Attitudinal Variables as Predictors of Voluntary Union Membership', *Personality and Individual Differences*, 37(2): 333–47.

Parry, G., Moyser, G., and Day, N. (1992) *Political Participation and Democracy in Britain*. Cambridge: Cambridge University Press.

Pastor-Satorras, R., and Vespignani, A. (2007) *Evolution and Structure of the Internet: A Statistical Physics Approach*. Cambridge: Cambridge University Press.

Pentland, A. (2014) *Social Physics: How Good Ideas Spread—The Lessons from a New Science*. New York: Penguin.

Pew Research Center (2005) 'The State of Blogging', 2 January, http://www.pewinternet
.org/2005/01/02/the-state-of-blogging/, accessed 22 May 2015.
—— (2012) 'Social Networking Popular Across Globe', http://www.pewglobal
.org/2012/12/12/social-networking-popular-across-globe/, accessed 22 May 2015.
—— (2014) 'Social Media Update 2014', http://www.pewinternet.org/2015/01/09
/social-media-update-2014/, accessed 22 May 2015.
Pfeffer, J., and Salancik, G. R. (1978) *The External Control of Organizations: A Resource
Dependence Perspective*. New York: Harper & Row.
Polsby, N. (1963) *Community Power and Political Theory*. New Haven: Yale University
Press.
Poteete, A., Janssen, M., and Ostrom, E. (2010) *Working Together: Collective Action, the
Commons and Multiple Methods in Practice*. Princeton: Princeton University Press.
Price, V., and Cappella, J. N. (2002) 'Online Deliberation and Its Influence: The Electronic
Dialogue Project in Campaign 2000', *Information Technology and Society*, 1(1):
303–29.
Price, V., Cappella, J. N., and Nir, L. (2002) 'Does More Disagreement Contribute to More
Deliberative Opinion?', *Political Communication*, 19(1): 95–112.
Pro Publica (2014) 'Deadly Force, in Black and White', 10 October, http://www
.propublica.org/article/deadly-force-in-black-and-white, retrieved 22 May 2015.
Public Administration Select Committee (2000) *Innovations in Citizen Participation in Gov-
ernment—Minutes of Evidence, Tuesday 11 January 2000*. HC79-v. London: HMSO.
Putnam, R. (2000) *Bowling Alone: The Collapse and Revival of American Community*.
New York: Simon & Schuster.
Rainie, L., and Smith, A. (2008) 'Beyond the Soundbite'. Washington DC: Pew Research
Center. http://www.pewinternet.org/2008/06/15/beyond-the-sound-bite/, accessed
27 May 2015.
Ramírez, R. (2005) 'Giving Voice to Latino Voters: A Field Experiment on the Effective-
ness of a National Nonpartisan Mobilization Effort', *Annals of the American Academy
of Political and Social Science*, 601(1): 66–84.
Reinstein, D., and Hugh-Jones, D. (2010) 'The Benefit of Anonymity in Public Goods
Games', University of Essex, Economics Discussion Papers 689, http://ideas.repec
.org/p/esx/essedp/689.html.
Rheingold, H. (2000) *The Virtual Community*. Cambridge, MA: MIT Press.
Rogers, E. M. (1995) *Diffusion of Innovations*. 4th ed. New York: Free Press.
Rotter, J. B. (1966) 'Generalized Expectancies for Internal Versus External Control of
Reinforcement', *Psychological Monographs*, 80(1): 1–28.
Ryan, T., and Xenos, S. (2011) 'Who Uses Facebook? An Investigation into the Relation-
ship between the Big Five, Shyness, Narcissism, Loneliness, and Facebook Usage',
Computers in Human Behavior, 27(5): 1658–64.
Sajuria, J., vanHeerde-Hudson, J., Hudson, D., Dasandi, N., and Theocaris, Y. (2014)
'Tweeting Alone? An Analysis of Bridging and Bonding Social Capital in Online Net-
works', *American Politics Research*, 28 November, doi:10.1177/1532673X14557942.
Salancik, G., and Pfeffer, J. (1977) 'An Examination of Need-Satisfaction Models of Job
Attitudes', *Administrative Science Quarterly*, 22: 427–56.
—— (1978) 'A Social Information Processing Approach to Job Attitudes and Task
Design', *Administrative Science Quarterly*, 23: 224–53.
Salganik, M., Dodds, P., and Watts, D. (2006) 'Experimental Study of Inequality and Un-
predictability in an Artificial Cultural Market', *Science*, 311(5762): 854–56.
Salganik, M., and Watts, D. (2009) 'Web-Based Experiments for the Study of Collective
Social Dynamics in Cultural Markets', *Topics in Cognitive Science*, 1: 439–68.

Sandler, T. (1992) *Collective Action: Theories and Applications*. Ann Arbor: University of Michigan Press.

Savage, M., and Burrows, R. (2007) 'The Coming Crisis of Empirical Sociology', *Sociology*, 41(5): 885–99.

Schattschneider, E. (1960) *The Semi-sovereign People*. New York: Holt, Rinehart and Winston.

Scheffer, M., Bascompte, J., Brock, W., Brovkin, V., Carpenter, S., Dakos, V., Held, H., van Nes, E. H., Rietkerk, M., and Sugihara, G. (2009) 'Early-Warning Signals for Critical Transitions', *Nature*, 461(7260): 53–59.

Schelling, T. (2005) *Micromotives and Macrobehaviour*. New York: Norton. 1st ed. 1978.

Schlozman, K. L., Page, B. I., Verba, S., and Fiorina, M. P. (2005) 'Inequalities of Political Voice', in L. Jacobs and T. Skocpol (eds.) *Inequality and American Democracy: What We Know and What We Need to Learn*, 19–87. Washington DC: Russell Sage.

Schultz, P. W. (1999) 'Changing Behavior with Normative Feedback Interventions: A Field Experiment of Curbside Recycling', *Basic and Applied Social Psychology*, 21: 25–36.

Segerberg, A., and Bennett, L. (2011) 'Social Media and the Organization of Collective Action: Using Twitter to Explore the Ecologies of Two Climate Change Protests', *Communication Review*, 14: 197–215.

Selfhout, M., Burk, W., Branje, S., Denissen, J., Van Aken, M., and Meeus, W. (2010) 'Emerging Late Adolescent Friendship Networks and Big Five Personality Traits: A Social Network Approach', *Journal of Personality*, 78(2): 509–38.

Shadish, W. R., Cook, T. D., and Campbell, D. T. (2002) *Experimental and Quasi-experimental Designs for Generalized Causal Inference*. Boston: Houghton Mifflin.

Shang, J., and Croson, R. (2006) 'The Impact of Social Comparisons on Nonprofit Fundraising', *Research in Experimental Economics Series*, 11: 143–56.

——— (2009) 'A Field Experiment in Charitable Contribution: The Impact of Social Information on the Voluntary Provision of Public Goods', *Economic Journal*, 119(540): 1422–39.

Shapiro, S. S., and Wilk, M. B. (1965) 'An Analysis of Variance Test for Normality (Complete Samples)', *Biometrika*, 52: 591–611.

Shirky, C. (2003) 'Power Laws, Weblogs and Inequality', http://www.shirky.com/writings/herecomeseverybody/powerlaw_weblog.html, accessed 30 May 2013.

——— (2008) *Here Comes Everybody: The Power of Organizing without Organizations*. New York: Allen Lane.

——— (2010) *Cognitive Surplus*. New York: Allen Lane.

Siegel, D. (2009) 'Social Networks and Collective Action', *American Journal of Political Science*, 53(1):122–38.

Silver, N. (2012) *The Signal and the Noise: The Art and Science of Prediction*. London: Penguin.

Simon, L., Corrales, J., and Wolfensberger, D. (2002) *Democracy and the Internet: Allies or Adversaries*. Washington DC: Woodrow Wilson Center Press.

Skitka, L., and Sargis, E. (2006) 'The Internet as Psychological Laboratory', *Annual Review of Psychology*, 57: 529–55.

Smith, A. (2013) 'Civic Engagement in the Digital Age'. Washington DC: Pew Research Center. http://www.pewinternet.org/2013/04/25/civic-engagement-in-the-digital-age/, accessed 20 December 2014.

Smith, J., John, P., Sturgis, P., and Nomura, H. (2009) 'Deliberation and Internet Engagement: Initial Findings from a Randomised Controlled Trial Evaluating the Impact of Facilitated Internet Forums', Paper presented at the ECPR conference, Potsdam, 10–12 September.

Spector, P. E. (1982) 'Behavior in Organizations as a Function of Employee's Locus of Control', *Psychological Bulletin*, 91(3): 482–97.

Stanley, H. E. (1987) *Introduction to Phase Transitions and Critical Phenomena*. Oxford: Oxford University Press

Straffin, P. (1977) 'The Bandwagon Curve', *American Journal of Political Science*, 21(4): 695–709.

Suleiman, R., and Rapoport, A. (1992) 'Provision of Step-Level Public Goods with Continuous Contribution', *Journal of Behavioral Decision Making*, 5(2): 133–53.

Sunstein, C. (2007) *Republic.com 2.0*. Princeton: Princeton University Press.

Suri, S., and Watts, D. J. (2011) 'Cooperation and Contagion in Web-Based, Networked Public Goods Experiments', *PLOS ONE*, 6(3): e16836.

Tangney, J. P. (1990) 'Assessing Individual Differences in Proneness to Shame and Guilt: Development of the Self-Conscious Affect and Attribution Inventory', *Journal of Personality and Social Psychology*, 59(1): 102–11.

Thaler, M., and Sunstein, C. (2008) *Nudge*. London: Penguin.

Tickle, J., Heatherton, T., and Wittenberg, L. (2001) 'Can Personality Change?' in W. J. Livesley (ed.) *Handbook of Personality Disorders: Theory, Research and Treatment*: 242–58. New York: Guilford.

Titmuss, R. M. (1970) *The Gift Relationship: From Human Blood to Social Policy*. London: Allen and Unwin.

Tolbert, C. J., and McNeal, R. S. (2003) 'Unraveling the Effects of the Internet on Political Participation?' *Political Research Quarterly*, 56: 175–85.

Truman, D. B. (1951) *The Governmental Process: Political Interests and Public Opinion*. New York: Knopf.

Valente, T. (1996) 'Social Network Thresholds in the Diffusion of Innovations', *Social Networks*, 18: 69–89.

Vanhanen, T. (1990) *The Process of Democratization: A Comparative Study of 147 States, 1980–88*. New York: Crane Russak.

—— (1997) *Prospects of Democracy: A Study of 172 Countries*. London: Routledge.

—— (2003) *Democratization: A Comparative Analysis of 170 Countries*. London: Routledge.

Van Vugt, M., Meertens, R. M., and Van Lange, P.A.M. (1995) 'Car versus Public Transportation? The Role of Social Value Orientations in a Real-life Social Dilemma', *Journal of Applied Social Psychology*, 25: 258–78.

Vecchione, M., and Caprara, G. V. (2009) 'Personality Determinants of Political Participation: The Contribution of Traits and Self-Efficacy Beliefs', *Personality and Individual Differences*, 46(4): 487–92.

Verba, S., and Nie, N. H. (1972) *Participation in America: Political Democracy and Social Equality*. New York: Harper & Row.

Verba, S., Scholzman, K., and Brady, H. (1995) *Voice and Equality: Civic Voluntarism in American Politics*. Cambridge, MA: Harvard University Press.

Volk, S., Thönib, C., and Ruigrok, W. (2011) 'Personality, Personal Values and Cooperation Preferences in Public Goods Games: A Longitudinal Study', *Journal of Personality and Individual Differences*, 50(6): 810–15.

Walt, S. M. (2011) 'Why the Tunisian Revolution Won't Spread', *Foreign Policy*, 16 January.

Ward, S., Lusoli, W., and Gibson, R. K. (2006) 'Reconnecting Politics? Parliament, the Public and the Internet', *Parliamentary Affairs*, 59(1): 1–19.

Warschauer, M. (2003) *Technology and Social Inclusion; Rethinking the Digital Divide*. Cambridge, MA: MIT Press.

Watts, D. (2003) *Six Degrees: The Science of a Connected Age*. New York: Norton.

—— (2004) 'The New Science of Networks', *Annual Review of Sociology*, 30: 243–70.

Watts, D., and Dodds, P. S. (2007) 'Influentials, Networks, and Public Opinion Formation', *Journal of Consumer Research*, 34(4): 441–58.

Watts, D., and Strogatz, S. (1998) 'Collective Dynamics of "small-world" Networks', *Nature*, 393(6684): 440–42.

Weaver, M., and McCarthy, T. (2013) 'Egypt on the Brink: "The Price Can Be My Life", President Morsi Says—as It Happened', *Guardian*, 3 July.

Weiman, J. (1994) 'Individual Behavior in a Free Riding Experiment', *Journal of Public Economics*, 54(2): 185–200.

Wenman, M. (2015) 'William E. Connolly: Resuming the Pluralist Tradition in American Political Science', *Political Theory*, 43(1): 54–79.

Westcott, N. (2008) 'Digital Diplomacy: The Impact of the Internet on International Relations', OII Working Paper 16, http://ssrn.com/abstract=1326476.

Whiteley, P. (2011) 'Is the Party Over? The Decline of Party Activism and Membership across the Democratic World', *Party Politics*, 17(1): 21–44.

—— (2012) *Political Participation in Britain: The Decline and Revival of Civic Culture*. London: Palgrave.

Whyte, A., Renton, A., and Macintosh, A. (2005) *e-Petitioning in Kingston and Bristol Evaluation of e-Petitioning in the Local e-Democracy National Project*. Edinburgh: International Teledemocracy Centre, Napier University.

Wiggins, J. S. (1996) *The Five-factor Model of Personality: Theoretical Perspectives*. New York: Guilford.

Wilcox, C. (2008) 'Internet Fundraising in 2008: A New Model?', *Forum*, 6(1): 6.

World Bank (2015) 'Mobile Cellular Subscriptions (per 100 People)', http://data.world bank.org/indicator/IT.CEL.SETS.P2.

Worstall, T. (2015) 'Eric Schmidt's Quite Right the Internet Will Disappear; All Technologies Do as They Mature', *Forbes*, 24 January, http://www.forbes.com/sites/timworstall /2015/01/24/eric-schmidts-quite-right-the-internet-will-disappear-all-technologies-do -as-they-mature/, accessed 22 May 2015.

Wright, S. (2012) 'Assessing (E-)democratic Innovations: "Democratic Goods" and Downing Street E-petitions', *Journal of Information Technology and Politics*, 9(4): 453–70.

Wu, B. (2015) 'Google's Eric Schmidt Predicts the Internet Will Disappear', *Science Times*, 27 January, http://www.sciencetimes.com/articles/2869/20150127/google-s-eric -schmidt-predicts-the-internet-will-disappear.htm, accessed 22 May 2015.

Wu, F., and Huberman, B. A. (2007) 'Novelty and Collective Attention', *Proceedings of the National Academy of Sciences*, 104(45): 17599–601.

Xenos, M., and Kyoung, K. (2008) 'Rocking the Vote and More: An Experimental Study of the Impact of Youth Political Portals', *Journal of Information Technology and Politics*, 5: 175–89.

INDEX